SAINT MARY'S SEMINARY LIBRARY
9745 Memorial Drive
Houston 24, Texas

THE THEORY OF COMMUNISM

THE THEORY OF COMMUNISM

AN INTRODUCTION

by

George H. Hampsch, Ph.D.

Assistant Professor of Philosophy
Member of Institute for Soviet and East European Studies
John Carroll University

PHILOSOPHICAL LIBRARY
New York

Copyright, 1965, by

Philosophical Library, Inc.

15 East 40th Street, New York 16, N.Y.

All rights reserved

Library of Congress Catalog Card Number: 65-21471

Printed in the United States of America

CONTENTS

FOREWORD   vii

Part I
Marxian Principles

I. Meaning of Communism   1
    Dictatorship of the Proletariat   1
    Socialism   3
    Communism: The Classless Society   4

II. Marxist Theory of Truth (Historical Materialism)   10
    Precedence of Matter over Spirit and Consciousness   10
    Precedence of Practical Truth over Speculation   14
    Historical Materialism   17
    Classes and the Class Struggle   26
    Marxist Concept of Social Class   29
    Marx's Notion of Class and Modern Sociology — Appendix II-a   33
    Peaceful Coexistence — Appendix II-b   42

III. Marxist Philosophy of Nature and Being (Dialectical Materialism)   58
    Marx's and Engels' View of their Ontology   58
    Influence of Hegel and Feuerbach on the Marxian View of Nature   59
    Parts of the Universe are Interrelated   66
    Laws of Matter   68
    Link between Soviet Science and Philosophy — Appendix III   77

IV. Marxist Theory of Man   89
    Origin of Man   89
    Pavlovian Psychology   91
    Freedom of Man   94
    Role of the Individual in History   97

V.	Marxian Ethics	104
	Ultimate Values: Marxist Economics and the Labor Theory of Value	104
	Moral Principles	111
	Attitude Toward Religion	116

Part II
Some Principles Applied

VI.	Communist Philosophy of the State and Law	131
	Theory of the State and Law	131
	Relationship of Law to Morality	137
VII.	Communist Philosophy of Education	150
	Education: A Superstructure and Weapon	150
	Polytechnism: Link between Education and Production	157
VIII.	Communist Aesthetics	173
	Role of Art	173
	Criterion of Beauty	175
	Socialist Realism	180
	Partisan Control of the Arts	183

Part III
Some Principles for the Future

IX.	The Classless Society and Political Order	197
	The "Withering" of the State	197
	Analysis of Political Order	202
X.	Social Power and the Classless Society	216
	Analysis of Social Power	216
	Pre-eminence of Comradeship and Social Justice	223
Index		239

FOREWORD

This work is presented as an objective study of the theory of communism. It is intended primarily for those readers of college caliber who have only a popular notion of the theoretical tenets of communism, and who wish to secure a deeper, more systematic knowledge of the subject — without being required to suffer the annoyance and possibly the indignity of being proselytized, one way or the other, in the process.

An underlying supposition throughout this work is that Leninism and the ideology invoked in the Soviet Union and throughout the communist world is basically Marxian. Although such a supposition is becoming less favored among non-Marxist interpreters of communist ideology, this author has found no conclusive argument to show that contemporary Soviet ideology, especially Soviet social philosophy, is not a proper and legitimate interpretation of Marx's thought — albeit an interpretation consonant with the Russian mind. To maintain this supposition is not to imply that the bolshevik interpretation is necessarily the only legitimate interpretation of Marx, or even the most fortunate one. It is maintained, however, that the movement initiated by Marx, developed by Engels, and in another way by Lenin, and finally actualized in contemporary communist countries, is the only interpretation of Marx viable at present. Hence this is the only exposition of Marxism in which the theory and the actual practice can be said to be unified.

To maintain that the bolshevik position is a legitimate interpretation of Marx is not to imply that it represents a monolithic dogma somehow extending undisturbed in its pure form from Marx to Khrushchev. Rather, it is held that there is a unity of theory and practice between the 19th century thought of Marx and the 20th century idealizations of the designs of the Communist Party. This unity is to be found within a theoretical evolution which began, perhaps, with Engels, extended down through

Lenin with his preoccupation with the problems peculiar to the Soviet Union, and continued through the Stalinist regime to the present Soviet Empire. That the notion of theoretical evolution is intrinsic to Marxist thought need hardly be argued. Any attempt to interpret present day history according to *Historical Materialism* in its pure 19th century form is certainly not Marxian. It is well to recall that Marx and Engels were quite emphatic on this point. They abhorred the idea that their words would ever become a stabilized dogma. (Engels, Letter to C. Schmidt, Aug. 5, 1890). What they felt they had discovered were some general patterns in the history of mankind — some universal laws by which future events could be properly interpreted and controlled. While their theories were to act as the basis for practical activity, it is also true that their findings and theories were to serve as guides to the *further* study of history (Engels, Letter to Schmidt; *Die Kommunisten und Karl Heinzen*, etc.).

In spite of certain tendencies of the Soviets in the past to dogmatize Marx and Lenin, all in all, the Bolsheviks have held true to this idea which they have termed the "creative advancement" of Marxist theory. One can trace this theoretical evolution in bolshevism back to Lenin himself. In capitalism, he saw for instance, a higher stage, called imperialism. Marx had hinted at this stage of imperialism in the last pages of volume I of *Das Kapital* but could not foresee it with any exactness at the time he lived. This advancement begun by Lenin was carried on under Stalin, for example, with the Lenin-inspired theory of "socialism in one country." Through this particular theory, the industrialization of the Soviet Union received priority over the completion of world revolution. In our own day, Khrushchev has extended the creative advancement of Marxism with his theory of "peaceful coexistence." Even within the Chinese camp an example of theoretical evolution can be found in the short-lived "Hundred Flowers" experiment of Mao Tse-tung.

It is the principle of "theoretical evolution" and another Marxian principle, that of "the unity of theory and practice," which justify the underlying assumptions that Soviet ideology is, in general, a legitimate interpretation of Marx given the historical conditions of the Revolution of 1917 and the culture of Russia. There is no obligation to further prove this position. On the contrary, the burden of proof lies with those who wish to hold that bolshevism does constitute a deviation from the thought of Marx. Indeed, notable attempts have been made in this direction. There exists an immense body of literature in defense of this position. Yet the evidence offered in these attempts has not been strong enough to convince this writer that bolshevism, *taken as a whole,* represents a deviation. Naturally, numerous isolated instances of official "deviation" might be pointed out. But this is to be expected. There has been no ideology or religion in the history of mankind in which the practice has ever approached the perfection of the theory. Communism is no exception.

It is through the principle of theoretical evolution inherent in Marxism that the author of this work justifies the use of such controversial writers as Bukharin, Stalin, Vyshinsky, etc., as documentary sources. The use of such authors does not necessarily imply that they in every instance held true to a legitimate Marxian position. It is maintained that in the area of Marxist theory in which they are cited, these authors are within that unified tradition of socialist thought which extends from Marx down to the contemporary Communist Movement. In a proper context they become qualified interpreters of Marxian theory.

The list of suggested readings following each chapter is not meant to exhaust the subject matter. Some will surely question the inclusion of certain titles and the exclusion of others. The selection is such as to include many different interpretations and viewpoints of the subject treated in each chapter. It lists those writers which the author has personally found most helpful. Other titles may well be substituted with equally satisfactory results.

A preliminary version of this work was used in several classes at John Carroll University. I am indebted to the students of these classes for their helpful suggestions and comments.

Prof. A. Robert Caponigri, Prof. Anton-Hermann Chroust and Prof. Nickolaus Lobkowicz of the University of Notre Dame, Rev. Paul A. Woelfl, S. J. and Prof. William E. Thirlkel of John Carroll University, and Prof. William S. Haymond of Georgetown University read all or portions of the text and made valuable comments and suggestions for improvement of the material. I am especially indebted to Prof. Caponigri for allowing me to use his manuscript, "An Introduction to Political Theory," which is in preparation for publication by Harper & Row. I am also grateful to Rev. Joseph O. Schell, S. J., Director of the Philosophy Department of John Carroll for his continued encouragement. To the Administration of John Carroll University, the Very Rev. Hugh E. Dunn, S. J., President, Rev. Wm. J. Millor, S. J., Academic Vice-President, Dr. Richard J. Spath, Coordinator of Research and the members of the Committee on Research I owe a debt of gratitude. Without their kind assistance, this work would not have come to print.

In proofreading and editing I had the valuable help of Mr. Wm. Douglas Bookwalter and Mr. Dale Leonard. Mrs. Elizabeth Catalano, Mrs. Rachel Baskind and Mrs. Charlotte Ward typed the preliminary and final drafts. I am grateful for their patience as well as their painstaking efforts. The Editorial Department of Philosophical Library has been very helpful in editing the manuscript. Mr. Philip R. Brodsky likewise provided valuable assistance to me.

Finally, I am indebted to my wife, Harriett, for her encouragement in this undertaking. Without her understanding and patience, the task would not have been accomplished.

GEORGE H. HAMPSCH

University Heights, Ohio

ACKNOWLEDGMENTS

Acknowledgment is gratefully made to the following publishers for permission to quote from their works:

Cooperative Publishing Society of Foreign Workers in the U.S.S.R.: *Karl Marx Selected Works*, V. Adoratsky, editor, C. P. Dutt, English edition editor.

Foreign Languages Publishing House: *Collected Works*, and *Selected Works*, by V. I. Lenin; *Economic and Philosophic Manuscripts of 1844*, by Karl Marx; *Problems of Leninism*, by Joseph Stalin.

Harvard University Press: *Soviet Legal Philosophy*, John N. Hazard, editor; *Political Control of Literature in the U.S.S.R.*, by Harold Swayze.

Henry Holt & Co.: *Communism*, by Harold J. Laski.

International Publishers Co., Inc.: *Historical Materialism*, by N. Bukharin; *Dialectics of Nature*, by Frederick Engels; *The German Ideology*, and *Selected Correspondence*, by Karl Marx and Frederick Engels; *The Role of the Individual in History*, by G. V. Plekhanov.

Charles H. Kerr Co.: *Capital*, and *A Contribution to the Critique of Political Economy*, by Karl Marx.

Alfred A. Knopf, Inc.: *Human Nature: The Marxian View*, by Vernon Venable.

Lawrence & Wishart, Ltd.: *Herr Eugen Dühring's Revolution in Science (Anti-Dühring)*, by F. Engels.

National Society for the Study of Education: *Modern Philosophies and Education*, Nelson B. Henry, editor.

Oxford University Press: *From Max Weber: Essays in Sociology*, H. H. Gerth and C. Wright Mills, editors.

Pantheon Books (Random House, Inc.): *On Socialist Realism*, by Abram Tertz.

Philosophical Library, Inc.: *Twentieth Century Sociology*,

Georges Gurvitch and Wilbert E. Moore, editors; *Soviet Education: Its Psychology and Philosophy*, by Maurice J. Shore.
Frederick A. Praeger, Inc.: *Dialectical Materialism*, by Gustav A. Wetter.
United States Dept. of State: *Soviet World Outlook*, 3rd ed.
University of Chicago Press: *Sociology*, by Joseph H. Fichter.
University of Pittsburgh Press: *Khrushchev and the Central Committee Speak On Education*, by George S. Counts.

I am grateful to the editors of the following journals for permission to quote from articles appearing therein:

Problems of Communism: "Totalitarianism Without Coercion?" by Herbert Ritvo.

Soviet Review: "When the State Has Withered Away," by G. Shaknozarov.

Survey: "Origins of Literary Control," by Ernest J. Simmons; "Marx On Education," by Horst Wittig.

A portion of Chapter II originally appeared in the *Duquesne Review;* a portion of Chapter III appeared in *The American Slavic and East European Review;* parts of Chapters V and VI appeared in the *Notre Dame Lawyer.* Acknowledgment is gratefully made to the editors of these journals for permission to reuse this material.

THE THEORY OF COMMUNISM

Part I

MARXIAN PRINCIPLES

CHAPTER I

MEANING OF COMMUNISM

In its wider signification communism refers to any social system in which all property, or at least all productive property, is socially owned and controlled. Thus understood, it comprises: (a) *communistic anarchism* which would abolish political authority as well as private property; (b) *socialism,* and (c) *communism,* in the strict sense. In its technical connotations, communism is distinguished from socialism — that is, social ownership of productive goods — in that it usually includes collective ownership of some or all forms of personal and consumptive goods as well. During the years of 1840-72 — due especially to the influence of Karl Marx and Frederick Engels — the term communism, in addition to a somewhat altered interpretation of this general, historical meaning, also came to imply revolutionary activity for the forceful overthrow of capitalism. Between 1872 and 1917 the terms socialism and communism were used as synonyms, or rather, the word communism disappeared. With the coming to power of Marxian Bolshevism in Russia the distinction between the terms was revived and continues to the present day.

Dictatorship of The Proletariat

For the Marxist, of course, the overthrow of all or any segment of capitalism is not the termination but rather the beginning of the process towards communism. This gradual transition from capitalism to communism has been variously interpreted. Some hold that it breaks into three stages[1], others two[2]. Apparently, there is strong enough evidence within the classics of Marxism for either position. In any case the distinction is of relatively minor importance. It is definitive in Marxism that once political power has been won by the proletariat or working class, the old society cannot be turned into a basically different one in a single stroke. It requires a long period of time for the remnants of capitalism — the institutions, ideas, mechanisms and traditions — to lose their influence in that society. Thus between the time that the workers overthrow capitalism and gain political control until the establishment of a perfect "classless society," there intervenes a period of social transformations which Marx has named "the dictatorship of the proletariat."[3]

This dictatorship is not merely the old capitalistic state in new hands. It is a new state based on new principles.[4]

The dictatorship of the proletariat is not a mere change of government, but a new state, with new organs of power, both central and local; it is the state of the proletariat which has arisen on the ruins of the old state, the state of the bourgeoisie.

The dictatorship of the proletariat arises not on the basis of the bourgeois order, but in the process of the breaking up of this order. . . .[5]

The form of government it is to take is that of a democratic republic.[6] Yet this state is democratic in a new way. It is to be patterned after the Paris Commune of 1871 and is simply the proletariat organized as the ruling class. The substantial difference between this state and all hitherto existing forms of the state is that formerly the class states have been dictatorships of an exploiting minority over the exploited majorities, whereas the dictatorship of the proletariat appears as a dictatorship of the worker majority over the bourgeois minority. Thus, in regard to the proletariat, it represents a new form of democracy in which the majority has political control, and the state functions for its goals. In relation to the owner class, the bourgeoisie, this form of state represents a "new" form of dictatorship under which the control of productive property is taken from it and administered by the state for the common benefit of the majority and the economic emancipation of labor.[7]

The dictatorship, therefore, represents "proletarian democracy."

Much like the Commune of Paris,[8] it will consist of elected councillors who function simultaneously as legislators and executives. There is to be universal suffrage, a citizen army, elected judges, police and officials subject to immediate recall; seizure of all closed factories and the eventual abolition of private ownership of productive property, universal education, and so on.[9] The dictatorship of the proletariat is still a political state, for some kind of organized force is still needed to maintain the proletariat in power and to resist the final onslaughts of the dying bourgeois class while radical transformations and new institutions are being introduced.

Socialism

When the transformation from bourgeois capitalist institutions to those of the proletariat is accomplished, the history of communist man begins. Yet the society that then prevails still fails far short of strict communism. It merely represents the first phase of communism and is generally called socialism by the Marxist. Whether socialism represents a stage in the transition to communism distinct from the dictatorship of the proletariat is susceptible to debate. In either case, it is certain that the dictatorship of the proletariat will remain during the phase of socialism along with its constitution, law, police, army, juridical and educational institutions.

Because the emergence of perfect communism requires a radical transformation of human motivation and value, the socialistic phase bears many of the faults of the old order. Although there is no private ownership of the means of production and since all are obliged to work, there is virtually only one class in the society, social distribution of the fruits of production, and so on, society still bears some of the economic, moral and intellectual features of capitalism.[10] Distribution of the fruits of production, for example, is based upon a utilitarian concept glorified under capitalism. Each worker receives in proportion to the intensity and value of his labor in relation to the production process — "from each according to his talents, to each according to his worth." Such distribution is made, moreover, only after a predetermined amount of commodities or their monetary worth is set aside for the replacement of capital, a reserve for accidents and the cost of state administration, education, medical care, etc. Marx admits a certain degree of justice in such distribution in that the workers receive in proportion to their contribution to society. Nevertheless, under the socialist system he maintains, some may still receive more than they need while others are receiving less than they and their families require for truly human existence. One cannot expect society to be any different as long as man's activities and motives are influenced by the remnants of capitalism and the imperfections existing within it.[11] But the new institutions of socialism will gradually produce new outlooks and new scales of value within society. With this transition of human nature will come the second or higher stage of communism, *the classless society*. The first or lower phase of communist society usually termed "socialism" can, according to Lenin, also properly be called "communism" insofar as the means of production have become common property. Yet he cautions that this lower phase is not complete communism. Only the future will bring this form of society. When it will come into being is a contingency not susceptible to prediction.[12]

Communism: The Classless Society

With the progress of time and man's thought, the classless society will appear. Perhaps the outstanding feature of this society in the eyes of Marx is that the principle of distribution is no longer based on the utility of the individual to society, but rather on fulfillment of needs — "from each according to his ability, to each according to his needs."[13] The individual is no longer enslaved by the division of labor and menial tasks. There is no division between mental and physical labors, for education and advanced technology will have lifted man from the degradation of unskilled labor and made labor the primary source of satisfaction of man's material and aesthetic needs. By means of labor the individual will become a fully developed and a fully free man.[14]

The state as the instrument and symbol of class exploitation will vanish with classes and their exploitation. The state as a government of *persons* will be replaced by the administration of *things* and by the regulation of the process of production. It is not abolished; it simply "withers away," since it is no longer of any use. As soon as there are no longer any classes to be held in subjection, as soon as the need for class exploitation and for economic aggression in the struggle for individual existence caused by the economic anarchy of capitalism no longer prevails, the need likewise ceases for a special organ to repress the collisions and excesses within the old system. As soon as the state really comes forward as the representative of all society and not as the representative of one of the classes, when it takes possession of the means of production in the name of all society, at that moment its existence is superfluous.[15]

The classless society will show forth man's true dignity. Gone will be the exploitation of man by man. The individual will no longer live merely for himself and his family, but for all mankind.[16] Society pools its labor, natural resources, capital and knowledge. It then enjoys the increased income resulting from this cooperation in a social manner according to real need. Men will no longer serve as mere commodities whose labor is bought and sold in the industrial marketplace for the sake of profit.[17] Men — their individual development, their intellectual expansion, their social and personal enrichment — are the primary concerns of the new society.[18] Such a society becomes then "an association in which the free development of each is the condition for the free development of all."[19]

Economic, political and moral freedom is not all that is predicted for the higher stage of communism. Technology will grant man a freedom of another species — a freedom based on man's ever-increasing mastery of his environment. Because of more efficient planning and better use of intellectual resources, science will have an unhindered growth. Men will no longer be subject to the blind forces of nature, but will act with full knowledge of the causes at work in nature as well as in themselves. Such knowledge represents freedom. As Engels points out, freedom does not consist in the dream of independence of the laws of nature, but rather *in the knowledge* of these laws and *in the possibility,* resulting from this knowledge, of systematically making the laws of nature work towards definite human goals. For freedom to the Marxist is *the realization of necessity*.[20]

The alienation of man from himself which reached its zenith under capitalism will disappear. Classless society, representing a form of social relationships most in keeping with man's deepest-felt needs symbolizes for the communist "the ascent of man from the realm of necessity to the realm of freedom."[21]

All the most significant tenets of modern communism were set forth previous to Marx in the history of social thought and reform. As V. I. Lenin points out,[22] Marxism was especially influenced by three sources of 19th century thought — German philosophy, and in particular that of Hegel and Feuerbach, English political economy as founded by Adam Smith and Ricardo, and French socialism, as represented especially in the thought of the so-called "Utopian Socialists," Count Henri de Saint-Simon, Charles Fourier and the Englishman, Robert Owen. Nevertheless, the communistic philosophy of Karl Marx and Frederick Engels represents a new synthesis and completeness, a new dynamism which caused it to triumph over all former varieties of socialism and communism. Even if one grants that Marxism is perhaps as much a result of previous currents of thought as the creation of the genius of Karl Marx, nonetheless it is necessary to concur with Professor Laski when he writes:

> The vital fact about him [Marx] is that he found communism a chaos and left it a movement. Through him it acquired a philosophy and a direction. Through him also, it became an international organization laying continuous emphasis upon the unified interest of the working-classes of all countries.[23]

This international organization made possible the seizure of power by the Bolsheviks under Lenin in the Russian revolution of 1917, the consequent survival of the Union of Soviet Socialist Republics, and the world-wide spread of Marxist communism in the present age.

Suggested Readings

CHAPTER I

Primary Sources

*Engels, F., *Socialism: Utopian and Scientific*, Part I.
Khrushchev, N. S., "Report to 21st Congress of C. P. S. U.," *Current Digest of the Soviet Press*, XI, No. 5 (March 11, 1959).
*Lenin, V. I., *The State and Revolution*, Chapters III and V.
———, *The Three Sources and Three Component Parts of Marxism*.
Marx, K., *Civil War in France*.
———, *Class Struggles in France*.
*———, *Critique of the Gotha Programme*.
———, *Eighteenth Brumaire of Louis Bonaparte*.
*Marx, K. and Engels, F., *Manifesto of the Communist Party*, especially Part III.
Stalin, J., *Foundations of Leninism*, Chapter IV.

Secondary Sources

*Berlin, Isaiah, *Karl Marx, His Life and Environment*, 2d ed., New York, Oxford University Press, 1959.
*Bober, M. M., *Karl Marx's Interpretation of History*, 2d. ed. rev., Cambridge, Harvard University Press, 1948, Chapter XIII.
Brinkley, G. A., "The 'Withering' of the State Under Khrushchev," *Review of Politics*, XXIII, No. 1 (1961), pp. 37-51.
Cole, G. D. H., *A History of Socialist Thought*, 4 vols., New York, St. Martin's Press, 1955, Vol. 1.
Jarrett, Bede, *Medieval Socialism*, London, Burns, Oates and Washburne, 1935.
Mayer, Gustav, *Friedrich Engels*, New York, Alfred A. Knopf, 1936.
Mehring, Franz, *Karl Marx*, London, Geo. Allen and Unwin, 1948.
*Wilson, Edmund, *To the Finland Station*, Garden City, N. Y., Doubleday and Co., 1947.
*Asterisk denotes the more essential reading.

FOOTNOTES TO CHAPTER I

1. See, for example, M. M. Bober, *Karl Marx's Interpretation of History*, 2d. ed. rev. (Cambridge, Mass., 1948), pp. 268-277.
2. See, for example, Chas. J. McFadden, *The Philosophy of Communism* (New York, 1939), pp. 157-172; R. N. Carew Hunt, *The Theory and Practice of Communism: An Introduction*, 5 ed. rev. (New York, 1961), pp. 158-163.
3. Karl Marx, "Letters to Joseph Weydemeyer, March 5, 1852," in *Karl Marx Selected Works*, ed. V. Adoratsky, 2 vols. (Moscow-Leningrad, 1935-1936), I, 377. Hereafter cited as *KMSW*. Cf. Marx, *The Class Struggles in France, KMSW*, II, 289; Lenin, *The State and Revolution* in *Lenin, Selected Works*, 2 vols. in 4. (Moscow, 1952), II, Part 1, 234, and *passim;* Joseph Stalin, *Foundations of Leninism*, in *Problems of Leninism* (Moscow, 1953), pp. 46-57.
4. K. Marx and Frederick Engels, preface to German edition (1872) of *Manifesto of the Communist Party, KMSW*, I, 190. Lenin, *The State and Revolution*, p. 234.
5. Stalin, *Foundations of Leninism*, pp. 50-51.
6. Engels, *Die Neue Zeit*, XX, Bd. 1 (1901-1902), 11.
7. Marx, *Civil War in France, KMSW*, II, pp. 498 f; Lenin, *The State and Revolution*, p. 234; Stalin, *Foundations of Leninism*, pp. 51-52.
8. Marx, *Civil War in France, KMSW*, II, 498-499. See also Marx and Engels, *Manifesto of the Communist Party, KMSW*, I, 227-228. Some of the reforms mentioned in the *Manifesto* were later considered by Marx and Engels to be subject to particular circumstances of time and place. Cf. preface to German edition of 1872 and preface to English edition of 1888, *KMSW*, I, 189-190 and 203.
9. Later in life Marx apparently did not limit the form of the proletarian state to that of the Paris Commune. Cf. Marx and Engels, *Selected Correspondence* (New York, 1942), p. 387. Lenin, moreover, states that the transition to communism will yield a variety of political forms under varied circumstances. *The State and Revolution*, pp. 234 and 257.
10. Cf. Marx, *The Critique of the Gotha Programme, KMSW*, II, 565; Lenin, *The State and Revolution*, pp. 294-298.
11. Cf. Marx, *The Critique of the Gotha Programme, KMSW*, II, pp. 562-565.

12. Lenin, *The State and Revolution*, pp. 299-300. The transition from socialism to the higher phase of communism began officially in the Soviet Union under N. S. Khrushchev. See, for example, his "Report to the 21st Congress of C.P.S.U.," *Current Digest of the Soviet Press*, XI, No. 5 (March 11, 1959).
13. Marx, *Critique of the Gotha Programme*, *KMSW*, II, p. 566.
14. *Ibid.*
15. Cf. Engels, *Socialism: Utopian and Scientific*, *KMSW*, I, p. 182.
16. Cf. Lenin, "A Great Beginning," in Lenin, *Selected Works*, II, Part 2, pp. 231-232.
17. Cf. Marx, *Wage-Labour and Capital*, *KMSW*, I, pp. 254-257.
18. Cf. Engels, *Herr Eugen Dühring's Revolution in Science* (*Anti-Dühring*) (London, 1940), pp. 310 and 322. Hereafter cited as Engels, *Anti-Dühring*.
19. Marx and Engels, *Manifesto of the Communist Party*, *KMSW*, I, p. 228.
20. Cf. Engels, *Anti-Dühring*, p. 128. This subject is treated further in Chapter IV below.
21. Engels, *Socialism: Utopian and Scientific*, *KMSW*, I, p. 186; *Anti-Dühring*, p. 312.
22. Lenin, *The Three Sources and Three Component Parts of Marxism*, *KMSW*, I, pp. 54-59.
23. Harold J. Laski, *Communism* (New York, 1927), p. 22.

CHAPTER II

MARXIST THEORY OF TRUTH
(HISTORICAL MATERIALISM)

Having had a glimpse at the historical meaning of Marxian communism, we may now apply ourselves to its intellectual content. The first task is to examine the communist approach to understanding reality, and in particular, the understanding of that reality in its relation to man.

Precedence of Matter over Spirit and Consciousness

"The basic question of all philosophy, especially of modern philosophy," says Engels, "is that concerning the relation of thinking and being."[1] This basic question resolves itself for Engels into the relationship of spirit to nature, that is, it resolves itself into the question of whether spirit or nature is primary, whether God created the world or whether the world has been in existence eternally, with the notion of God having been created in the material brain of man. On this question all of philosophy has split into two camps:

> Those who asserted the primacy of spirit to nature and, therefore, in the last instance, assumed world creation in some form or other . . . comprised the camp of idealism. The others, who regarded nature as primary, belong to the various schools of materialism.[2]

Engels proceeds to equate materialism (matter over spirit) with an epistemological realism (the world exists independently of our knowing it, independently of consciousness). In fact it is this epistemological position that is signified by the term "materialism" for the Marxist more often than an ontological position. It is found not only in Engels[3] but in Lenin and Stalin as well. Lenin for example proclaims:

> Materialism in general recognizes objectively real being (matter) as independent of the consciousness, sensation, experience, etc., of humanity. . . . Consciousness is only the reflection of being, at best an approximately true (adequate, perfectly exact) reflection of it.[4]

And Stalin adds forcefully:

> Contrary to idealism, which asserts that only our consciousness really exists, and that the material world being, nature, exists only in our consciousness, in our sensations, ideas and perceptions, the Marxist materialist philosophy holds that matter, nature, being, is an objective reality existing outside and independent of our consciousness; that matter is primary, since it is the source of sensations, ideas, consciousness and that consciousness is secondary, derivative, since it is a reflection of matter, a reflection of being. . . .[5]

Anyone who rejects idealism becomes a materialist in the eyes of the Marxist. All arguments in contemporary thought that tend towards an epistemological realism are used by him as proof for the materialistic thesis. Apparently the Marxist refuses to consider the possibility of holding a realistic position in epistemology without in any way denying non-material being.

Matter is primary in respect to its origins, and consciousness only arises later from matter. The proof of this assertion, claims the Marxist, lies in the realm of concrete experience. From common experience it is seen that sensation is associated only in the higher forms of matter. It is only in the evolution of matter that sensation comes about. Sensation is somewhat potentially contained in matter[6] which must go through some dialectical "leaps," or qualitative changes, at a definite stage in the historical development of matter. A high level of sensation is called *consciousness*, which is basically a reflection, a mirroring internally by ghly organized matter of processes occurring inside and outside of itself. Objective physiological processes are accompanied in the nerve centers by their inner, subjective expression which takes the form of consciousness. That which in itself is an objective matter process is at the same time, for an organism equipped with a brain, a subjective mental act.[7] Just as there is a qualitative distinction between inorganic and organic matter, between sensate and non-sensate matter, so also there is a qualitative distinction to be made between human and animal consciousness. The most essential distinction between human and animal intellect is the fact that only human understanding is capable of dialectical or progressive thought, resulting from the ability to investigate the nature of concepts themselves.[8] This ability of man represents a special property of the highly organized matter of the human brain. How the transition to this higher order of intellectual activity took place, the Marxist considers to be a yet unsolved problem. Engels felt he saw the beginnings of human consciousness in higher animal life. The dog, for instance, must possess generic concepts since it is able to distinguish quadrupeds and bipeds; it must be able to analyze unknown objects since it can identify unseen objects by sound, and finally, it must synthesize its thoughts as when it performs artful tricks.[9] Soviet scientists consider that they have found the beginnings of intellect among some anthropoid apes who are able to reach a food-target by means of alternate routes and the employment of certain objects as tools.[10] Likewise there is the claim of detecting "primary abstractions" among chimpanzees in their ability to separate colored properties from those of size and shape.[11] Nevertheless, the Marxist insists that these animal manifestations of intellect represent only the pre-history of the human intellect. An essential or qualitative difference separates the human mind from mere animal thought processes.

As has been seen, Marxism adheres to an epistemological realism. Not only does matter have a priority over knowledge, but it is possible for this matter *to be known*. Of course, all materialistic philosophies have held that the eternal world is knowable and reflected in human consciousness. Lenin remarks:

> The "naïve realism" of any healthy person who has not been an inmate of a lunatic asylum or a pupil of the idealistic

philosophers consists in the view that things, the environment, the world, exist *independently* of our sensations, of our consciousness, of our *self,* and of man in general. The same *experience* . . . that has produced in us a firm conviction that *"independently"* of us there exists other people, and not mere complexes of my sensations of high, short, yellow, hard, etc. —this same *experience* produces in us the conviction that things, the world, the environment exist independently of us. Our sensation, our consciousness is only *an image* of the external world and it is obvious that an image cannot exist without the thing imaged, and that the latter exists independently of that which images it. Materialism *deliberately* makes the "naïve" belief of mankind the foundation of its theory of knowledge.[12]

Yet pre-Marxian materialism conceived of knowledge as a passive contemplation of reality, a reflection of the world in consciousness by a purely mechanistic process. It over-simplified the process of knowledge and failed to appreciate its dialectical nature. Marxism counters this with its "copy-theory" of knowledge, first propounded by Engels and later expanded by Lenin.

According to this theory, things exist independently of our consciousness and our perceptions. Our representations and concepts of them arise through the operations of the external world upon our sense organs. These representations depict or "mirror" the world outside. They are "pictures," "mirror-images," "copies" of the objects without. Further, there is no difference in principle between the phenomenon and the thing-in-itself. This reflection of reality in consciousness is not to be thought of as a momentary act or as a static photograph of reality. Just as the external world is a process—a process of development—so knowledge too is a process in which we move from a state of ignorance to a state of knowing whereby things are transferred from things-in-themselves into things-for-us. Our knowledge is not ready made and unalterable, but just as knowledge emerges from ignorance so, too, inexact knowledge becomes ever more complete and more exact.[13]

Human knowledge is dialectical. Its contradiction is found between the unlimited character of things to be known and the definite limitations of human knowledge in any one historical epoch. The dialectical process leads us from matter unknown to consciousness as it occurs in our sensation, from thence to abstract thought transcending sense. From abstract thought, one then rises to practice. This is the complete dialectical road to knowledge of the truth, to knowledge of objective reality.[14] Sense perception merely reflects the appearance of things, their outer generality and their outer connectedness. Sense knowledge fails, however, to grasp the relationships and laws involved, or the element of causal connection. This is the work of abstractive knowledge which penetrates into the essence of things, seeks out the inner unity behind the outward resemblance, discovers the "general" in the singular, extracts the essential from the mass of accidental particulars.

The ascent from singular appearance to general essence — provided it is correct — does not get farther away from the truth even though it does move farther from the concrete things themselves. Abstract knowledge, rather, comes closer to the truth; it presents a deeper, more faithful, more complete, scientific reflection of reality.[15] The Marxist is seen to take a middle ground between a complete empiricism on one hand and a complete rationalism on the other. Against the strict empiricists such as Hobbes, Locke and Feuerbach, who hold that sense perceptions are the only source of knowledge, and likewise against the rationalists such as Descartes, Spinoza and Leibniz, who thought it possible to attain knowledge of the world by speculation without regard to sense knowledge, the Marxist looks upon both types of knowledge as essential stages in the knowing process.

But the copy theory alone does not suffice to furnish all the necessary ingredients of the knowledge process.

Precedence of Practical Truth over Speculation

There is a further important aspect to be considered in the Marxist theory of truth, and this is the role of "practice" in the process of manifesting truth. For though the knowing process begins in sensation and advances to abstract thought, it only completes itself "on the basis of the development of socio-historical practice, which emerges in the class-society as the practice of a particular class."[16] Material reality is perfectly reflected only in social consciousness. The knowing subject must be conceived, not in an abstract idealist fashion as "consciousness," "soul" or "thought," not as a logical or psychological "subject," nor as "man as such," but rather as man the socially active being, the representative of a particular class.[17] "Practice" is the material activity of man — above all the production of goods, but also the class-struggle and the political, scientific and artistic life of men. As such, practice serves in a twofold capacity in regard to human knowledge. First, it serves as the foundation of knowledge; secondly, as the "third stage" of the knowing process, it serves as the criterion of truth.[18]

It is the socio-historical practice in any epoch which sets the context or the social environment in which the act of knowledge in the individual takes place. It is within this particular social environment that the sensations and abstract thought take place. Thus practice is the very "foundation of the entire knowing-process, from beginning to end."[19] The Soviet philosopher, Rutkevich, sees this as flowing from the social character of human thought:

> ... dialectical materialism views the individual act of thought in any one of the innumerable human heads as a particle of the historical process of knowledge embracing the world as a whole, in which this particle is organically incorporated. Our thinking is not, therefore, that of an isolated individual. And since our knowing is a socio-historical process, it is also conditioned by the development of social practice.[20]

But social practice also functions as the criterion of truth. Marxism looks at truth as the correspondence of thought with reality, but the proof for this correspondence is not found exclusively in the contemplative apprehension of the world, but more surely in the struggle to change it.[21] In practice man must prove the truth, that is, he must prove the reality and power of his thinking. Especially by experiment and industry can man show the correctness of his conception of natural processes by reduplicating the process himself and by making it serve his own purpose.[22] Experiment is not the only source of verification, however. The Marxist does not reduce practice to experiment. Naturally, there are certain observations where experimental verification is not possible. But even beyond this, there is a more decisive form of criterional practice. This is the role played by the workers in the production process and their political activity in the class-struggle.[23] The more completely the interests of the working class find expression in social practice, the more surely will the objective and universal laws of reality be made manifest to the human mind. As will be seen, it is the subjective interests of the working class, according to Marx's conception of history, that best represent the objective laws of reality in their present phase of development. This is the perfect unity of theory and practice.

Objective truth, then, for the Marxist is the content of human thought as tested in practice, and in conformity with objects independent of the knowing subject and humanity in general.[24] It is discovered in the historical development of the knowledge of social man. As such, it is not a static thing, but a process. Man cannot grasp the full extent of objective truth in one and the same instant; he can only seek to come increasingly closer to it by gradual steps.[25] This progressive accumulation of truth is termed, "relative truth." Relative truth represents a moment or stage in the knowledge of truth. This is not to imply mutability in the object of knowledge. Still, at any given historical stage a phenomenon is reflected in man's consciousness with only an approximate, relative accuracy, and only to a certain degree of depth.[26] It is still capable of unlimited further exactness. Within relative truth, however, there is, for Lenin, an "absolute truth."[27] Absolute truth consists in:

> . . . an absolutely exact agreement of thought with its object, *i.e.*, a content of our knowledge such that neither now nor in the future, in consequence of the further development of knowledge, can ever be proved false.[28]

Examples of such absolute truths are, for the Marxist, the fundamental theses of communist philosophy such as the economic theory of history, the class struggle, the collapse of capitalism, the triumph of socialism, the material nature of the universe and its dialectical motion, as well as many lesser tenets. These truths have been confirmed in practice and nothing in the future can ever refute them.[29]

The unity of speculative knowledge with practical activity is understandable only in the light of the Marxist conception of history wherein intellectual activity is construed as a function of economic practice. If reality is most truly reflected in social consciousness, then it is this sociological truth that is most vital, most meaningful to man. Such truth is to be found in the proper interpretation of man's history, an interpretation which shows forth the dynamic of that history.

Historical Materialism

Marx's theory of history was not meant to be a mere speculative hypothesis, a prophetic revelation, or just an opportunist weapon in the hands of revolutionaries. It was, for him, the practical, scientific generalization of laws flowing from the investigation of historical facts. It was to be the statement of scientifically derived laws governing the process of social evolution, laws to be observed in the transformation of human nature from one historical epoch to another. The cornerstone of the theory is this. Men make their own history, and yet, in another sense they do not make their own history because they do not do so spontaneously under conditions they themselves have chosen. They make history upon terms already determined and handed down to them.

As Engels puts it:

> . . . we have seen that the many individual wills active in history for the most part produce results quite other than those they intended — often quite the opposite; their motives therefore in relation to the total result are likewise of only secondary significance. On the other hand, the further question arises: What driving forces in turn stand behind these motives? What are the historical causes which transform themselves into these motives in the brains of the actors?[30]

These historical causes are represented in the inner laws of the economic development of mankind. Of all the factors determining historical development, the decisive element is pre-eminently the production and reproduction of life and its material requirements. The first premise of human existence and, therefore, of all history is that man must be able to live in order to make history. The first historical act is hence the production of the means to satisfy these essential needs. Economic necessity is the foundation upon which all other parts of the social structure must be built. The ultimate determinant of social change is to be found in the mode of production and exchange of material necessities by which men live. Economics is the foundation or the substructure of society on which a superstructure of laws and political institutions is based, as well as philosophy, art, literature, morality and religion. The entire superstructure of a society is the result of the economic methods of production in use at that time.

> In the social production which men carry on they enter into definite relations that are indispensable and independent of their will; these relations of production correspond to a definite stage of development of their material forces of production. The sum total of these relations of production constitutes the economic structure of society — the real foundation, on which rises a legal and political superstructure and to which correspond definite forms of social consciousness. The mode of production in material life determines the social, political and intellectual life processes in general.[31]

History shows this to be true, claims Marx. Feudal society, for example, transformed all its institutions to suit its economic needs. Law was such as to fix men into a landholding system which revolved to the benefit of landlords. Even the Church adopted itself to the economic needs of feudalism. Instead of being the prophet of equality, it neatly adjusted its doctrines to the social hierarchy feudalism needed. As medieval society declined, the merchant class arose and with it a state which in its law emphasized the inviolability of private property. Little by little it cleared away the concepts and institutions which were part of the medieval social structure and replaced them with others built upon the notion of contract. The individual took on new importance. This was reflected in the sphere of religion as well as politics. Protestantism, with its emphasis upon the individual and his conscience as the legitimate spiritual authority, replaced Rome. The petty sovereignties gave way to the concept of nationalism, because a national government was better suited to help commerce by the promotion of order and legal simplicity. And so on, throughout every age, the student of history finds not a free flow of human events, but concrete necessities set by an economic environment which makes them inevitable. "It is not the consciousness of men that determines their being, but on the contrary, their social being that determines their consciousness."[32]

Though the production of the means of life, "the economic base," is the decisive factor in historical movement and social transformation it is by no means for Marx and Engels the only element operating causally. Political, juridical, philosophical, religious, literary, artistic development is based on economic development, to be sure. But all these also react upon one another as well as on the economic base itself. It is not as though the economic mode of production is the only active cause while everything has only a passive effect. Rather, there is an interaction on the basis of economic necessity, which ultimately must assert itself.[33]

> The economic situation is the basis, but various elements of the superstructure . . . also exercise their influence upon the historical struggles and in many cases preponderate in determining their *form*. There is an interaction of all these elements in which, amid all the endless *host* of accidents . . . the economic movement finally asserts itself as necessary . . . there are innumerable intersecting forces, an infinite series of parallelograms of forces which give rise to one resultant — the historical event.[34]

At each stage of history one finds in it a sum of productive forces, historically caused relations of individuals to the environment and to one another which are handed down to each generation from the previous one. These relations are indeed modified by the new generation, yet they at the same time prescribe the conditions of life, and determine the special character of their further modification and development. Men are products of circumstances. Yet it must never be forgotten that these circumstances are the result of previous generations of men and their activity, and that these very circumstances will themselves be changed by men.[35] Thus, the Marxian concept of history is basically this. Man changes history and is thereby himself changed. All history, then, is nothing other than a continual transformation of human nature.[36]

Throughout their numerous writings, Marx and Engels engaged in considerable analysis and dissection of economic production in order to demonstrate that humanity, in any one historical period, is ultimately determined by the mode of production present in that particular epoch. Yet because historical materialism is above all an ideology, and hence a philosophy of action *(praxis)*,[37] Marx is primarily interested, not in why man can in abstraction be said to be what he is, but rather in why concretely he changes within the progression of history.[38] Since for Marx, human nature in any period is determined by the underlying mode of production, it follows that the concrete changes in man can only be referred ultimately to the concrete sequences of change in the modes of production.

The ultimate determinant of human behavior, and hence the primary conditioning factor in the transformation of human nature is for Marx, modes of production which are employed in the maintenance of human life. The mode of production is a definite form of human activity, a definite manner of life.[39] In fact it is the central expression of human life. As individuals express their life, so they are. What they are coincides with their production, both with *what* they produce and with *how* they produce. The nature of humans thus depends on the material conditions determining their production.[40] If it is true that human nature is determined by the character of its productive activities, then the general conditions of production — that is, the conditions without which production could not take place — are likewise the primitive determinants of man's nature. For Marx, human nature is not an abstraction inherent in, or assigned to, each single individual. For him it is, rather, the *ensemble* of all social relations that constitutes the human essence in any historical epoch.[41] Yet it should be remembered that Marx did not reduce human nature just to

20

this class nature. He made a distinction between constant "fixed drives which exist under all circumstances and which can be changed by social conditions only as far as form and direction are concerned" and "relative drives which owe their origin to a certain type of social organization."[42]

A mode of production may be said to be composed of the "factors of production." These are four in number. Naturally, production presupposes the existence of a needful organism, that is, it presupposes a subject of production, mankind.[43] This then is to be the first factor in the process of production. Since production is essentially an activity carried on for the satisfaction of human wants, it also presupposes the existence of that which is needed, *viz.*, "the object, nature."[44] Production then is the fitting of natural substances to human wants. Thus a second condition of production, and one which, along with human needs, serves as an instrument in determining the particular mode of production is the character of the natural environment in which the needs arise. The way in which men produce their means of subsistence depends primarily on the nature of the actual means they find in existence and have to reproduce.[45]

If the subject, mankind, involves externally a relation with nature in determining its production, it likewise involves within itself a relation that can properly be called "social," *i.e.*, a relation involving mutual and cooperative human activity toward an end.[46]

> In production, men not only act on nature but also on one another. They produce only by cooperating in a certain way and mutually exchange their activities. In order to produce, they enter into definite connections and relations with one another and only within these social connections and relations does their action on nature, their production, take place.[47]

For Marx, as for Aristotle, man is a *zoon politikon,* a social animal. All production is an appropriation of nature by the individual only within and through a definite form of society. Since the social relations described constitute an element of production which in its turn delimits the nature of individuals, Marx does not hesitate to conclude that man is an animal which can develop from organism to individual only in society.[48] True production by an individual outside the forces of society would be as great an absurdity as the idea of the development of language without community life and communication.[49] Production is social, man is social, the myth of the social contract and the *laissez-faire* economists notwithstanding.[50]

This social relation no less than the relation to natural environment is a condition of production, and hence, in its own particular way, a determinant of human nature.

A fourth and final condition of productive activity is the instrument of labor. The instruments of labor comprise the realm of tools and industrial technique. They are, for Marx, that ". . . which the labourer interposes between himself and the subject of his labour, and which [serve] as the conductor of his activity."[51] As such, they join the human being to nature and, secondly, through them his activity is transferred to nature.[52] Nature's material becomes adapted to the needs of man; labor and nature become identified in a *product*.[53] Human labor has incorporated itself with nature: "the former is materialized, the latter transformed."

Tools and technique, however, likewise serve to separate man from direct contact with nature. It is the instrument of labor that man directly controls and manipulates, not nature; it is the tool that acts on nature.[54] In this sense, tools can first be said to separate man physically from the object of his work.

In another aspect, too, there is a separation of man and nature. Most instruments of labor, being neither a gift of nature, nor inventions of the immediate users, nor even the direct creative manipulation of nature by any one generation of workers,[55] are the result of hundreds of labor processes that lie between them and nature, from whence sprung their raw material.

For Marx and Engels, these four factors are the structural components of the production process wherever, whenever and in whatever form it historically appears. The two factors, human labor and its social milieu constitute the subjective side of the process. On the objective side, the other two factors, the natural object of labor, and the instruments, together compose for Marx, "the means of production."[56] Speaking in the abstract, these four general conditions of production — labor, its social organization, its instruments and its object — are all co-responsible but, may, in differing circumstances exercise unequal causality.[57] Which factor is dominant cannot be decided *a priori*, but is to be found only through empirical and historical investigation. Any attempt to generalize or predict conclusions in this area is a misconstruction of the productive process.[58]

Yet it can be known *a priori* that the relation between the factors is one of interdependence, interaction and mutual transformation. For the Marxist knows in advance that humanity will both modify and be modified by nature, society and the instruments it employs, and that each of these and the processes which involve it with human nature will acquire its specific characteristics from the character of the total historical milieu of which these factors and their interdependent relationships are integral parts.[59]

What conditions must prevail in order that the various changes in the modes of production come about? What took place in the history of man that caused the various modes of production — communal ownership in the primitive ages, slavery in the classical world, feudalism of the middle ages and finally capitalism — to develop and grow each in its turn, only to be supplanted by another? In every case, Marx and Engels felt, a point in the development of the mode of production has been reached when certain subjective factors and certain objective factors have come into conflict within the economic system. This conflict has become so irreconcilable that the only possible outcome is the complete destruction of the system in a sudden revolutionary manner and its replacement with a new one. Up until this point has been reached, these factors have been in opposition to one another, but have by their opposition actually fomented the maximum development and fruitfulness of the productive forces — for no social order ever disappears before all the productive forces in it have been developed.[60] After this point of maximum development has been reached, the opposition ceases to be constructive, the conflict becomes such that there is a complete rupture within the system and its superstructure. Political forms, laws, mores, beliefs and behavior patterns of men are transformed. A new mode of production and a new form of society with a transformed human nature comes into being.

At a certain stage of their development, the material forces of production in society come in conflict with the existing relations of production, or—what is but a legal expression for the same thing—with the property relations within which they have been at work before. From forms of development of the forces of production these relations turn into their fetters. Then begins an epoch of social revolution. With the change of the economic foundation the entire immense superstructure is more or less rapidly transformed.[61]

Some of the factors of production develop more rapidly than do others. The former, Marx refers to as "the forces of production," the latter, "the relations of production." As long as a system of production is in a stage of expanding or progressive development, all the factors of production, the human, the social, the natural and the technical are able to be considered forces of production. As the system becomes senile and approaches its violent end, some of these same factors cease to be forces of production.[62] What are these factors which are no longer forces of production? What are these laggard relations of production? Although the phrase "relations of production" is used ambiguously in the writings of Marx and Engels, the term in this context refers simply to the property relations or the system of ownership of the forces of production which prevails in any one system. It is these property or ownership relations which eventually clash with the forces of production. The forces of production are inevitably more powerful, the restrictive property relations are destroyed and the factors of production appear in a totally new form.

How do these abstractions show themselves concretely in present society? Under capitalism, how and why do the productive forces stand in opposition to property ownership? To the Marxist, the conflict within capitalism can be expressed as one of essential incompatibility between social production and capitalistic or individual appropriation.[63] In the medieval period of the artisan, production was for the most part individualistic. The laborer was responsible for the completion of the whole product from raw material to the finished product. As a rule, the raw material belonged to him; he fashioned this with his own tools by means of his own labor or that of his family. His ownership of the product was based on his own labor, therefore. The production of the product was relatively individualistic and the ownership rightly belonged to the sole producers. As long as the means of production were owned by their individual users, appropriation of the product could justly remain private. Yet by the very fact of individual ownership of the means of production, the potential development of them was greatly restricted. The only way they could develop and become enlarged into the modern gigantic system of production of the present day was to come under a new system of productive relations which allowed for a great concentration of ownership in the hands of a few. Historically, this was accomplished by the bourgeois revolution and the ensuing capitalistic system.

Under capitalism, the relations of production substituted a highly concentrated for a highly diversified ownership of the forces of production. Moreover, modern production took on a social character. Instruments of modern industry as well as the workers who use them are gathered together in large concentrations, and the division of labor is highly developed. No one man is responsible for the completion of the whole product, but shares responsibility for it with perhaps thousands who are likewise engaged in the productive enterprise. No one can say of the finished product: "This is my product; this is what my labor has fashioned for human use." No worker can at the termination of the day's labor appropriate even one article at the end of the assembly line without being liable for theft. And rightly so, says the Marxist, for the production is no longer individual but social.

The contradiction of capitalism lies in the fact that in spite of the social character of production the appropriation is still individual and private. The owner of the instruments of labor continues to appropriate the product as under the artisan system although it is no longer his product, but exclusively the product of others' labor.[64] The individuals who privately appropriate the product of social labor are often those who contribute little or nothing to the labor process, but in virtue of inherited stock certificates, for example, allow others to perform the tasks of producing and distributing the products they now own. This very contradiction between social production and individual appropriation contributed to the rapid development of man's economic potential in the early stages of capitalism. And this, of course, was a significant step away from the stifling conditions present under feudalistic economies. Capitalism in the eyes of the Marxist, represents a progressive leap in the history of mankind — a throwing off of the repressive feudal bonds.[65] But now the development has ceased and capitalism is in its death-throes. The relations of ownership have ceased to be forces of production but have become fetters on the further economic development of mankind. Progress has become subordinated, or merely serves as a means to personal advantage and profit. These ownership relations must be destroyed to be replaced by others. Mankind is now ready, claims the Marxist, to complement social production with social appropriation, by which those who produce the products by their combined labor will also collectively own the product as well as the instruments of labor. By means of the complete overthrow of capitalism, a sweeping away of the old conditions of production, man will enter a new era of socialism where each will receive in proportion to his contribution. These conditions will in time gradually give way to a higher stage of communism where each will contribute to the labor process according to his ability and receive according to his needs.

Classes and the Class Struggle

A comprehension of the factors of production and their coordinating causality yet falls short of satisfactorily explaining the historical materialist theory of human causality and its role in the search for truth. What has been seen at this stage is that human nature at any given period is determined by the underlying mode of production, and that the mode of production undergoes various changes when certain specified conditions prevail. Now if human nature is determined by the mode of production then it follows obviously that change in human nature should rightly be attributed to the sequence of changes in the modes of production. As was mentioned previously, this aspect of humanity, *viz.*, its actual historical change is that which is of utmost importance to the practical and ideologically bent minds of Marx and his disciples. Thus, the central principle to be discovered by Marx and Engels in their life-long historical investigations and consequent inductions and synthesis, is precisely the proximate principle of the actual historical development of productive systems. How, specifically, is the revolutionary overthrow of productive systems accomplished? As V. Venable has forcefully pointed out, the answer for Marx and Engels is not to be found in the dialectic — as though it were some blind motive force in history moving people to confiscate feudal estates, to operate publicly bourgeois factories, to overthrow the opposing class, and so on. "The dialectic has nothing to do whatever with the matter. The dialectic for Marx and Engels is not a thing, but merely the formal structure of actual processes, both social and natural."[66] Rather, the agent cause of the process of social revolution is simply the human element of production, namely man, and his motive is nothing other than human need. It is man and not the dialectic with its contradictions of production that is the maker of history.

If the collective dictates of individual human needs brings about results that are consonant with dialectical principles and Marxian predictions, so much the sounder Marxism and dialectics. But the result is not the cause. If the revolutionary rupture of restrictive property relations liberates the forces of production along with the human beings who have been oppressed by them, so much the better for these forces, but it was the humanly intolerable state of the oppressed classes not their abstract desire to remove a dialectical impasse from the current economy that was the primary cause.[67]

Thus for Marx and Engels the dynamics of history is not to be sought in the terms of contradiction between the expanding forces of production and their restrictive relations, but as they state so clearly in the beginning of the *Communist Manifesto*,[68] it is to be sought in terms of class conflicts — those continuing, deadly struggles which are the genitors of the social evolution that constitutes history. This is not to imply that the class struggle and the contradictions among the forces of production are unrelated. The productive forces are the result of practical human energy.

Yet this energy is itself conditioned by the circumstances in which men find themselves because of productive forces already won in the struggles of former generations.[69] The existence of the particular classes "is bound up with particular, historic phases in the development of production."[70] It is the production process that ultimately determines which classes exist in society; determines, through division of labor, who belongs to them; and determines too, the direction of their ensuing struggle. Yet it is only by means of the human struggle that the restrictive aspects of the production process can be overcome, that a new mode of production as well as all the economic relations which are the necessary conditions of that particular mode of production can come about, and that a new class structure can result. For the Marxist it is the class struggle which can truly be called the motor of human history.

In the present epoch, society is divided into two great groups, the capitalists or bourgeoisie, and the wage-earners or proletarians. The outstanding distinction between the two is the fact that one lives by owning, the other lives by and is dependent upon wages. About minor features of distinction, Marx is not concerned. Some wage-earners may own investments, some capitalists may manage their interests. But in whatever way the classes are subdivided, the essential point is that one class is united to itself by the fact it lives primarily on the sale of its labor, and the other by the fact that it owns the means of production. These two classes, the bourgeoisie and the proletariat, are, like the opposing classes of every age, with the exception of the age of primitive communism, engaged in a struggle from which will arise a new mode of production and a new society.

But the present struggle is unique in that it is the final struggle —for there is to arise from this, as from no other class struggle, the abolition of all classes and the creation of a free and equal society. In a preface to the *Communist Manifesto,* Engels writes:

> . . . all history has been a history of class struggles, of struggles between exploited and exploiting, between dominated and dominating; classes at various stages of social evolution; . . . this struggle, however, has now reached a stage where the exploited and oppressed class (the proletariat) can no

longer emancipate itself from the class which exploits and oppresses it (the bourgeoisie), without at the same time forever freeing the whole of society from exploitation, oppression and class struggles. . . ."[71]

This golden age of classless society does not come about immediately upon the proletariat gaining political supremacy over the bourgeoisie by revolution. "In developments of such magnitude, twenty years are more than a day — so later on days may come in which twenty years are embodied."[72] In the meantime, the proletariat is forced by circumstances to form its own dictatorship as the bourgeoisie had, for all practical purposes, done before them. By striving with every means known to man to destroy all control by the bourgeoisie and to put all instruments of production under the supervision of the proletarian state, the state will finally "wither away" and all men will live harmoniously as brothers in a classless society ever developing and strengthening its freedom.[73]

The Marxist Concept of Social Class

A cardinal point in the Marxist social theory of truth is that it is classes which, through the actions of past societies of men, determine in considerable measure the character of the general environment into which an individual is born. It is classes which set the pattern of his social environment. It is classes which, by assigning him a specific role in the division of labor, determine the manner in which he will deal with that environment. It is classes which, in their revolutionary struggle, overthrow productive systems, transform ownership relations, establish new classes, new divisions of labor and actually change human nature. For Marx it is classes, in the last analysis, that have stamped men with their behavior patterns, institutions and cultures. And since the nature of the individual is to be determined by the position that he occupies in the social relations of production,[74] that is by his class, change in human nature is determined in the long run by what new social relations and new classes, the conflict of classes produce. Thus the whole process of human socialization as we now know it, and as it has been known in all historical ages, with the exception of the primitive stage of communal ownership, has been causally determined to a great extent by class and class activity. *A fortiori,* all social control, as the state and law which serve as instruments of the dominant class, become determined by class and class conflict. It is ultimately class conflict through which social "leaps" take place, and which consequently is to be considered the dynamic of history.

Moreover, it is the ideas of the ruling class that are in every phase of history the ruling ideas. The class which is the dominating economic force of society is at the same time its ruling intellectual force. In having the means of material production at its disposal this class has control at the same time over the means of mental production, so that thereby the ideas of those who lack the means of mental production are subject to it.[75] Thus even the value choices of a society are for Marx, class-controlled.

With such emphasis by Marx on the great initiative power and influence of the social class, we would do well to come to some clear understanding of what he meant by class.

In the last pages of the last volume of *Capital,* Marx begins what was intended to be his definitive analysis of classes,[76] but he was able to complete only three paragraphs. However, this fact cannot be said to deprive us of a possible understanding of his meaning, for scattered throughout his and Engels' works there are frequent discussions of it. His theory seems to be as follows. Conflict or basic incompatibility of interest is of the essence of class. Classes are simply the distinctions that may be made among men on the basis of their position in society in terms of the *relations* of production. And since relations of production are definable in terms of ownership and non-ownership of the forces of production such as labor, natural resources and the instruments of labor, the class to which any man belongs may be discovered by determining what forces of production he owns relative to the general distribution of ownership within the system. Under the capitalist mode of production, therefore, the bourgeois class is composed of those who, having deprived workers of a portion of the value of their labor, hold title to the raw materials, auxiliary materials and the tools or instruments of labor used in the production process — that is, it is composed of those who own the "constant capital," those means of production which in the Marxian analysis, do not in the process of production, undergo any quantitative alteration of value. The proletarian class is composed of those who, while not owning constant capital, contribute labor-power or "variable capital" to the production process and consequently cause the value increase resulting from production. Since the bourgeoisie own the constant capital by means of depriving the worker of some of the value-increment arising from his labor,[77] the distinction of class in terms of ownership must always presuppose a more basic distinction resting on a relationship of exploiter to exploited. Nonetheless, the Marxist, N. Bukharin, correctly defined the social class when he termed it ". . . the aggregate of persons *playing the same parts in production, standing in the same relation towards other persons in the production process, these relations being also expressed in things* (instruments of labor)."[78]

Classes, then, are to be distinguished by their role in production, a role expressed in the property relations of the society. Production, in turn, implies the need for distribution of the products resulting therefrom. The forms of distribution will correspond to the forms of production. Thus, the position of the class in production will determine its position in distribution. It seems that it is in the arena of distribution that the antagonism between the classes arises. Although as Marx makes quite clear,[79] the criterion of class is ownership, not relative income, nonetheless, the conflict does not seem to arise directly because the one class is monopolizing the tools and natural resources while the other possesses nothing of the means of production. Rather, the antagonism appears to come about because of the contradiction in income, that is, in a contradiction between the shares held by each class in the product manufactured. The immediate basis of the class conflict, therefore, in Marxian theory, is the efforts of the classes to increase or conserve their share in the distribution of the total mass of products. This is the most primitive and general expression of class interests. Marx attempts to show that under the wage system of capitalism there is necessarily periodical resistance on the part of the workingmen against a reduction of wages, and periodical attempts at getting a rise in wages. Since he also shows that a general rise in wages would result in a fall in the general rate of profit, and vice versa, he concludes that there must be an incessant struggle between capital and labor in the area of distribution of the product.[80] Of course, the economic basis for this conflict under capitalism is to be found in Marx's surplus-value theory.[81] Class struggles in the ancient world took the form chiefly of a contest between debtors and creditors.[82]

If ownership of the forces of production comes about by the deprivation of value-increment of one class by the owner class, and this, in turn, results in an antagonistic distribution of the products to the non-owner class, then in the system of class society, the process of production, for Marx, is a process of exploitation — above all, economic exploitation, but political and moral oppression as well.

In the bourgeois-proletarian society, for instance, the proletariat produce a greater share of the product than they receive, for a twofold reason. First, a portion of the product or of its value is accumulated by the owners of the means of production for extending the productive process. Second, the proletariat, in working for the owners of the capital and tools is actually supporting them. In so doing, the worker is the victim of exploitation; he becomes, in a sense, an economic semi-slave.[83] The bourgeois class, although a numerical minority, becomes dominant and free thereby from exploitation. Its main effort is to maintain and extend the opportunities for economic exploitation. The effort of the proletariat is directed principally towards liberation from this exploitation. This can come about only through the construction of a new form of society in which the proletariat becomes the dominant exploitative class. But this class-controlled society too, must give way in time to one in which no class conflict and, consequently, no exploitation is possible. Such a society, for Marx, must be classless, propertyless and stateless as well.

Since ownership of the means of production makes possible the exploitation of the labor power of the non-owner, or to look at the other side of the coin, frees the owner from such exploitation by others, a man's class can also be determined by the extent he is free to exploit and free from being exploited. In the anticipated social system of the Marxist, the restrictive, lagging property relations as represented by private ownership, will be drastically altered. With this modification will come about as a consequence, the disappearance of the unequal distribution of freedom. All forces of production are to be socially owned; that which is socially produced is to be socially distributed. No one is free to exploit; freedom from exploitation is universal. There are, therefore, no classes.

It is precisely the exploitation of man by man in class society that makes such a form of society degrading to man, and makes a complete structural revision of present society imperative for the Marxist. For him it is only in a classless society completely free of all economic, political and moral oppression that man can recognize his full dignity and his full creative and technological potential. The class structure of society must be overcome, but this is to be accomplished only by the proletarian class becoming dominant and exploiting the bourgeoisie to the point of extinction. Only then will the diverse forms of exploitation begin to wither away and the new history of mankind begin.

Marx's Concept of Class and Modern Sociology — Appendix II-a

To what extent does the concept of class envisioned by Marx coincide with such concepts as the *category,* the *class,* the *group,* etc. current in modern sociological analysis?

From the Marxist notion of class given above, it is seen that to some degree it embraces the modern sociological concept of category, and to some degree not. A social category may be defined as a plurality of persons who are *thought of* as a social unit because they are actually similar in some way. Unlike the persons in a group, persons in a category need have no contact with each other, no reciprocal relations, no communication or self-identification.[84] As such, the Marxist concept of class would seem able to be considered a category, especially as perceived in the present epoch of history in which the former multiplicity of class distinctions has currently simplified itself into the single class distinction of bourgeoisie-proletariat.[85] Yet we must be mindful of the different shades of meaning that may be present in the term "class" and the analogous use of the word resulting therefrom.

First, it seems evident that the term "class" and that of "category" would not be synonymous. "Category" certainly would be the wider term and would serve as the genus. For Marx reduced the number of classes in the present epoch to two, with the principle of unity being social position in respect to ownership of the forces of production and exploitation. Still, it is not likely that he would fail to distinguish other categories in society based, for example, on identity of skills, marital status, intelligence, types of dwellings inhabited, etc., whether in the present class-exploited society or even in the class*less* society of the future.

However, there is another difficulty of greater import. Marx looks to the class apparently as the source of conflict and change within society. It is classes that have been responsible for the institutions and cultures of the past and present, and it is through the agency of the proletarian class that classless society will eventually be realized. Yet the social category represents merely a unity which the mind sees in plurality because of some extrinsic similarity. Hence it would seem to follow that no social category *qua* category can be considered a principle, however remote, of social activity.

N. Bukharin is most probably correct when he denies that the Marxist concept of class is embraced by the notion of social category, at least, as it is defined above. It will be remembered that Bukharin referred to the notion of class as an aggregate of persons playing the same part in the production process. Yet he would wish to make a clear and exclusive distinction between that which he terms a "logical aggregate" and a "real aggregate."[86] An aggregate in general, for Bukharin is simply a total quantity or a compound unit existing apart from the various units composing it and considered as a unit in itself.[87] Hence, a forest, a class, human society, or even the number of male infants born within a certain interval of time is a valid example of an aggregate for him.

From these examples, it can be shown that aggregates are of different kinds, namely imaginary or logical, and real.

In the case of the male infants, we realize that these individuals are not found together in real life. One lives in one place and another lives elsewhere. Each is a separate individual who does not have any influence on another. It is the human mind that combines them; it is the human mind that makes the aggregation. It is a mental aggregate, not a living or real aggregation. Such artificial classifications may be called logical aggregates.[88] This idea of *logical* aggregate we see corresponds quite closely with that of social category defined above. The *real* aggregate, on the other hand, is something of an entirely different order.

When we consider a society, or a forest, etc., the case is more complex. The union of the component parts is not merely mental. The forest, for example, with its trees, bushes, wild vegetation and so on, comprises an actual living unit. The forest is something other than the sum of its component parts. All of these various parts are continuously interacting on one another. Thin out some of the trees and perhaps the others will wither because of less moisture, or perhaps they will better survive because of the increase of sunlight. There is an interaction of the parts on each other, and this interaction is a real, existing fact — not merely imagined by the mind. Such an interaction of parts furthermore is of long duration and continues as long as the whole continues to exist. Such aggregates Bukharin calls *real aggregates*.[89]

This, then, is the nature of the real aggregate. Its properties are twofold. First, there is a real interaction of the parts on each other and on the whole, independently of the mind perceiving the interaction. Second, this interaction is permanent and continual. With such properties, the "real aggregate" of Bukharin is directly opposed to the concept of "aggregate" as used in modern sociology. For in present day social analysis, the aggregate takes a position midway between the social group and the category. It is similar to the group in that its constituent members are united by a commonness of values or goals. Like the category, its members need not have direct, but only oblique communication, while it differs from both the group and the category in that it is quite transitory and usually short-lived.[90]

In Bukharin's analysis, the class for Marx would be a *real aggregate*. Its unity lay, not merely in the minds of men, but in the uninterrupted fixed relations between real living persons found within the existing mode of production. The function of men in production and the ownership in the interests of production — that is, the distribution of persons and the distribution of the means of production — are existing, abiding phases in production and serve as the basis of class relations and class distinctions. A class, consequently, is a plurality of persons united by a common role in the production process.[91] As such, the Marxist notion of class, in the eyes of Bukharin, far transcends the social category, as it has been described. For him, that which the term social category designates, would be closer to a mere *logical* aggregate. J. H. Fichter, however, insists that the social category is not merely mental or imaginary but based on real similarities, common characteristics, identity of status, etc. For him, a scientifically valid category must have a real existing basis in external and objective human beings. Yet he would not demand necessarily an interaction between the constituent parts.[92]

It must be kept in mind, however, that to the Marxist, *class* and *real aggregate* are not coextensive. The class is defined always and only, according to a production criterion, for it is productive relationships that are basic to men. Yet, as is evident in every society, totalities of persons differ from others by reason of politics, religion, ideology, personal wealth, and so on. These totalities, based on actual social relationships, can each be considered a *real* aggregate. Nonetheless, these social relationships can always be ultimately determined, in Marxist analysis, by the position of classes in the process of production. The class as a *real* aggregate, occupies an unique and radical position which serves as the "base" and cause of the other social real aggregates, which rest, in turn, as dependent "superstructures" on this somewhat fixed foundation.

One may very well be tempted to find a closer identification of the Marxist concept of class with the term "class" as commonly used in modern sociological analysis. On examination, however, one must agree with A. W. Green that there seems to be a prevalent lack of unanimity as to how this term is to be defined.[93] E. A. Ross would characterize the class as a tangent group, having its distinctive public opinion, creed, personal ideals, moral standards, mass suggestions, etc., — that is, having a more or less complete apparatus of control.[94] C. H. Cooley would see the class as any persisting social group, other than the family, existing within a larger group.[95] J. S. Roucek,[96] J. H. Fichter,[97] A. M. Rose,[98] H. M. Johnson,[99] W. L. Warner[100] and others would identify the class with a section of the population having the same status or prestige in relation to the other members of a society. For R. E. Park and E. W. Burgess, the class is a permanent crowd having the psychological bond of identical interests.[101] K. B. Mayer would characterize the class as an aggregate of individuals and families in similar economic positions.[102]

It may be observed that the class for Marx could, at least in part, fall within the limits of each of these notions. Still, the class for him, is somehow all of this, and yet more.

That which most characterizes the Marxist concept of class is its being that which is the principle of exploitation and social conflict, and consequently, the principle of historical movement. It is not as social category or as class, as characterized above, that it can be this principle. It seems that there is only one source of unification that can properly account for social activity, whether this activity takes the form of exploitation, social conflict, progress, recession or stagnation. This principle of unity is to be found in the unity of value. Yet it is only individuals or groups which can make the necessary preferential choices,[103] which constitute values. Groups are said to be capable of valuational decisions because the group decision is in the last analysis, the decision of human individuals in some pattern of interaction.[104] This is not to say that the group valuational decisions are the sum total of the individual values of the persons comprising the group, or that the individuals in the group are necessarily responsible for its valuational decisions. Thus, the values of a group may possibly have been arrived at long before any of the present members belonged to it. Yet these persons can be identified as members of the group because they accept and adhere to the group values — even though they do so as individuals. Furthermore, it is not even necessary that an individual member of a group realize which of the values he adheres to are those of the group, which values constitute him as a member, or which values characterize his particular function within the group.[105] One does not look to what a particular member, or even the group as a whole, thinks the values of the group to be to find those goals by which the group is defined. Yet these goals will always be found to be the goals of the members in some pattern of interaction. The class, then, for Marx would seem to be individuals and/or groups having the same values or goals, resulting from the relations of production, without necessarily having social contact or reciprocal relations with each other, and which may be *thought of* as a social unit because of the unity of social activities following upon common goals. As such, the class would be more than a social category, insofar as it can be considered, in some way to be the source of social activity. Yet it would not necessarily constitute a group that would actually be existing outside and completely independent of the minds of men. Strictly speaking, the class *qua* class could not be the principle of social activity, but its integral parts, the persons and groups composing it considered in their unity of purpose, could so be designated. This, then, would be the class for Marx. Its strength lay in its singleness of purpose; its weakness lay in its lack of reciprocal relations among its members. Thus, it should ever strive for more and more "class consciousness" — that is, in the eyes of Marx, it must become ever increasingly identifiable, not only to outside observers, but more importantly, to its own members. Likewise, the members must seek to become more identifiable to each other by a strong feeling of solidarity through close adherence to common values, greater identification of behavior patterns and, if possible, as in the case of the dominant class, the creation of institutions for the sake of class permanency and for the attainment of the common values through exploitation. The class must strive for mutual or reciprocal contact and communication among the members, through which each individual can enact his particular role towards the attainment of the common values and, thereby, assume the status or position he is to occupy relative to the other social positions in the collectivity. In other words, the class should seek to become strong or dominant. It does this insofar as it attains the essential characteristics of a status *group,* that is, insofar as it becomes "an identifiable, structured, continuing collectivity of social persons who enact reciprocal roles according to social norms, interests and values in pursuit of common goals."[106]

Marx was conscious of two different stages of evolution in actual existing classes. First, there is the situation where the class discharges a definite function in the process of production, yet has no class consciousness of its peculiar position, or of the hostility of its interests to the other classes. This Marx calls *class "an sich,"* a class "in itself." When the class becomes conscious of its social role, knows what it wants, feels it has a mission and unites, it becomes *class "für sich,"* a class "for itself."[107] The class *für sich* would appear to have many of the same characteristics as a "group" for Marx, while the class *an sich* would appear to resemble more closely a form of "category." However, Marx would still insist on the use of the term "class" as a designation for both stages of evolution. While the class *für sich* is better able to fulfill its role in history, it is not its consciousness of its role that makes it a class. As Marx and Engels point out: "It is not a question of what this or that proletarian or even the whole proletariat, conceives to be the goal for the moment — it is a question of *what it is* and what it will historically be driven to do in accordance with its being."[108] Yet the very insistence on greater class consciousness among the proletariat, in order that it might more surely carry out its historical role through reciprocal relations among the workers, makes evident that Marx, at least implicitly, looked to concurrent action by individuals having the same values as the source of social activity — although the end result of this activity may not be, necessarily, in accordance with their wills.[109]

When the proletarian class becomes the one dominant political *group,* its institutions become the culture of the society, and its values the ruling ideas. Later, when the proletariat becomes the only vast political group, it need no longer be considered a class, that is, a principle of conflict, for there is no exploitation. The group becomes the society; its members have identical relations to the forces of production; complete bi-lateral freedom from exploitation prevails, and hence, the class*less* society comes into existence.

It has been argued, and with justification, that Marx failed to consider the difficulty of such a large plurality as the proletariat becoming identified as a group, and consequently as a principle of social activity. Certainly, history testifies that the revolutionary movements of the past produced a much smaller group through which change was brought about in existing societies. In the American Revolution, the "Founding Fathers," in France, the Jacobin clubs, and in the Russian Revolution, the extreme left revolutionary party, the Bolsheviks, became the fundamental organizers of the new society. In such cases, the so-called working class seemed to serve more in the role of a mob, an instrument manipulated by a political party or hard-core group, than as a *per se* principle of social activity.

So it would seem that the Communist Party has been substituted for the proletariat as the cause of social movement.[110] This serves to corroborate the position that only groups and individuals can serve as principles of social activity, including exploitation, and the class can be so designated a principle only if by the term "class" is meant the groups and individuals which comprise it as they act through a commonness of values.

Bukharin objects strongly to any attempt to find an opposition between the party and the class.[111] He looks to the inequality within the class as the reason for the existence of the party. In the modern working class much inequality exists as to brain power and ability. Likewise, proletarian "age" must be taken into consideration. There is much difference between a peasant who has just begun work in a factory and the worker who has been there since childhood. Finally, there are inequalities in respect to class-consciousness, with some workers more aware of their mission than others. Yet for all the differences, a class is more or less a unit as compared with the other classes.

> The working class, therefore, *as to their class-consciousness, i.e.,* their permanent, general, not their personal, not their guild or group interests, but as to the interests of the class as a whole, is divided into *a number of groups and sub-groups, as a single chain consists of a number of links of varying strength.*[112]

If the working class were perfectly equal, it could act as a source of social change without a permanent group or organization of leadership. Since in existential circumstances this is never the case, naturally one would expect to find the entire class led by that section of it that is most advanced, best schooled, most united. In the instance of the proletarian class, this *avant-garde* group, it goes without saying, is the Communist Party.[113]

The party is not the class. In fact, it is usually but a small part of the class, as the brain is but a relatively small portion of the body. But to the thinking of the Marxist, this does not allow for an attempt to find such an opposition between the party and the class as to see only the party as the cause of social transformation, and the class merely its instrument. "We may *distinguish* between class and party, as we distinguish between the head and the entire body, but we cannot *discuss them as opposites,* just as we cannot cut off a man's head, unless we wish to shorten his life."[114] Whether this constitutes an adequate rebuttal to the above denial of the possibility of a large class such as the proletariat operating as an active principle in the revolutionary struggle, is ultimately decided, in all probability, by one's breadth of vision and his loyalties.

The attempt to evaluate the Marxian concept of class still leaves unsolved some knotty philosophical problems to be faced by the Marxist. One such problem may be stated as follows: If social action is dependent on value, and if value is realized through preferential choice, then it is ultimately only the concrete individual as an initiative agent that can be the principle of the preferential choices by which he becomes a member of a class. However, this seems to be in conflict with the impersonalism and anti-individualism of Marx who looked upon the individual as only "a point of interaction of socio-economic relationships." Perhaps this problem was, at root, the cause of unrest in Berdyaev, Bogdanov and others who, at one time, had an affinity for the Marxian theory.[115]

For the Marxist to cite his patriarch to the effect that the human organism becomes a "person" only through society[116] — which, seen from another vantage, is to say that all human values are socially derived — still does not offer a solution to the difficulty at hand. If we may grant that human values are socially derived, that man is, as Aristotle insists, essentially a political animal, nonetheless it is only through the "internalization" of these values by the individual, their dynamic acceptance by an initiative agent capable of indetermined preferential choice that allows for the designation of a human being as a member of a "class-conscious" collectivity, and a principle of social activity. Yet, in the Marxian philosophy of man, no place is allowed for an indeterminate principle of value acceptance or rejection in the individual.[117] Hence, the difficulty remains.

A second problem might be proposed to the Marxist as to who, or what, will constitute the principle of social activity and preferential choice control in the classless society when the state and, eventually, the Communist Party, will have withered away.

Peaceful Coexistence — Appendix II-b

A discussion of peaceful coexistence may proceed from any one of several viewpoints. The basis of Sino-Soviet differences has been placed in various causes. Some political scientists and historians have the tendency to see the conflict as simply another example of "power politics," founded on excessive nationalism, oriental racism, expansionism, a long-standing antipathy of the two countries due to ancient territorial disputes, etc. Economists often see the conflicting positions of the two communist camps to be the result of adventurous domestic economic policies. Other scholars place the foundation of the dispute in the aggressive military policies advocated by the Chinese. While all these causes must undoubtedly be taken into account in arriving at an adequate understanding of the Russian-Chinese conflict, it is by no means clear that any one or all of the above is the primary source of the altercation. It is well to keep in mind that the disputants themselves always tend to argue in terms of theory. Whether ideology is the deepest root of the conflict, or merely a subterfuge for more pragmatic goals, need not be argued at this juncture. The point to be emphasized is that the question is debatable. However, it is only a consideration of coexistence from a theoretical point of view that has meaningfulness within the context of this work. The following analysis will be limited to this aspect alone.

Theoretically, the positions of both the Soviet-Yugoslav camp and that of the Chinese-Albanians surprisingly enough have rather strong foundation in the writings of Marx, Engels and Lenin.

The Soviets maintain that while the struggle of the classes must continue unhesitatingly with the bourgeoisie eventually being eliminated and world-wide socialism replacing the imperialist nations, nevertheless the proletarian revolutionary struggle must adjust to the flow of history.[118] Because of the advance of science and technology, the world, both communist and imperialist, is in a nuclear age. Consequently, a thermo-nuclear global war is not only possible, but at times quite probable. The threat of such a war is a much greater danger to the socialist revolution than it is to imperialistic forces. For capitalism is already in its death-throes as is evidenced by the collapse of colonialism, and by the desperate attempt of Western Europe predicted over fifty years previously by Lenin[119] to unite itself into an economic United States of Europe, *i.e.,* the common market, in order to prolong its inevitable collapse. Hence the capitalist powers, *in a sense,* have nothing to lose in a nuclear war and the socialist nations have, *in a sense,* nothing to gain. Yet such a catastrophe could within minutes, wipe out a hundred years or more of human progress towards the higher type of society envisioned by the Marxists, if not wipe human life off the face of the earth. Hence the primary concern of communists should be to prevent a nuclear war at all costs. This is in the present age the best, and in fact, the only way to bring about the revolutionary demise of capitalism and the success of communism. It is by means of an active struggle for peace, democracy and national liberation, and not through nuclear conflict, that the people of the world can best weaken imperialism and limit its sphere of action.[120]

Now a cursory study of the classic works of Marx, Engels and Lenin might lead one to think that the attitude of peaceful coexistence is contrary to the tenets of Marxism-Leninism. With a deeper study of these men, one may very well be encouraged to modify his opinion. As has been mentioned,[121] Marxism is a philosophy that has as its hallmark, the notion of *theoretical evolution.* Marx abhorred the idea that his words would ever become a stabilized dogma, as Engels argues quite pointedly in a letter to Conrad Schmidt.[122] "All I know is that I am not a Marxist," declared Marx, recalls Engels. What Marx meant to convey by these words was his revulsion for a movement that had arisen among some French followers who tended to look upon his work as the culmination of philosophical and historical endeavor, in much the same fashion as many Germans in Marx's own youth looked upon the philosophy of Hegel as the terminus of philosophy. In contrast, Marx considered his ideas to be merely the result of empirical investigation from which were derived some *general* trends to be noted in human history. He refused to enter into any intricate discussion of the outcome of future history, but referred to it usually in very vague and generalized terms. He felt that any attempt to predict particular conclusions about the distant future was a misconstruction of the general laws discovered by him. Marx and Engels felt that what they had discovered were some general patterns in the history of man, some universal laws by which future events could be properly interpreted and controlled.[123] True, they insisted that their theories were to act as the basis for practical activity. What is often forgotten or ignored however, is that Marx also considered, as Engels points out, that his findings and theories were to serve as guides to the *further* study of history.[124]

In spite of tendencies within bolshevism to dogmatize Marx, and especially Lenin, all in all the modern Communist Movement has held true to this idea which they have termed the "creative advancement" of Marxist-Leninist theory.[125] One can trace this theoretical advancement back to Lenin himself who saw in capitalism a higher stage called imperialism, through Stalin with his theory of "socialism in one country," to Khrushchev with his theory of "peaceful coexistence," and Mao Tse-tung with his "Hundred Flowers" experiment and the "Great Leap Forward."

If peaceful coexistence is looked upon as the application of Marxian principles of history to the particular problems of the nuclear age, one can find in the theory of peaceful coexistence a good deal of conformity with the mind of Marx. Moreover, the Soviets would insist that peaceful coexistence is not a complete novelty of the nuclear age. They find a basis for their theory in the writings of Lenin where he insisted that the inevitability of war with imperialism was always conditioned by the concrete particular circumstances regarding the strength of the opposing forces. Hence, as long as the socialist nations were in danger of losing a war with capitalism, peaceful relations with the imperialistic powers would do more to bring about the decay of capitalism than a war of folly.[126] Lenin for example, looked to the treaty of peace signed with bourgeois Estonia in February, 1920 as being of historical significance in that it strengthened the security of the Soviet state and allowed for greater concentration of internal problems.[127] While in power, he thus formulated a foreign policy based on a long-lasting coexistence of the Soviet state with the capitalist nations surrounding it.

This tendency for coexistence persisted during the time of Stalin. Although those communists who are offended by the theory of coexistence are often referred to as "Stalinists," there is much in the actions of Stalin that give support to the coexistence theory.[128] Certainly, the position of Stalin in relation to Trotsky can be termed one of coexistence. Whereas Trotsky looked to war and world revolution as inevitable and therefore to be undertaken immediately, Stalin preferred to strengthen the internal economic and political security of the Soviet state while carrying on diplomatic relations with imperialistic powers. He even went so far as to enter into a non-aggression pact with a nation representing the extreme ideological contrary of bolshevism, Nazi Germany, in the summer of 1939. And if this period of peaceful coexistence lasted less than two years, it is well to remember that it was Hitler, not Stalin who broke this pact. It is also reported that following World War II, Stalin advised the Chinese Communist Party not to start a civil war with Chiang Kai-shek, but rather to attempt to form a coalition government.[129] In 1949, he sought to bring an end to the Communist uprising in Greece[130] — merely another example of coexistence. Khrushchev then, according to the Soviets, is but carrying out the theoretical evolution of the notion of "class-struggle by peaceful means" into the *nuclear* age.

The Chinese-Albanian camp would look upon Khrushchev's theory in a somewhat different light. Among Chinese theoreticians the principle of peaceful coexistence is viewed as "revisionist."[131] This revisionism derives from the fears of the Soviets and Yugoslavs — fear of imperialism and fear of war.[132] They have thereby sunk from a position of revolutionary struggle against imperialism to that of "reformism," i.e., to the theory of the peaceful growing of capitalism into socialism.[133] Chinese Communists, on the other hand, are not afraid of either imperialism or war. They are in favor of a radical settlement of accounts between the world of socialism and that of capitalism by means of a revolutionary clash. If this means war, it will be a just war. One should not be afraid of it or renounce it, because the sacrifices made, however great, will soon be recompensed.[134] To speak today about using peaceful means to bring about the transition from capitalism to socialism is unrealistic, the Chinese go on to say, for the proletariat can never overcome counter-revolutionary violence other than by means of revolutionary violence. At a time when the strength of the socialist nations is growing so rapidly these countries should not renounce the possibility of settling accounts with imperialism, and should not run away from war.[135]

The Chinese feel that this position is the one that conforms most fully with the mind of Lenin. Lenin held that imperialism necessarily breeds war. These wars will eventually have to be waged against the socialist revolution, that is, against those nations that embrace socialism. Hence war is inevitable, because of imperialism's own inner laws.[136] The capitalists will not relinquish their control, their institutions, their way of life without a *physical* struggle. To realize this is to live in reality. Thus, socialist nations should not conduct their affairs in such a manner as to prevent the inevitable. To do so is to betray the class struggle and to renounce Marxism-Leninism.[137]

One has but to look at the past actions of the Soviet Union to see how successful forceful action on the part of socialism can be, claim the Chinese. Because of the use of military might and strong diplomatic pressures following World War II, the prewar bourgeois and fascist states of Eastern Europe easily fell into the socialist camp to become worker republics. Although the Western powers alone possessed the atomic bomb, they proved to be mere "paper tigers" under the threat of war.[138] It is in the continuation of these policies, not in revisionist peaceful coexistence, that the socialist revolutionary movement is to progress.

Which of these two positions is the correct interpretation of

Marxist revolutionary principles? If a definitive answer could be given to this question, perhaps the Sino-Soviet conflict would not exist.[139] The reason no clear-cut answer can be given is that the matter is so treated in the classics of Marxism-Leninism that it allows for more than one possible legitimate interpretation. The solutions offered will never reach any degree of scientific certitude, will possess only varying degrees of probability and hence, will never advance beyond the arena of opinion.[140] Without this ideological certitude, the opinion which the various Communist Parties throughout the world eventually embrace will undoubtedly be an emotive response to "power politics," racism, historical loyalties and antipathies, or purely economic considerations. In what manner the Russians and Chinese will at last solve this serious ideological problem, probably only future generations will know.

Suggested Readings

CHAPTER II

Primary Sources

Engels, F., *Ludwig Feuerbach and the Outcome of Classical German Philosophy*, Part II.
———, "On Historical Materialism."
———, *Socialism: Utopian and Scientific*, Part III.
Khrushchev, N. S., *On Peaceful Coexistence: A Collection*, Moscow, Foreign Languages Publishing House, 1961.
*Lenin, V. I., *Materialism and Empirio-Criticism*, Chapters I and II.
Mao Tse-tung, "Hundred Flowers" speech.
———, "Imperialism and All Reactionaries are Paper Tigers."
Marx, K., Preface to *A Contribution to the Critique of Political Economy*.
*Marx, K. and Engels, F., *The German Ideology*, Part I.
*———, *Manifesto of the Communist Party*.
The New Communist Manifesto, Declaration of Rep. of 81 Communist Parties, Moscow, Nov.-Dec., 1960.
Stalin, J., *Dialectical and Historical Materialism*.

Secondary Sources

Bendix, R. and Lipset, S. M., "Karl Marx's Theory of Social Classes," in R. Bendix and S. M. Lipset (eds.), *Class, Status and Power*, Glencoe, Ill., The Free Press, 1953.
*Bober, M. M., *Karl Marx's Interpretation of History*.
Bukharin, Nikolai, *Historical Materialism: A System of Sociology*, New York, International Publishers, 1925.
*Chambre, Henri, *From Karl Marx to Mao Tse-tung*, trans. by Robert J. Olsen, New York, P. J. Kenedy and Sons, 1963, Chapter IV.
Cornforth, Maurice, *Historical Materialism*, New York, International Publishers, 1954.

*――, *The Theory of Knowledge*, 3rd. ed., New York, International Publishers, 1963.
Hunt, R. N. Carew, *The Theory and Practice of Communism*, 5th ed. rev., New York, Macmillan and Co., 1961, pp. 30-56.
Jacobs, Dan N. and Baerwald, Hans H. (eds.), *Chinese Communism: Selected Documents*, New York, Harper and Row, 1963, especially pp. 145-214.
Kardelj, E., *Socialism and War*, in *The New Communist Manifesto and Related Documents*, ed. Dan N. Jacobs, 2nd. ed., New York, Harper and Row, 1962, pp. 183-212.
Laski, Harold J., *Communism*, New York, Henry Holt and Co., 1927, Chapter II.
"George Lucas on Co-Existence," *Soviet Survey*, No. 10 (1956).
*McFadden, Chas. J., *The Philosophy of Communism*, New York, Benziger Bros., Inc., 1939, Chapters III, IV, XI and XII.
*Venable, Vernon, *Human Nature: The Marxian View*, New York, Alfred A. Knopf, Inc., 1945, Chapters II, VII and VIII.
*Wetter, Gustav, *Dialectical Materialism*, trans. Peter Heath, rev. ed., New York, Frederick A. Praeger, 1958, pp. 281-295 and 488-517.
――, "The Soviet Concept of Coexistence," *Soviet Survey*, No. 30 (1959), pp. 19-34.

FOOTNOTES TO CHAPTER II

1. F. Engels, *Ludwig Feuerbach and the Outcome of Classical German Philosophy* (hereafter cited as Engels, *Ludwig Feuerbach*), in *Karl Marx Selected Works*, ed. V. Adoratsky, 2 vols. (Moscow-Leningrad, 1935-36), I, 430. Hereafter cited as *KMSW*.
2. *Ibid.*, 431.
3. *Ibid.*
4. V. I. Lenin, *Materialism and Empirio-Criticism*, in *Collected Works* (Moscow, 1960-1963), XIV, 326.
5. J. Stalin, *Dialectical and Historical Materialism*, in *Problems of Leninism* (Moscow, 1953), p. 721.
6. Lenin, *Materialism and Empirio-Criticism*, p. 46.
7. M. B. Mitin, *Dialektichesky materializm*, p. 115, as cited in Gustav A. Wetter, *Dialectical Materialism*, trans. Peter Heath, rev. ed., (New York, 1958), p. 491. Hereafter cited as Wetter, *D.M.*
8. Engels, *Dialectics of Nature* (New York, 1940), pp. 203-204.
9. *Ibid.*, p. 203.
10. Cf. N. Y. Voytonis, *Predistoriya intellekta* (Moscow-Leningrad, 1949), pp. 157ff, as cited in Wetter, *D.M.*, p. 492.
11. Cf. M. A. Leonov, *Ocherk dialektichesky metod* (Moscow, 1947), p. 521, as cited in Wetter, *D.M.*, p. 493.
12. Lenin, *Materialism and Empirio-Criticism*, pp. 69-70.
13. *Ibid.*, p. 103.
14. Lenin, *Philosophical Notebooks*, as cited by Wetter, *D.M.*, p. 501.
15. *Ibid.*, p. 505.
16. F. I. Khaskhachikh, *Materiya i soznanie* (Moscow, 1951), p. 145, as cited in Wetter, *D.M.*, p. 506.
17. Cf. V. Ral'tsevich, *Bol'shaya Sovetskaya Entsiklopediya*, 1st ed., XXII, col. 198, as cited in Wetter, *D.M.*, p. 506.
18. Editorial postscript, *Voprosy filosofii*, 1955, 1, pp. 147f.
19. M. N. Rutkevich, *Praktika-osnova poznaniya i kriteriy istiny* (Moscow, 1952), p. 125, as cited in Wetter, *D.M.*, p. 507.
20. *Ibid.*, p. 121, in Wetter, *D.M.*, pp. 507-508.
21. Cf. Marx, *Theses on Feuerbach*, XI, in *KMSW*, I, p. 473.
22. Cf. Engels, *Ludwig Feuerbach*, in *KMSW*, I, p. 432.

23. Cf. Rutkevitch, *Praktika-osnova*, p. 167, as cited in Wetter *D.M.*, p. 511.
24. *Ibid.*, p. 142, as cited in Wetter, *D.M.*, p. 513.
25. Cf. Lenin, *Philosophical Notebooks*, cited in Wetter, *D.M.*, p. 513.
26. Rutkevitch, *Praktika-osnova*, p. 179, in Wetter, *D.M.*, p. 515.
27. Cf. Lenin, *On Dialectics, Selected Works*, 12 vols. (New York, 1943), XI, p. 378.
28. Rutkevitch, *Praktika-osnova*, p. 179, in Wetter, *D.M.*, p. 514.
29. *Ibid.*, p. 183, in Wetter, *D.M.*, p. 515.
30. *Ludwig Feuerbach*, in *KMSW*, I, p. 458.
31. Marx, *A Contribution to the Critique of Political Economy*, preface, in *KMSW*, I, p. 356. Hereafter cited as Marx, *Critique of Political Economy*.
32. *Ibid.*
33. Cf. Engels, "Letter to H. Starkenburg, Jan. 25, 1894," in *KMSW*, I, p. 392.
34. Engels, "Letters to Joseph Bloch, September 21, 1890," in *KMSW*, I, pp. 381-382.
35. Cf. Marx, *Theses on Feuerbach*, III, in *KMSW*, I, p. 472.
36. On this point, see Vernon Venable, *Human Nature: The Marxian View* (New York, 1945), pp. 28-34. Hereafter cited as Venable, *Human Nature*.
37. Marx, *Theses on Feuerbach, KMSW*, I, pp. 471-473.
38. *Ibid.*
39. Marx and Engels, *The German Ideology*, ed. R. Pascal (New York, 1947), p. 7.
40. *Ibid.*
41. Cf. *Theses on Feuerbach*, VI, in *KMSW*, I, pp. 472-473.
42. Criticizing Bentham's utilitarianism, Marx says, "He that would criticize all human acts, movements, relations, etc., by the principle of utility must first deal with human nature in general, and then with human nature as modified in each historical epoch." *Capital*, 3 vols. (Chicago, 1909), I, 668n.
43. Marx, appendix to *A Contribution to the Critique of Political Economy* (Chicago, 1904), p. 269. Hereafter cited as *Appendix to Critique of Political Economy*.
44. *Ibid.*
45. Marx and Engels, *The German Ideology*, p. 7.
46. *Ibid.*, p. 18.
47. Marx, *Wage-Labour and Capital*, in *KMSW*, I, p. 264.
48. *Appendix to Critique of Political Economy*, p. 268.
49. *Ibid.*

50. *Ibid.,* p. 267. See also Engels, *Dialectics of Nature,* p. 282.
51. Marx, *Capital,* I, 199.
52. *Ibid.*
53. *Ibid.,* p. 201.
54. *Ibid.,* p. 199.
55. *Ibid.,* p. 202.
56. *Ibid.,* p. 201.
57. Cf. Venable, *Human Nature,* Chapter VII, especially pp. 89-97.
58. Cf. Engels, "Letter to Conrad Schmidt, August 5, 1890," in Marx and Engels, *Selected Correspondence,* trans. Dona Torr (New York, 1942), pp. 472-473.
59. Cf. Venable, *Human Nature,* p. 97.
60. Cf. Marx, *Critique of Political Economy,* preface, in *KMSW,* I, pp. 356-357.
61. *Ibid.,* p. 356. For a further exposition of the Marxist position on the conflict of ownership relations with other forces of production, see Venable, *Human Nature,* pp. 104-111.
62. Cf. Marx, *Capital,* I, p. 400. On this point, also see Venable, *Human Nature,* pp. 105-107.
63. Cf. Engels, *Socialism: Utopian and Scientific,* in *KMSW,* I, p. 169.
64. *Ibid.*
65. *Ibid.,* pp. 165-166. See also Marx, *Capital,* I, part IV.
66. Venable, *Human Nature,* p. 111.
67. *Ibid.,* pp. 111-112. Cf. Marx, *Economic and Philosophic Manuscripts,* trans. Martin Milligan (Moscow, 1961), pp. 164-165.
68. *KMSW,* I, pp. 204-218.
69. Cf. Marx, "Letter to P. V. Annenkov, December 28, 1846," in *KMSW,* I, pp. 372-377. See also, G. Plekhanov, *Fundamental Problems of Marxism,* ed. D. Riazanov (New York, 1929), pp. 57-58.
70. Marx, "Letter to Joseph Weydemeyer, March 5, 1852," in *KMSW,* I, p. 377.
71. Preface to German edition (1883) of *Manifesto of the Communist Party, KMSW,* I, p. 193.
72. Marx, *Briefwechsel,* III, p. 127, as quoted by Lenin in "Karl Marx," *KMSW,* I, p. 49.
73. Cf. Marx and Engels, *Manifesto of the Communist Party, KMSW,* I, p. 228.

The following section appeared in a slightly altered form as an article in the *Duquesne Review,* Vol. IX, No. 1 (1963). Reprinted with permission.

74. Cf. *Theses on Feuerbach,* VI, in *KMSW,* I, pp. 472-473.
75. Cf. Marx and Engels, *The German Ideology,* p. 39.
76. Cf. Venable, *Human Nature,* p. 113.

77. Cf. Marx, *Capital,* I, especially Chapters VII-IX. Also see Marx, *Value, Price and Profit, KMSW,* I, pp. 282-337.

78. Nikolai Bukharin, *Historical Materialism: A System of Sociology* (New York, 1925), p. 276. Hereafter cited as Bukharin, *Historical Materialism.* Although Bukharin eventually lost favor with Stalin and was eliminated in the purges of the late 1930's, nevertheless the above mentioned work still represents a valid and, perhaps, the best detailed analysis of the Marxist concept of "class." However, one should keep in mind the remarks of Lenin concerning the "scholastic" tendencies of Bukharin. On this, see Lenin's "Testament" in Dan N. Jacobs (ed.), *The New Communist Manifesto and Related Documents,* 2d. ed. (New York, 1962), p. 133.

79. Marx, *Capital,* III, pp. 1031-1032. Cf. R. Bendix and S. M. Lipset, "Karl Marx's Theory of Social Classes," in R. Bendix and S. M. Lipset (eds.), *Class, Status and Power* (Glencoe, Ill., 1953), p. 29.

80. Marx, *Value, Price and Profit,* Chapters XIII and XIV, *KMSW,* I, pp. 325-337. See also, Bukharin, *Historical Materialism,* p. 285.

Of course, for Marx, the conflict in the area of distribution is always a consequence of the inequalities in the ownership of the means of production. Thus, the root of the class conflict is the same as that by which the classes are distinguished. Marx, *The Critique of the Gotha Programme, KMSW,* II, p. 567.

81. See Chapter V, below.

82. Cf. Marx, *Capital,* I, p. 152.

83. Even some eminent non-Marxist sociologists are willing to grant this point of semi-enslavement. See Ferdinand Tönnies, *Fundamental Concepts of Sociology (Gemeinschaft und Gesellschaft),* trans. and suppl. Charles P. Loomis (New York, Cincinnati, etc., 1940), pp. 114-115.

84. A. Robert Caponigri, "Introduction to Political Theory" (book in preparation for publication), Chapter I. See also, Joseph H. Fichter, *Sociology* (Chicago, 1957), p. 63.

85. Marx and Engels, *Manifesto of the Communist Party, KMSW,* I, pp. 205-206. The bourgeois and proletarian classes of the present epoch are more easily identified with "category" than the manifold gradations and subordinate gradations of social rank in earlier periods. For oftentimes the class was, at one and the same time, the result of economic conditions, thereby strictly to be designated a class, and likewise a *legal-political* "caste" (*sic* Bukharin, p. 279) having self-identification and communication. Thus, in much of the feudal period, the landholders were at once *landlords* as to their class, and *nobles* as to their *political-legal* status. Both classifications were mutually inclusive.

86. Bukharin, *Historical Materialism,* pp. 84-85.

87. *Ibid.,* p. 84.
88. *Ibid.*
89. *Ibid.,* pp. 84-85.
90. Caponigri, "Introduction to Political Theory," Chapter I. Common examples of aggregates would be, a crowd at a football game, a crowd watching a parade, or a mob in the streets of a rebellious city.
91. Bukharin, *Historical Materialism,* pp. 278-279. Cf. Marx, *The Eighteenth Brumaire of Louis Bonaparte, KMSW,* II, p. 415.
92. Fichter, *Sociology,* pp. 63-64. This recalls the differentiation made by the scholastic philosophers of *ens rationis cum fundamento in re* (an entity of the mind having the basis for its construction by the mind in the real world) from both a strictly logical entity and a real being. The category for Fichter would fall somewhere between what, for Bukharin, is a *logical aggregate* and his *real aggregate.*
93. Arnold W. Green, *Sociology: An Analysis of Life in Modern Society,* 3d. ed. (New York, 1960), p. 174.
94. Edward Alworth Ross, *Social Control: A Survey of the Foundations of Order* (New York, 1904), p. 400.
95. Charles Horton Cooley, *Social Organization: A Study of the Larger Mind* (New York, 1915), p. 209.
96. Joseph S. Roucek, "Social Classes," *Social Control,* ed. Joseph S. Roucek, 2d. ed. (Princeton, N. J. and New York, 1956), p. 149.
97. Fichter, *Sociology,* p. 73.
98. Arnold M. Rose, *Sociology: The Study of Human Relations* (New York, 1957), p. 222.
99. Harry M. Johnson, *Sociology: A Systematic Introduction* (New York and Burlingame, 1960), pp. 469-470.
100. W. Lloyd Warner, "American Caste and Class," *American Journal of Sociology,* XLII (September, 1936), p. 234.
101. Robert E. Park and Ernest W. Burgess, *Introduction to the Science of Sociology,* 2d. ed., (Chicago, 1924), p. 206.
102. Kurt B. Mayer, *Class and Society,* revised edition (New York, 1955), p. 23.
103. Behavior is preferential when it takes one path rather than another while having this other in view, more or less clearly, as intrinsically possible. Preferential behavior, therefore, always involves a conscious decision.
104. A group may, for the present, be defined simply as "human beings in reciprocal relations." Cf. Fichter, *Sociology,* p. 109.
105. Thus, the father of a family may very well perform his functions as such without realizing which of his functions within the family group characterize him as the head of the family.

106. Fichter, *Sociology*, p. 110.
107. Marx, *The Poverty of Philosophy*, (New York, 1963), p. 173. See also Bukharin, *Historical Materialism*, pp. 292-293; Bendix and Lipset, "Karl Marx's Theory of Social Classes," p. 33.
108. *The Holy Family*, as quoted in *KMSW*, I, preface, xviii-xix.
109. On this point, see Engels, *Ludwig Feuerbach*, *KMSW*, I, pp. 457-459; Lenin, *Economic Content of Narodism and the Criticism of It in Mr. Struve's Book, Selected Works*, XI, pp. 624-626; Plekhanov, *Fundamental Problems of Marxism*, pp. 58-59.
110. Some would hold that existentially it is the bolshevik state, the instrument of the Communist Party, that instigates social activity within the U. S. S. R. Cf. Waldemar Gurian, *Bolshevism: An Introduction to Soviet Communism* (Notre Dame, Ind., 1952), pp. 20-21. Milovan Djilas would identify the motive force in Soviet society with the political bureaucracy. However, he then proceeds to characterize this bureaucracy as a "class." Cf. *The New Class* (New York, 1957), especially pp. 37-69.
111. Bukharin, *Historical Materialism*, pp. 304-307.
112. *Ibid.*, p. 305.
113. Lenin, *The State and Revolution*, in *Selected Works*, VII, 26.
114. Bukharin, *Historical Materialism*, pp. 305-306. See also Lenin, *"Left-Wing" Communism: An Infantile Disorder, Selected Works*, X, pp. 79ff. Stalin, *Problems of Leninism*, pp. 164-188; N. S. Khrushchev, "For a Close Tie of Literature and Art with the Life of the People" in *Soviet World Outlook*, 3rd. ed. (Washington, D. C., 1959), p. 36.
115. George L. Kline, "Current Soviet Morality," *Encyclopedia of Morals*, ed. Vergilius Ferm (New York, 1956), pp. 569-570.
116. Marx, *Appendix to Critique of Political Economy*, p. 268.
117. Cf. I. P. Pavlov, *Selected Works* (Moscow, 1955), p. 484; T. I. Oyzerman, "Marxistsko-leninskoe reshenie problemy svobody i neobkhodimosti," *Voprosy filosofii*, 1954, 3, p. 27, as cited in Wetter, *D.M.*, pp. 389-390.
118. *The New Communist Manifesto*, Declaration of 81 Communist Parties Meeting in Moscow, Nov.-Dec., 1960, in *The New Communist Manifesto and Related Documents*, pp. 28-29. Cf. E. Kardelj, *Socialism and War*, *ibid.*, p. 197.
119. Lenin, *Imperialism, The Highest Stage of Capitalism*, in *Selected Works*, V, pp. 95-96.
120. *The New Communist Manifesto*, pp. 26-29.
121. See above, Foreword.
122. Engels, "Letter to Conrad Schmidt, August 5, 1890," *Selected Correspondence*, pp. 472-475.
123. *Ibid*.

124. Ibid., p. 473. Cf. Engels, *Die Kommunisten und Karl Heinzen,* as cited in *KMSW,* I, xv; Lenin, "Our Program," *Handbook of Marxism,* ed. E. Burns (New York, 1935), pp. 571-574; *KMSW,* I, p. 436n.
125. *Voprosy filosofii,* 1954, No. 2, p. 5. Cf. Stalin, *Marxism and the Problems of Linguistics* (Moscow, 1955), pp. 70-71; N. S. Khrushchev, "Report of the Central Committee to the 21st Party Congress," *Soviet World Outlook,* p. 36; "Declaration of the Twelve Communist Parties in Power," Moscow, November, 1957, in Jacobs, *The New Communist Manifesto,* pp. 177-178.
126. Cf. Lenin, *"Left Wing" Communism, An Infantile Disorder,* in *Selected Works,* X, p. 111; *Compromises, ibid.* VI, pp. 208ff. Kardelj, *Socialism and War,* pp. 185ff.
127. Cf. Kardelj, *Socialism and War,* pp. 186-187. In Lenin's *Selected Works* see Vol. VIII, p. 393n. For Lenin's position on concessions, see *Selected Works,* VII, pp. 279ff. IX, pp. 161ff. and 378ff.
128. Cf. Marshall D. Shulman, *Stalin's Foreign Policy Reappraised* (Cambridge, Mass., 1963), pp. 1-12, and *passim.*
129. Cf. Milovan Djilas, *Conversations with Stalin* (New York, 1962), p. 182; Shulman, *Stalin's Foreign Policy Reappraised,* pp. 106-107.
130. Djilas, *Conversations with Stalin,* pp. 181-182; Shulman, *Stalin's Foreign Policy Reappraised,* pp. 71-72.
131. Cf. Lu Ting-yi, *Unite Under Lenin's Revolutionary Banner,* in *Chinese Communism: Selected Documents,* ed. Dan N. Jacobs and Hans H. Baerwald (New York, 1963), pp. 172ff. The Chinese also seek a type of peaceful coexistence, but in the current controversy, it has a different meaning for them than for the Soviets. See introduction, *ibid.,* p. 7n; Wu Chiang, "Our Age and Edward Kardelj's 'Dialectics,'" *ibid.,* pp. 212-213; Jacobs, *The New Communist Manifesto,* introduction, p. 5.
132. Lu Ting-yi, *Unite Under Lenin's Revolutionary Banner,* p. 176.
133. *Ibid.,* p. 174.
134. *Ibid.,* p. 176; Sung Tu, "Answers to Readers' Queries on War and Peace," in Jacobs and Baerwald, *Chinese Communism,* pp. 164ff.
135. Lu Ting-yi, *Unite Under Lenin's Revolutionary Banner,* pp. 174-176; Sung Tu, "Answers to Readers' Queries on War and Peace," pp. 161-167.
136. Cf. Lenin, *Materials on Revision of Party Programme* (1917), in *Selected Works,* VI, p. 106; *War and Peace, ibid.,* VII, p. 302; Sung Tu, "Answers to Readers' Queries," pp. 161-163.
137. Cf. Lu Ting-yi, *Unite Under Lenin's Revolutionary Banner,* pp. 172-173; Wu Chiang, "Our Age and Edward Kardelj's 'Dialectics,'" pp. 206-207.
138. Cf. Mao Tse-tung, "Imperialism and All Reactionaries Are Paper Tigers," in Jacobs and Baerwald, *Chinese Communism,* pp. 147-157,

especially pp. 151-153; Sung Tu, "Answers to Readers' Queries," p. 167.
139. D. N. Jacobs and H. H. Baerwald among others, hold that difference in the interpretations of theory is not the cause of the conflict, although the dispute tends to be argued out in terms of theory. Cf. *Chinese Communism,* introduction, p. 8. See also, Jacobs, *The New Communist Manifesto,* introduction, p. 7.
140. It is possible to show an interesting analogy between this dispute within bolshevism and a major dispute within Christianity. The author intends no sacrilege and hopes it offends no one.

The Sino-Soviet ideological conflict is in some respects quite similar to the Catholic-Protestant conflict within Christianity. For over 450 years, Catholics and Protestants alike have insisted that their interpretation of the meaning of the words of Christ and Scripture were correct. Both traditions ultimately base their position on the Scripture itself. Both traditions present arguments which are viable enough to convince millions of their correctness, and yet are apparently not strong enough to convince millions of others. After four centuries of debate, the controversy continues. Only recently has there been a sincere effort to come to some appreciation of the other's position. Yet if there is to be a return to a Christian unity, it seems that it will have to come about through some higher principle than that of reasoned arguments based on an interpretation of Scripture.

Analogously, if the Russians and Chinese are to solve their ideological difficulties, they will not be able to do so simply by quoting Marx or Lenin in support of their position. Neither side has definitive arguments. The solution must be found through other means.

CHAPTER III

MARXIST PHILOSOPHY OF NATURE AND BEING (DIALECTICAL MATERIALISM)

Marx's and Engels' View of Their Ontology

If, as V. Venable points out, historical materialism states the laws of the development of human history, then dialectical materialism states the laws of all history whatsoever. It is the Marxian philosophy of change.[1] It constitutes the Marxian metaphysics.

However, the Marxist would feel more at ease if a term other than "metaphysics" be used to designate his philosophy of being, for next to the word "bourgeoisie," perhaps no other term is as obnoxious to the followers of Marx as "metaphysics." To them metaphysics stands for those philosophical positions that Marx and Engels have cast aside forever. It is the antithesis of science and truth, the antithesis of dialectics. Metaphysics represents all irresponsible speculation divorced from fact and experience, all indifference to the canons of scientific procedure. It was metaphysicians who refused to view the heavens with Galileo's telescope lest Aristotle's speculations be proved wrong; it was Descartes turned metaphysician, who raised the universal doubt; it was the metaphysician Kant who attempted to kill metaphysics by formulating the categories. Even Hegel, the first exponent of the dialectic, turned metaphysician to the extent he mystified and idealized it.

Moreover, metaphysics represents in Marxist eyes any philosophical world view which renders objects static, atomistic, subsistent, isolated or severed from one another. In other words, metaphysics represents any view that ignores the dynamic and interacting "whole" of reality, and substantializes the static parts.[2] No, the Marxist would not wish to call dialectical materialism his metaphysics. Yet it does represent the Marxian ontology, the Marxian philosophy of natural reality seen in its ultimate principles. Dialectical materialism for Marx and Engels constituted neither a dogmatic pronouncement, a set of *a priori* principles from which the various concrete data of the universe could be logically deduced, nor a philosophical "system" by which men could properly interpret these empirical data. For the Marxist the laws of reality are merely guides to further study and empirical investigation,[3] as well as guides to action, practice and changes in human history.[4] "Communism proceeds not from principles, but from facts. It is no doctrine, but rather a movement."[5] For Marx and Engels, dialectical materialism represented the most highly detailed account possible of the most general laws that could be discovered in all change known to man in their day. It represented the laws of all process, both human and natural, which had been observed up to that period by empirical investigation; it described the ontological structure of development. Its laws represented the laws of ultimate reality; yet these laws were neither innate to man, nor infused by higher beings. There is no human knowledge of them prior to man's discovery of them in his actual experience with reality.[6] They are not built into nature by man, but discovered in it and evolved from it.[7]

Marx and Engels did not consider themselves fully responsible for the discovery of the dialectical laws of reality. The early Greeks, and especially Aristotle, analyzed the most essential forms of dialectical thought. Later Descartes, Spinoza, Diderot and Rousseau all brilliantly expounded dialectics.[8] Above all, of course, it was Hegel who first presented dialectics in a completely conscious manner.[9]

Influence of Hegel and Feuerbach on the Marxian View of Nature

At the time Marx entered the University of Berlin, all German universities were obliged to teach the philosophy of Hegel, who had recently died. This philosophy of deep abstractions was known as dialectical idealism. It was called idealism because it was concerned with thought, ideas, spirits, minds. Reality, said Hegel, is not things but ideas. It was called dialectical because it described the method by which thoughts or ideas developed — that is, by contradiction.

Hegel develops a series of concepts called "logical categories" consisting of quantity, quality, essence, appearance, possibility, accident, necessity, reality, and so on. These conceptions, having self-sustaining, eternal existence independent of man, much resemble the platonic world of forms except for one important difference. They are not static but dynamic. The totality of these dynamic forms he refers to as *the Idea* or *the Absolute*. The *Absolute* is the ultimate reality, the source of nature — and through nature — the source of mind. The connection between the categories is dialectical; that is, the connection is such that if any one of them is sufficiently examined, it will be found to lead on to another either as a reaction to its incompleteness and one-sidedness or as a transcending of its contradictions. The *Absolute* is not only the totality of thought, but also of all experience. History, the passage of human events, will show forth the same dialectical process as the dynamic forms. All elements of human behavior as well as all human institutions have an essential tendency to beget the contrary and, as a result, to transform themselves into new things — syntheses which include and yet surpass the first two antagonistic terms. Every synthesis is a conquered or resolved contradiction. In the synthesis, the thesis and its contradictory antithesis are said to be transposed, sublimated, transfigured. Yet the dialectical law also applies to any newly created synthesis which, in its turn as thesis, begets a new antithesis. Hence, for Hegel nothing possesses complete reality except the *Absolute,* and it is insofar as a thing is seen in its relation to the *Absolute* that it possesses, to a greater or lesser degree, reality, reasonableness and truth.[10]

As has been mentioned, dialectics did not originate with Hegel. The term itself comes from a Greek word meaning to argue or discuss. Among the early Greek philosophers it signified an art of discussion whereby apparently contrary or contradictory positions held by the disputants were altered by their precise exposition and rebuttal so that a position was arrived at that was both closer to the truth and mutually acceptable. This art of dialectics is seen in its near perfection in the Socratic dialogues of Plato. Plato, however, is responsible for an added imposition of meaning to the term because dialectics, for him, also designates the science which arrives at a knowledge of the nature of ideas.

To the Scholastics of the Middle Ages, dialectics had at least two meanings. First, it was used as a synonym for "logic," the science of right thinking; secondly, it referred to that particular aspect of logic as found in Aristotle's *Topics* wherein the syllogisms produce conclusions which are not demonstrative because of their content or matter, but are true only in varying degrees of probability, *i.e.,* their contradictions cannot be demonstrated false. These conclusions, because of their mere probability, are always open to further discussion and greater certitude. In all instances, the word "dialectics" somehow referred to the art or science of statement and counter-statement from which emerged a fuller grasp of the truth.

Hegel was quick to notice that dialectics is always productive of a more developed idea, richer in its content of truth. This completed idea, he contended, is always arrived at through a series of three stages. The first stage is to assert the positive truth contained in the original idea. This he calls the *thesis*. The thesis contains within itself its own contradictory. This, the second stage of development of the idea, Hegel calls the *antithesis*. The antithesis is not the annihilation of the thesis. Rather, it qualifies or limits the original concept by negation of a portion of its content. The antithesis is an attack on the error inherent in the thesis and, in a sense may be said to possess indirectly a positive content of truth. The continued negation of the thesis brings into existence the third stage that represents the developed idea which Hegel terms the *synthesis*. This consists of the unification of the truth found in the thesis and antithesis. For Hegel the development of the idea results from the very nature of the idea itself. Since the idea contains its own contradiction, the mere positing of the idea or thesis brings the antithesis into existence, and thence the synthesis. This process, insofar as it represents only a portion of the Absolute, is capable of continuing indefinitely. The developed idea, the synthesis, may in its turn become the thesis of a new dialectical process from which will emerge a more fully developed idea.[11]

The followers of Hegel divided themselves into two schools following his death. There were those who were impressed by his idealism, and certainly Marx was not one of these. The other group to which Marx belonged in his youth was known as the "Left" Hegelians. This group rejected Hegel's idealism as well as a certain anti-dialectical tendency of his system that presented itself as the summit of philosophical development and the Prussian monarchy as the final incarnation of the Spirit. It was impressed by his dialectics with its denial of the permanence of truth and the immutability of principle, in which everything appears to be continually on the move in the process of endless becoming. In addition, Marx respected the immense power of synthesis in Hegel's system by which the whole range of human knowledge is apprehended in its living unit — the idea of a world-embracing, universal, living interconnection of all things with one another.[12] These aspects of Hegelianism were to have a permanent place in his philosophy.

About the time he received his doctorate, Marx was also deeply influenced by the materialistic philosophy of Ludwig Feuerbach, who in his controversial work, *The Essence of Christianity,* attempted to destroy Christianity by affirming that matter is the basic reality. Feuerbach then applied the Hegelian dialectic to deduce his conclusion that religion was an illusion formed in the brain of man that alienated him from his fellow men and from himself. This was much to the liking of Marx. Feuerbach had dealt a deathblow to the idealism of Hegel and had placed materialism on the throne once more.[13]

Whereas Hegel looked to the infinity of diversity and contingency in nature as a weakness in nature showing forth its subserviency in relation to spirit, Feuerbach *(Critique of the Hegelian Philosophy)* reversed this relationship to affirm not that material reality is inadequate to the concept but that the concept is inadequate to reality. Hence, Hegelianism may justify history but is not capable of explaining the world of nature, for true reality is composed of the diverse parts of nature. Only the sensory individual is real, and the universal concept is merely an illusion on the part of man. Hegel considered the idea to be the true reality and nature as the external guise. Feuerbach *(Outlines for a Philosophy of the Future)*, inverting the Hegelian thesis, held that the idea is not a real entity but merely a duplication and at best a pale reflection of nature.[14] Thus, Feuerbach terminated in a full-fledged materialistic philosophy.

Now Marx arrived at the idea of taking the dialectical method that Hegel had applied to ideas and applying it to Feuerbach's basis of reality, *i.e.,* matter, in a more consistent way than Feuerbach had done. In their investigations both Hegel and Feuerbach had hit upon important truths. Hegel had seen that reality is a process of self-development in accordance with the dialectical method, but, in thinking that dialectics was the self-development of the concept, he had "mystified" this method and made it unusable. Feuerbach had re-established once more the truths that reality was matter and that man was the center of that reality, but in spite of his somewhat superficial use of the Hegelian dialectic, he had fallen into the same errors as previous materialists. First, he had taken a too mechanistic view of the universe by explaining vegetable, animal and even human organisms in terms of purely mechanical causes. Secondly, in failing to escape from the realm of abstraction, he was unable to comprehend the universe as a process — as matter developing in an historical process. His materialism had an excessively abstract, "metaphysical" character which conceived of man as an absolute entity remaining unchanged regardless of his historical development and concrete situation. Thirdly, his humanism was too religious, for Feuerbach had done no more than replace the religious link between God and man by an equally religious relationship between men themselves.[15]

In a sense Marx and Engels synthesized Hegel and Feuerbach. Whereas Hegel saw the dialectical development in nature and human events as only a mere shadow of the self-movement of the concept going on from eternity independent of the human brain, Marx and Engels reversed this ideology. They held that concepts are comprehended in men's minds materialistically and that dialectics reduces itself to the science of the general laws of motion of both the external world and of human thought.[16]

From the contradictories of Hegel's idealist dialectic and Feuerbach's materialism, there arose *Dialectical Materialism,* the ontology of communism. From now on Marx would see contradiction at the very heart of matter. There is no need of a God to explain matter and causality, for matter contains motion within itself. Matter develops and evolves by contradiction, struggle, opposition. Reality is revolutionary; being is matter becoming and in some fashion united to itself as a whole.

Joseph Stalin perhaps sums up the ontology of Marxism most adequately as follows:

(a) Contrary to metaphysics, dialectics does not regard nature as an accidental agglomeration of things, of phenomena, unconnected with, isolated from, and independent of each other but as a connected and integral whole, in which things, phenomena are organically connected with, dependent on, and determined by, each other. . . .

(b) Contrary to metaphysics, dialectics holds that nature is not a state of rest and immobility, stagnation and immutability, but a state of continuous movement and change, of continuous renewal and development, where something is always arising and developing, and something always disintegrating and dying away. . . .

(c) Contrary to metaphysics, dialectics does not regard the process of development as a simple process of growth where quantitative changes do not lead to qualitative changes, but as a development which passes from insignificant and imperceptible quantitative changes to open fundamental changes, to qualitative changes; a development in which the qualitative changes occur not gradually, but rapidly and abruptly, taking the form of a leap from one state to another; they occur not accidentally but as the natural results of an accumulation of imperceptible and gradual quantitative changes. . . .

(d) Contrary to metaphysics, dialectics holds that internal contradictions are inherent in all things and phenomena of nature for they all have their negative and positive sides, a past and a future, something dying away and something developing; and that the struggle between these opposites, the struggle between the old and the new, between that which is dying away and that which is disappearing and that which is developing, constitutes the internal content of the process of development, the internal content of the transformation of quantitative changes into qualitative changes.

The dialectical method, therefore, holds that the process of development from the lower to the higher takes place not as a harmonious unfolding of phenomena, but as a disclosure of the contradictions inherent in things and phenomena, as a "struggle" of opposite tendencies which operate on the basis of these contradictions. "In its proper meaning," Lenin says, "dialectics is the study of the contradictions within the very essence of things."[17]

As we have seen, the Hegelian dialectic was the portion of idealism upon which Marx based his materialism. It afforded a sound basis for a materialistic philosophy because it provided materialism with an energizing principle it so badly needed. Marx and Engels acknowledged that the Hegelian dialectic was the basis of all dialectic and stated that they were going to turn it right side up and apply it to the materialistic conception of nature,[18] for nature is the test of dialectics. Modern natural science has provided the materials by which nature's process in the last analysis is proved to be dialectical and not metaphysical.[19] For Hegel it was the *idea* that was composed of contradictory elements. For Marx *matter* is composed of contradictory elements. The contradictory elements in matter account for Marxian development. In Hegel's dialectic the idea was self-sufficient; its contradictory nature provides it with a motive force of development. For Marx, matter is self-sufficient; its contradictory nature provides it with an immanent principle which dispenses with the need of any cause external to itself.[20] As Marx points out:

> To Hegel, the life process of the human brain, *i.e.,* the process of thinking, which, under the name of "the Idea," he even transforms into an independent subject, is the demiurgos of the real world and the real world is only the external, phenomenal form of "the Idea." With me, on the contrary, the idea is nothing else than the material world

reflected by the human mind, and translated into forms of thought.[21]

And Engels adds:

> According to Hegel . . . the dialectical development apparent in nature and history . . . is only a miserable copy of the self-movement of the concept going on from eternity, no one knows where, but at all events independently of any thinking human brain. This ideological reversal had to be done away with. We comprehended the concepts in our heads once more materialistically — as images of real things instead of regarding the real things as images of this or that stage of development of the absolute concept.[22]

Parts of the Universe are Interrelated

The application of the dialectic to material reality gave Marx both a new approach to the understanding of individual reality and a concept of the universe as a constantly developing process in which all things are interrelated and interacting. The conception of the universe as a process was a logical and necessary deduction of Hegelianism. In contrast, the materialism of the 18th century had fallen into the practice of analyzing each individual reality in itself and ignoring its relationship to everything else. This was primarily due to the fact that materialism had allied itself with the natural sciences of that period which were mostly concerned with classifying individual things.[23]

The analysis of Nature into its individual parts, the grouping of the different natural processes and natural objects into definite classes, the study of the internal anatomy of organic bodies in their manifold forms — these were the fundamental conditions of the gigantic strides in our knowledge of Nature which have been made during the last four hundred years. But this method of investigation has also left us as a legacy the habit of observing natural objects and natural processes in their isolation, detached from the whole vast interconnection of things; and therefore not in their motion, but in their repose; not as essentially changing, but as fixed constants; not in their life, but in their death . . . , and this is so because in considering individual things it loses sight of their connections; in contemplating their existence it forgets their coming into being and passing away; in looking at them in rest it leaves their motion out of account. . . .[24]

Marx and Engels believed that Hegelianism in contrast to natural science and previous materialism had maintained the proper outlook on the universe by viewing it as a vast constantly developing process. When science minutely analyzed the individual particle, it failed to consider that that which it analyzed never existed in such a manner in the real world. In the world of nature, it is a part of the whole acting upon the other realities and other realities upon it. If an adequate grasp of the individual is to be had, this fact must be taken into consideration. Natural science and 18th century materialistic philosophy had failed to do this. With the inversion of Hegelianism and the subsequent application of the dialectic to materialism, Marx and Engels arrived at what to them was the true viewpoint of the universe. Instead of matter being regarded as inert, characterized only by mechanical motion caused externally, dialectical materialism conceives it as essentially active. Things are no longer to be considered as merely a totality of so many distinct and independent entities, but rather as parts of one great process in which all things are related and interacting. "The world is not to be comprehended as a complex of ready-made *things,* but as a complex of *processes.* . . ."[25] No phenomenon can be understood if taken by itself, but only if considered in its inseparable connection with surrounding phenomena.[26]

This viewpoint forms the basis of dialectical materialism. Ideologically, it forms the foundation and guidepost of the Marxist approach to science. Without appealing to any cause external to nature itself, this analysis of nature affords the Marxist scientist an overall explanation of all natural phenomena.

The Laws of Matter

A better understanding of this dialectical approach to nature can be had if an examination is made of what may be termed the fundamental laws of matter. Although these laws have been stated in various ways by the different commentators of Marxism, they may be correctly reduced to the same three fundamental laws of the dialectic as formulated by Hegel in his *Logic*. These laws have become known as: *The Law of the Transition from Quantity to Quality, The Law of the Unity and Struggle of Opposites,* and *The Law of the Negation of the Negation.*

The Law of the Transition from Quantity to Quality attempts to explain the appearance of new qualities in natural things and the subsequent consequences of their appearance. The content of this law is that the development of things and phenomena in the world proceeds up to a certain point or "node" as a gradual quantitative change. As the quantitative change advances beyond the limits prescribed by the nature of the thing in question, a sudden leap from quantitative to qualitative change takes place; there is a fundamental alteration of the subject. It ceases to be what it is and becomes something else. A new quality has emerged.[27]

By "quality" the dialectical materialist means the immediate determinateness of a given thing which distinguishes it from other objects. As such, quality is not to be confused with the "property" of a thing which signifies its quality in its relation to other things.[28] Whereas quality may be described as the determinateness of a thing immediately identical with its being, "quantity" is not identical with the being but external to it; its changes, within certain limits, have no effect on the quality of the thing.[29]

To summarize, quality refers to the relative stability of the thing, its inner unit; quantity expresses its capacity for certain changes which do not disturb the basic stability. In the course of quantitative change the invariance of quality is only relative to certain limits. Once quantitative change reaches this limit, there is a sudden transition from the previous quality to a new one. The organic unity of qualitative and quantitative determination is referred to by the dialectical materialist as "measure." Measure denotes the limits in which quantitative alterations do not result in qualitative changes. The points of transition from one measure to another are termed "nodes."[30]

There are many examples offered by science as proof of the law of transition from quantity to quality. The most obvious for Engels is offered by molecular chemistry where so often a quantitative addition or diminution of atoms will give a new element with totally different qualities.[31]

How different is laughing gas (nitrogen monoxide N_2O) from nitric anhydride (nitrogen pentoxide N_2O_5)! The first is a gas, the second at ordinary temperatures a solid crystalline substance. And yet the whole difference in composition is that the second contains five times as much oxygen as the first, and between the two of them are three more oxides of nitrogen NO, N_2O_3, NO_2), each of which is qualitatively different from the first two and from one another.[32]

More recent physics has strengthened the Marxist assurance of the actuality of this law. Within the periodic system of the elements, a change in atomic number tends to coincide with a new qualitative state of an element. The law applies equally to the organic world. In the field of biology, as early as Darwin, it was alleged that the accumulation of insignificant quantitative changes in organisms eventually results in a new species.[33] Even man is not exempted. Comparative physiology shows the striking similarity of structure of man with other vertebrates. Man represents a qualitative leap in a previous quantitative series.[34]

Certainly the law of transition makes clear that dialectical materialism is a philosophy of evolution. But unlike some theories of evolution, Marxism insists that new forms are never the result of mere gradual change. While it is true that gradual quantitative development precedes the emergence of the new form and that it is quantitative development which ultimately accounts for the emergence of the new forms, nevertheless the actual emergence of the new reality is always the result of a "leap," a sudden change in nature. "In spite of all intermediate steps, the transition from one form of motion to another always remains a leap, a decisive change."[35] Thus the emergence of all new forms, including man, is to be explained as a leap in nature, a sudden production of a qualitatively new reality resulting from a quantitative development in an already existing thing. The insistence upon a *sudden* production of new forms when carried over to the social sciences shows itself in the form of a necessity for *violent revolution* in that field.

The Law of the Unity and Struggle of Opposites asserts both the essentially contradictory nature of reality and that the very contradictions thus revealed exist in unity. The dialectical method holds that the process of development from the lower to the higher does not take place as a harmonious unfolding of phenomena but rather as an indication of the contradictions inherent in things and phenomena, and as a struggle of opposite tendencies which operate on the basis of these contradictions. These internal contradictions are inherent in all things and all phenomena of nature. Each has its negative and its positive side, its past and its future, something disintegrating and something developing. The struggle between these opposites, between the old and the new, between that which is dying away and that which is coming to be, between that which is disappearing and that which is developing, constitutes the internal content of the process of development and the internal content of the transition of quantitative changes into new qualities.[36]

Science, itself, provides the basic proof of the unity of opposites.[37] It has shown that attraction and repulsion are properties of every body. Similarly, science has shown positive and negative charges are essential to the nature of electricity. Magnetism is made up of positive and negative poles. Man's personality is composed of the selfish and the altruistic, antisocial and social traits within the same entity. One of the strongest proofs that reality is a unity of opposites has been proffered by science in recent decades. The atom is composed of protons and electrons — the basic unit of all reality is shown to be a unity of opposites. Energy and matter have always been regarded as opposites. Yet modern science in apparently reducing the atom to positive and negative charges of electricity, would have us hold that matter is energy and that energy constitutes matter. This is another indication, argues the Marxist, that reality is a unity of opposites.

From Hegelianism came the concept that the contradiction inherent in the idea provided the idea with an inherent motive force towards development. In dialectical materialism the contradiction in matter provides matter with an immanent motive force driving it on to development. Thus, in the whole of nature, development does not proceed as the result of God or any external agent, or by teleological designs, but it comes about because of the inherent contradictions contained in the universe. Contradiction is for the Marxist, as for Hegel, the root of all motion and of all life. Reality, by its very makeup, is a unity of opposites; all things contain an immanent contradiction within themselves. This furnishes the key to the "self-movement" of everything existing. It furnishes the key to the "leaps," to the "break in continuity," to the "transformation into the opposite," to the extinction of the old and the coming to be of the new.[38] Contradiction is necessarily productive of motion, needing no agent outside the material universe itself to account for motion. Motion is merely the mode of existence of matter arising from the very nature of matter itself.

The real connection between matter and motion . . . is simple enough. *Motion is the mode of existence of matter.* Never anywhere has there been matter without motion nor can there be. . . . All rest, all equilibrium, is only relative, and only has meaning in relation to one or other definite form of motion. . . . Matter without motion is just as unthinkable as motion without matter. Motion is therefore as uncreatable and indestructible as matter itself.[39]

As long as we view the realities about us as static and lifeless, each one as by itself, we do not see the contradiction in them — except for, perhaps, certain qualities that are partly diverse to one another. If on the other hand, claims Engels, we look at reality as it exists in nature; if "we consider things in their motion, their change, their life, their reciprocal influence on one another," then we do become immediately involved in contradictions. Even simple mechanical local motion can come about only by a body being both in one place and another at the same instant. It is the continuous assertion and simultaneous solution of this contradiction that precisely constitutes motion.[40]

Contradiction is not limited to inorganic matter. Life itself is a contradiction, just as is the development of human thought and social life. In fact, the law of opposites was originally discovered by Marx as a law of social development. Engels, through his investigations in the realm of natural sciences, confirmed it as an ontological law of being. As such it has now universal application for the Marxist.[41]

The Law of the Negation of the Negation in the opinion of Soviet philosophers can be understood only on the basis of the first two laws. The law of the unity and struggle of opposites is concerned with the nature and origin of change and development. The law of transition expresses development as a transformation from quantitative to qualitative change. The law of negation of negation relates to the tendency and to the direction of that development. The law of opposites expresses *why* development occurs; the law of transition tells *how* it occurs; and the law of negation, tells *whither* it is going.

The law of negation of negation states that a sudden change to a new quality according to the law of transition necessarily implies the negation of the previous quality. But development does not cease with this negation. The new quality becomes in its turn the starting point for a further process of development which once again is negated. The previous quality is "transcended" *(aufgehoben)* by a new one.

Marxism presents this law, then, as its explanation of the progressive character of reality. This law, as the other two, is a direct inversion of Hegel. In Hegelianism, the idea developed by way of a three-fold dialectical process — a thesis, an antithesis and a synthesis. This is, in effect, the positing of an assertion, its negation, and the negation of the negation. Marx, by applying this Hegelian law to material reality, made "negation" and "negation of negation" phases of development of matter rather than phases of development of the idea.[43] Thus the nature of matter and motion is such that a thing in motion necessarily progresses towards its own negation. This motion, however, no sooner negates than it is itself in turn negated. Motion continues on, but always on a higher plane, always towards development.

> The dialectical method therefore holds that the process of development should be understood not as movement in a

circle, not as a simple repetition of what has already occurred, but as an onward and upward movement, as a transition from an old qualitative state to a new qualitative state, as a development from the simple to the complex, from the lower to the higher.[44]

Despite the negation, dialectical development retains its connection with the past. It does not truly abolish or annihilate what has previously transpired. The law of negation of the negation implies no immediate cancellation of the past; rather it is a denial which conserves that which is positive and true in what had previously been attained.[45]

The law of negation is a law of nature. It operates in nature in only one way in reference to each individual. To properly understand this law, one must closely observe nature and see how it negates each particular reality in order to produce development. When a particular entity is not interfered with, nature negates it in its particular manner, and development is realized. Any other form of negation is not the proper negation of the thing as it should be negated under normal conditions in the world of nature. The classic example of natural negation and unnatural negation is given by Engels in reference to the grain of barley. It can be destroyed by brewing and so consumed or allowed to die in the soil and thus germinate and develop thirty-fold.[46]

It is by the observation of reality that the dialectical laws of nature are to be discovered and understood. This holds as true in the search for sociological truth as it does for the truths of physics, chemistry or biology. It is only in the observation of all nature that the Marxist can understand himself and his world. This is undoubtedly what Paul Langevin, the renowned French Marxist physicist, had in mind when he wrote concerning education:

> The school should unite with nature and with life, often leaving the walls of the classroom to return laden with experience and with observations, to enrich itself with reflection and meditation, to learn how to record the expression and the representation of things seen, lived or felt. It should feel itself part and parcel of the outside world. . . . Thus the child's

field of vision will widen progressively along with his discovery of his immediate world. This will enable him to find his place there as well as in an ever widening circle. He will follow the true way of culture which goes from the near to the far, from the particular to the general, from the concrete to the abstract, from individuality to generality, from egocentric to altruistic interest. This is as true of his contact with men as it is of his contact with things.[47]

This, then, is the Marxian philosophical view of nature. The Marxist will approach science with these philosophical convictions which will serve to integrate his scientific knowledge while at the same time acting as guiding lights for his research into new and undiscovered areas of science. By the law of transition, he knows that his own mind is of a material nature and is just an emergent, a product of a qualitative leap which occurred in nature after organic matter had evolved to a very high degree. He knows that the matter which the scientist investigates is a composite of contradictory elements, a unity of opposites. He knows that such contradiction is necessarily productive of motion, that the subject of his investigation is by its very nature autodynamic and that "the last vestige of a creator external to the world is obliterated."[48] He knows that the motion proper to the matter under the scientist's microscope produces the development of it and that this being tends towards its own negation in a manner which results in its continuous development.

The Marxist also realizes that these laws are absolute in the sense that nothing in the yet undiscovered realm of science will in any way contradict them. Rather, new discoveries will only serve to strengthen them. Any scientific theory, ancient or modern, that stands opposed to the Marxian concept of nature can be presumed false and can be rejected *ipso facto*. In the field of astronomy, as one instance, the now generally accepted theory of the expanding finite universe of Abbé Lemaitre must be rejected by the communist.

This theory of a closed but expanding universe has offered explanation of many difficulties confronted by astronomers of the past. It explains, for example, why distant galaxies exhibit a redshift in their spectral lines; it is simply an instance of the so-called

"Doppler effect." It is caused by recessional velocity. This means that our universe is in a rapid state of dispersion. It was Albert Einstein who first dismissed the once popular infinite universe theory. He showed that the universe could be infinite only if the mean density of matter is zero. But there is no physical basis for this in experience. Rather for Einstein, there is a closed, curved, yet unbounded universe.[49] De Sitter, in turn, constructed a spherical universe devoid of matter and managed to get rid of Einstein's troublesome absolute, straight-line time direction. A. Friedmann, using Einstein's original relativist gravitational equations, arrived at a dynamic model of the finite unbounded universe with a varying radius. Finally, Lemaitre showed that both the Einstein and De Sitter universe models were basically unstable. That is to say, as soon as matter condenses in Einstein's universe, or as soon as matter is introduced into De Sitter's universe, it expands. Thus was born the expanding finite universe theory. The present size of the universe shows mathematically that it is from four to six billion years old.[50]

The Marxist feels bound to reject this theory as being opposed to his basic concepts of nature, for the Marxian view obviously implies the eternal existence of matter. Engels indicates that the world is an infinite and eternal process, using the word "infinite" in its strictest connotation.

> Eternity in time, infinity in space, mean from the start, and in the simple meaning of the words, that there is no end in *any* direction, neither forwards nor backwards. . . . It is clear that the infinity which has an end but no beginning is neither more nor less infinite than that which has a beginning but no end. . . . The material world . . . is an infinite process, unrolling endlessly in time and space.[51]

Thus, any estimation of "the age of the universe" or a finite time scale is backsliding towards the religious idea of creation by God.[52] A finite expanding universe would contradict Engels' formulation of the finite to the infinite. The material world is "an infinite process unrolling endlessly in time and space"; the finiteness of Lemaitre's material world leads to the contradiction of its infiniteness.[53]

The communist cosmologist must hold Einstein and his successors guilty of placing astronomical studies in a geometric strait jacket. Their theory is just another example of idealistic and mathematical symbolism or formalism. It is reactionary because it tends towards subjectivism and anthropomorphism.[54] Secondly, the relativist cosmologists have fallen into the error of extrapolation. The theory of relativity is valid only for portions of the universe.[55] The extension of the relativist physical laws to the universe, as a whole, is unscientific. There is no strict proof that the mathematico-physical laws which appear valid on a local scale, can be applied to the universe as a whole, given the experimental inaccessibility of much of the heavens. Finally, the very fact that the expanding finite universe theory has received the blessings of Pope Pius XII is just further proof that this theory is fundamentally religious and, therefore, unscientific.[56]

For the communist cosmogonist, the universe has no creator and, therefore, no beginning in time. The universe contains innumerable worlds in infinite space existing eternally and undergoing perpetual change. There is no heat death of the universe but rather an unending succession of worlds whereby extinct stars fall into one another producing tremendous heat from collision and then evolving into new stars.[57] What appears to the bourgeois astronomer to be solid proof for receding velocity—the red spectral shift because of the Doppler effect—is explained by the Marxist astronomer as a phenomenon caused by the slight loss of energy in aging photons passing through a gravitational field. This is the cause of the color shift.[58] The infinity of the universe cannot be denied philosophically. It is only religion and idealism that bind the bourgeoisie to a finite universe.

In all other fields of science likewise the communist can accept only theories that coincide with his principles. In genetics, he must reject *Mendelism-Morganism* as reactionary and unscientific. The *chance* assortment of chromosomes is mythical nonsense. To the Marxist, science is the enemy of chance. He holds that heredity and its effects can be changed merely by a change of metabolism.[59] This is based on the dialectical laws of matter and, therefore, must be true. In quantum mechanics he must reject the "complementarity principle" of the Copenhagen school, in chemistry he discounts the "resonance theory" of Pauling. And so it goes. All science must be firmly based on the dialectical laws of nature. In them is to be potentially found all truths of science. The communist must approach science with this firm conviction or his study is in vain.

The Link Between Soviet Science and Philosophy — Appendix III

It is a particularly difficult task to discover in the Soviet philosophic doctrine a precise formulation of a "philosophy of science" or a "philosophy of nature."[60] The reason is threefold. First, there is the ambiguity found in the Marxist classics, especially in the writings of Engels who, more than anyone, was responsible for the construction of a *doctrina naturae* from the mutual insights of Marx and himself. Second, there is the inherent necessity of dialectical materialism or any materialistic position to identify its philosophy of nature with its ontology despite the loud outcry of the Soviet philosophic camp against any attempt to identify its position with that nauseous word, "metaphysics." Finally, there is a condition of flux in the positions of contemporary Soviet philosophers on several important facets of a current philosophical problem — the relation of philosophy to the natural sciences.

An attempt will be made, however, to present a relatively definitive exposition and occasional critique of the elements of this relationship between different approaches within the field that are construed as stabilized. By so limiting our consideration, we necessarily undermine our chance at obtaining an integrated understanding of the link between the special sciences — especially those newest among them, for example, mathematical physics — and philosophy.

The present role of philosophy as an independent intellectual discipline as well as its relationship to the special sciences has resulted from a successful struggle against exponents of two extremist views concerning the position of philosophy amongst the bolshevists themselves. One group, called the mechanists, insisted that the Marxist "world outlook" should be found and embodied in the latest findings of the experimental sciences. The second group, the "menshevizing idealists," were those accused of reducing the materialistic dialectic to a methodology, a system of concepts, an *a priori* logic of thought divorced from the real, natural world. It is extremely interesting to come face to face so often with the obvious and pervading influence of Kant on Western thought — an influence that has even seeped into an interpretation of materialistic realism! It must be remembered at the same time that most of the tendencies towards idealism and romanticism which are found occasionally amongst Marxists can be traced more surely to the Hegelian soil in which the materialistic dialectic is rooted than to any other one source.

The official Soviet view of dialectical materialism is that it is neither a methodology exclusively nor simply a general theory of matter built on the experimental evidence of the positive sciences; rather it is a combination of both — a world outlook and a methodology. Insofar as it is a world outlook, that is, an overall theory of reality, it deals with the same subject matter as the special sciences. But this, of course, immediately raises the question of how philosophy is to be distinguished from the other sciences if the subject matter is the same.

According to Russian philosopher Kedrov,[61] it was Marx and Engels who first found a satisfactory solution. Whereas the natural sciences confine their inquiries to a particular portion of reality and investigate the laws operative in that field, philosophy looks to laws operative in reality as a whole. Hence, there is no antagonism or even subordination between philosophy and the sciences; rather there is a mutual supplementation. Philosophy provides a general *method* of scientific knowledge and an ultimate *interpretation* of the factual knowledge obtained by the sciences. The sciences supply the concrete *facts* from which philosophy can derive the generalizations of the laws of reality.

Such a theory appears to be basically sound although we may question its origin in Marx and Engels. However in failing to distinguish between metaphysics and natural philosophy the Marxist not only limits the scope of reality and therefore the scope of philosophy and truth but errs grievously when he applies the laws of matter to derive an explanation of the social, historical, legal, religious and aesthetic problems. His so doing involves, in addition, a bit of circular reasoning as we shall investigate presently. In this dual-function conception of philosophy, the Soviets seem to be breaking with an anti-philosophical attitude which is found in certain portions of Engels' writings if not in those of Marx. Engels does not hesitate at times to glorify the positive sciences in the fashion of the 19th century while relegating philosophy to the role of a logic or a methodology only.

> As soon as each separate science is required to get clarity as to its position in the great totality of things and of our knowledge of things, a special science dealing with this totality is superfluous. What still independently survives of all former philosophy is the science of thought and its laws — formal logic and dialectics. Everything else is merged in the positive science of Nature and history.[62]

However, as has been mentioned, Engels is ambiguous on this point. In another place in *Anti-Dühring,* Engels seems to recognize philosophy as including the general laws of being as well as those of the mind.

> [Dialectics is] nothing more than the science of the general laws of motion and development of Nature, human society and thought.[63]

The ambiguity in Engels as we have seen has been a source of no small internal conflict even among the bolshevists, not to mention the struggle within the broader realm of Marxist philosophy itself. But whatever the ambiguity, without question the official Soviet philosophy reappears as a science of the laws of being. However, because it does purport to explain the laws of all reality, it also claims to offer to science a universal methodology. The dialectic, too, becomes an instrument of scientific investigation; while serving in this capacity, it itself becomes enriched by the attainments of the natural sciences. Precisely because the dialectic provides all science with a unitary method it becomes the "science of sciences," an "organon" of the sciences, standing above them and showing them how they should approach phenomena and in what manner they are to investigate them.

Now such a restriction of method is in itself legitimate, for a scientific method is, indeed, a *conditio sine qua non* of any theory of science. Marxism, though, attempts to unify or rather identify its science of thought and its ontology. This it can do without hesitation for, if thought is at root material, it necessarily follows the laws of matter.

However, the Soviet philosophy does not stop at the restriction of method; it actually commits the sciences *a priori* to specific positions or assertions about reality much as a theology sets down its principles as infallible and irreproachable. The basis for the seeming authoritarianism in this respect is founded in the "partisan character" of philosophy as formulated by Lenin. This partisanship was stated by Lenin in the following words:

> Materialism includes, so to speak, partisanship, which enjoins the direct and open adoption of the standpoint of a definite social group in any judgment of events.[64]

Such an approach to philosophy at first appears almost scandalous. For philosophy must above all be a science, and therefore objective. A partisanship in philosophy would appear to be so foreign to the philosophic spirit that one could immediately question the integrity of a Soviet philosopher both in his strict *a priori* interpretations of the physical facts established and predicted by modern science and, especially, in the retractions of his opinions found to be contrary to the Communist Party "line." Yet we can begin to understand how such a philosophic spirit can be advanced in all earnestness if we call to mind the important maxim of dialectical materialism which goes back in origin to Marx himself — the demand for a unity of theory and practice. Philosophy must be actualized, brought out of the realm of pure thought into that of practice. The speculative truth is worthless unless it has a direct utilitarian relationship to human exigency. A philosophy is Philosophy only if it is first of all an ideology. But more than that. This ideology must be found in class-consciousness for it is only the class and not the individual that serves as a basis for value. All philosophy, including bourgeois philosophy, is a class-interested philosophy — even if it endeavors to hide its ideology under the mask of objectivity.[65] But of all class ideologies, it is the philosophy of the proletarian class — its *par-*

tisan philosophy — that reflects in its *subjectivism* the true *objective* laws of reality. The more completely the interests of the working class find expression in philosophy, the more completely and profoundly will the philosophy expose these objective laws of being, for it is the subjective interests of the proletariat, according to Marx's conception of history, that coincide with the objective laws of development. It is at this point that the Marxist reasoning becomes involved in some circularity which may be briefly summed up as follows. The apparent starting point in philosophy for Marx is with man — communal man — that is, society. But knowledge of society must come from a study and interpretation of history, that is, actualized philosophy. In order to offer what he considered a correct interpretation of history, he posited his well-known theory of *historical materialism,* which, in the words of Sorel and Croce, is actually a "metaphysics of economics." This theory presupposes two philosophical positions — the Hegelian dialectic and the material nature of reality. Using these two suppositions, Marx, with the help of Engels, proceeded to the position that history with its economic determinism eventually leads to the bourgeoisie-proletariat class struggle. Each class has its own ideology, but only the proletarian partisan philosophy reflects reality and the objective laws of being. These laws are then discovered to be dialectical, and reality material. Using these laws of matter, the proletariat can further philosophize about society, and so on. Thus, it is evident that the suppositions are used to advance a theory which serves as the principle by which the suppositions are proved. The suppositions are then used as principles to strengthen the original hypothesis.

If it is granted that objective reality is to be found in partisan philosophy, the question still to be answered is: who or what is to interpret the *de facto* interests of the proletariat? Who, reply the Soviets, could possibly be better fitted for the role than the Communist Party, the *avant-garde* of the working class, its outspoken defender and its most progressive segment, the repository of the revelation recorded in the Marxist classics and the tradition of the workers' struggle towards their present state of socialism.

The Communist Party fulfills its function as official interpreter in two ways. First, by properly applying the Marxist-Leninist theory to the practical aspects of everyday life; second, in generalizing the experiences of the working-class in their struggle, thus becoming the perpetual developer of the philosophy, the responsible cause of its theoretical evolution. The resolutions of the Party must therefore be regarded as ". . . classical examples, not merely of the application of Marxist-Leninist theory to life . . . but also of the creative advancement of Marxist-Leninist theory."[66]

In the field of philosophic endeavor, the scholar must adhere to the party line as the infallible norm of truth. Any conclusions which obviously conflict with this norm may be presumed to be contrary to the objective laws of reality. Even if his opinion does not appear to conflict with the norm, he must still hold his judgment in abeyance pending possible condemnation by the Party. This loyalty to the Party is expected not only of the philosopher but of scientists in all fields of endeavor, for the same reasons. Very recent history has shown these principles to be conspicuously in operation, especially in the fields of logic, astronomy, biology and quantum physics.

Finally, the partisan character of philosophy requires of the scholar an uncompromising criticism of the reactionary interpretations given by bourgeois intellectuals to the latest discoveries in science and, at the same time, acceptance and preservation of everything of objective value produced by modern bourgeois science.

We are now in position to summarize the link between the positive sciences and philosophy under the Communist Party. Philosophy is conceived as an independent intellectual discipline. As a philosophy of nature, it is at one and the same time an ontology and a logic. As ontology, it serves as a supplemental interpreter of the factual knowledge of the natural sciences, for they have the same subject matter. As a logic, in applying the laws of the thought-process, *i.e.*, the laws of the dialectic, it provides the sciences with general principles of operation.

The Soviet "partisan spirit" in philosophy appears as a logical result of fundamental Marxist principles. As such, it adds a finishing touch to a philosophy of natural science that presents itself as both complete and inviting to an unanalytic and materialistically-bent mind.

Suggested Readings

CHAPTER III

Primary Sources

Conference on the Philosophical Problems of Science, Academy of Sciences and Ministry of Education, Moscow, October, 1958, in *Daedalus*, Vol. 89 (1960), No. 3, pp. 632-647.
Engels, F., *Dialectics of Nature*.
*———, *Herr Eugen Dühring's Revolution in Science (Anti-Dühring)*.
———, *Ludwig Feuerbach and the Outcome of Classical German Philosophy*.
*———, *Socialism: Utopian and Scientific*, Part II.
Feuerbach, Ludwig, *Essence of Christianity*.
Hegel, G. W. F., *The Science of Logic*.
Lenin, V. I., *Materialism and Empirio-Criticism*, Chapters III-V.
———, *On Dialectics*.
*Marx, K., *Theses on Feuerbach*.
*Stalin, J., *Dialectical and Historical Materialism*.
———, *Problems of Leninism*.

Secondary Sources

Bochenski, J. M., *The Dogmatic Principles of Soviet Philosophy*, Dordrecht, Holland/Stuttgart, Germany, D. Reidel Publishing Co., 1963, especially nos. 4-10.
Chambre, Henri, *From Karl Marx to Mao Tse-tung*, Chapter VIII.
Cook, Robert C., "Walpurgis Week in the Soviet Union," *The Scientific Monthly*, Vol. 68 (1949), 6, 367-372.
Cornforth, Maurice, *Materialism and the Dialectical Method*, 2d. ed., New York, International Publishers, 1960.
*Hook, Sidney, *From Hegel to Marx*, New York, The Humanities Press, 1958.
*Hunt, R. N. Carew, *Theory and Practice of Communism*, pp. 16-30.
*McFadden, Chas. J., *The Philosophy of Communism*, Chapters II and X.

Mikulak, Maxim W., "Soviet Cosmology and Communist Ideology," *The Scientific Monthly*, Vol. 81 (1955), No. 4, pp. 167-172.

Müller-Markus, S., "Diamat and Einstein," *Survey*, No. 37 (1961), pp. 68-78.

Somerville, John, "Dialectical Materialism," in D. D. Runes (ed.), *Twentieth Century Philosophy*, New York, The Philosophical Library, 1947.

Turkevitch, John, "Soviet Science in the Post-Stalin Era," *The Annals of the American Academy of Political and Social Science*, Vol. 303, January, 1956, pp. 139-151.

Venable, V., *Human Nature: The Marxian View*, Chapter IV.

*Wetter, G., *Dialectical Materialism*, pp. *250-365, 366-369, 518-535.

———, "Ideology and Science in the Soviet Union: Recent Developments," *Daedalus*, Vol. 89 (1960), No. 3, pp. 581-603.

FOOTNOTES TO CHAPTER III

1. Vernon Venable, *Human Nature: The Marxian View* (New York, 1945), p. 35. Hereafter cited as Venable, *Human Nature*.
2. F. Engels, *Herr Eugen Dühring's Revolution in Science* (*Anti-Dühring*), (London, 1940), pp. 27-28. Hereafter cited as Engels, *Anti-Dühring*.
3. Engels, "Letter to Conrad Schmidt, August 5, 1890," in *Karl Marx Selected Works*, ed. V. Adoratsky, 2 vols., (Moscow-Leningrad, 1935-36), I, 380. Hereafter cited as *KMSW*.
4. K. Marx, *Theses on Feuerbach*, in *KMSW*, I, pp. 471-473.
5. Engels, *The Communists and Karl Heinzen*, *KMSW*, I, preface, xv.
6. Venable, *Human Nature*, p. 38.
7. Engels, *Anti-Dühring*, p. 17.
8. *Ibid.*, p. 26; Engels, *Socialism: Utopian and Scientific*, *KMSW*, I, pp. 155-156.
9. Engels, *Anti-Dühring*, pp. 30-31.
10. R. N. Carew Hunt, *The Theory and Practice of Communism*, 5th ed. rev., (New York, 1961), pp. 16-19.
11. *Ibid.*, pp. 19-20; Charles J. McFadden, *The Philosophy of Communism* (New York, 1939), pp. 28-33.
12. Gustav A. Wetter, *Dialectical Materialism*, trans. Peter Heath, revised ed., (New York, 1958), pp. 6-7. Hereafter cited as Wetter, *D.M.*
13. Engels, *Ludwig Feuerbach and the Outcome of Classical German Philosophy*, in *KMSW*, I, p. 428. Hereafter cited as Engels, *Ludwig Feuerbach*.
14. Wetter, *D.M.*, pp. 10-11.
15. Marx, *Theses on Feuerbach*, I, *KMSW*, I, p. 471; Engels, *Ludwig Feuerbach*, *ibid.*, pp. 434-438, and 442-450. See also, Wetter, *D.M.*, pp. 14-15.
16. Engels, *Ludwig Feuerbach*, *KMSW*, I, p. 452.
17. J. Stalin, *Dialectical and Historical Materialism*, in *Problems of Leninism* (Moscow, 1953), pp. 714-718. Hereafter cited as Stalin, *DHM*.
18. Engels, *Anti-Dühring*, p. 15.
19. *Ibid.*, p. 29; Engels, *Ludwig Feuerbach*, *KMSW*, I, pp. 454-455.

20. McFadden, *The Philosophy of Communism*, pp. 33-34.
21. Marx, preface to the second German edition of Volume I of *Capital*, 3 vols., (Chicago, 1909), I, p. 25.
22. Engels, *Ludwig Feuerbach, KMSW*, I, p. 452.
23. *Ibid.*, 454.
24. Engels, *Anti-Dühring*, pp. 27-28.
25. Engels, *Ludwig Feuerbach, KMSW*, I, p. 453; McFadden, *The Philosophy of Communism*, pp. 35-37.
26. Stalin, *DHM*, pp. 714-715.
27. *Ibid.*, pp. 715-717; Wetter, *D.M.*, pp. 319-333.
28. B. M. Kedrov, *O kolichestvennykh i kachestvennykh izmeneniyakh v prirode* (Moscow, 1946), pp. 13-15, as cited in Wetter, *D.M.*, pp. 320-321.
29. *Ibid.*, p. 26, in Wetter, *D.M.*, p. 321.
30. G. F. Alexandrov, *Dialektichesky materializm* (Moscow, 1954), pp. 160f., as cited in Wetter, *D.M.*, p. 321.
31. Engels, *Anti-Dühring*, pp. 142-143.
32. Engels, *Dialectics of Nature*, (New York, 1940), p. 31.
33. Wetter, *D.M.*, p. 323.
34. Marx, "Letter to Engels, July 14, 1858," in *Historisch-Kritische Gesamtausgabe*, ed. D. Rjazanov and V. Adoratski, (Frankfort-Berlin, 1927-33), Abt. 3, Bd. 2, pp. 326-327.
35. Engels, *Anti-Dühring*, p. 77.
36. Stalin, *DHM*, pp. 717-718. Cf. Engels, *Socialism: Utopian and Scientific, KMSW*, I, pp. 158-159.
37. Engels, *Anti-Dühring*, pp. 18-19; *Socialism: Utopian and Scientific, KMSW*, I, p. 159.
38. V. I. Lenin, *On Dialectics, Selected Works*, 12 vols., (New York, 1943), XI, p. 82.
39. Engels, *Anti-Dühring*, p. 70. See Lenin, *Materialism and Empirio-Criticism, Collected Works* (Moscow, 1960-63), XIV, pp. 266-273.
40. Engels, *Anti-Dühring*, p. 135.
41. Wetter, *D.M.*, p. 342.
42. M. F. Vorobiev, "O soderzhanii i formakh zakona otritsaniya otritsaniya," *Vestnik Leningradskogo Universiteta*, 1956, 23, p. 57, as cited in Wetter, *D.M.*, pp. 355-356.
43. Wetter, *D.M.*, pp. 355-364; McFadden, *The Philosophy of Communism*, pp. 44-48.
44. Stalin, *DHM*, p. 716.
45. Lenin, *Philosophical Notebooks*, as cited in Wetter, *D.M.*, p. 356.
46. Engels, *Anti-Dühring*, p. 152.

47. Paul Langevin, *La Pensée*, I, No. 1, as quoted in Robert S. Cohen, "On the Marxist Philosophy of Education," *Modern Philosophies and Education*, ed. Nelson B. Henry (Chicago, 1955), pp. 201-202.
48. Engels, *Anti-Dühring*, p. 18.
49. A. Einstein, *The Meaning of Relativity*, 4th. ed., (Princeton, N. J., 1953), p. 99.
50. Cf. Maxim W. Mikulak, "Soviet Cosmology and Communist Ideology," *The Scientific Monthly*, LXXXI (1955), No. 4, p. 168. Hereafter cited as Mikulak, *SCCI*. See also Wetter, *D.M.*, pp. 436-442.
51. Engels, *Anti-Dühring*, pp. 59-61.
52. *Pod Znamenem Marksizma*, 1940, 7, p. 123 as cited in Mikulak, *SCCI*, p. 169. Cf. N. P. Barabashev, *Bor'ba s idealizmom v oblasti kosmogonicheskikh i kosmologicheskikh gipotez* (Kharkov, 1952), pp. 116f., as cited in Wetter, *D.M.*, p. 438.
53. Actually Engels' theory of the infinite dialectical process and the finite ever-expanding theory of Lemaitre are quite similar, but philosophically contradictory.
54. *Pod Znamenem Marksizma*, 1940, 6, p. 126; 7, p. 119, as cited in Mikulak, *SCCI*, p. 169.
55. *Ibid.*, 1940, 8, p. 67, in Mikulak, *SCCI*, p. 169. Cf. A. A. Zhdanov, *On Literature, Philosophy and Music* (New York, 1950), p. 73. See Wetter, *D.M.*, pp. 437-438.
56. *Izvestia*, Jan. 28, 1953, as cited in Mikulak, *SCCI*, p. 171.
57. Engels, *Dialectics of Nature*, pp. 21-25, 201-202. The contemporary, scientifically sophisticated interpretation of Engels' theory of stellar origin is to be found in V. A. Ambarzumyan, "Problema vozniknoveniya zvezd v svete novykh rabot sovetskikh astrofizikov," *Vestnik Akademii Nauk SSSR*, 1953, 12, pp. 49-60, and summarized in Wetter, *D.M.*, pp. 439-440.
58. A. F. Bogorodsky, *Pod Znamenem Marksizma*, 1940, 7, p. 128, as cited in Mikulak, *SCCI*, p. 171. Cf. Barabashev, *Bor'ba s idealizmom*, p. 117, cited in Wetter, *D.M.*, pp. 437-438.
59. T. D. Lysenko, *The Science of Biology Today*, as cited by Robert C. Cook, "Walpurgis Week in the Soviet Union," *The Scientific Monthly*, LXVIII, (1949), No. 6, 370. Cf. Wetter, *D.M.*, pp. 455-469.
60. This section of Chapter III appeared in a slightly altered form in *The American Slavic and East European Review*, XX (1961), No. 1. Reprinted with permission. On this subject, see, Wetter, *D.M.*, pp. 249-274, from which the author has borrowed extensively.
61. B. M. Kedrov, "O klassifikatsii nauk," *Voprosy filosofii*, 1955, 2, pp. 49-68, as cited in Wetter, *D.M.*, p. 250.
62. Engels, *Anti-Dühring*, p. 31. See also p. 155.

63. *Ibid.*, p. 158.
64. Lenin, *The Economic Content of Narodism and the Criticism of It in Mr. Struve's Book, Collected Works*, I, p. 401.
65. Cf. Lenin, *Materialism and Empirio-Criticism*, pp. 342-343, 348 and 358.
66. "Edinstvo teorii i praktiki," *Voprosy filosofii*, 1954, 2, p. 5, as cited in Wetter, *D.M.*, p. 273.

CHAPTER IV

THE MARXIST THEORY OF MAN

One of the arguments used by Marx in attempting to prove production to be the basic force of history was that man differs from other animals by the fact that he has the ability to produce tools, something unknown in the rest of the animal kingdom. This ability makes man vastly superior to the animal; yet he is still at root animal, material and subject to the dialectical laws of nature.

We may distinguish men from animals by consciousness, by religion, by anything you please. They themselves begin to distinguish themselves from animals as soon as they begin to produce their own means of subsistence . . . a step conditioned by their physical organization.[1]

The whole of nature, from the smallest element to the greatest, from grains of sand to suns; from protista to men . . . is in a ceaseless flux, in unresting motion and change.[2]

Man, for the Marxist, is entirely of a material nature. No part of him, even that which seems most supra-sensuous, his mind, transcends matter — the only reality.[3] As such, man must have originated from the unending evolution of matter.

Origin of Man

Although modern science in the West looks to the evolutionary account of human origin as a highly probable hypothesis, Soviet scientists — keeping within the precedence of Marx who accepted Darwin's thesis of natural selection as the basis in natural science for his own historical view[4] — have accepted human evolution as an established scientific fact.[5] Man has developed through a dialectical process involving three stages:[6]

a. a stick-wielding herd of monkeys
b. primitive man
c. men united in clans.

The australopithecoids represent the first stage. These creatures were essentially apes who, because of climatic changes at the end of the Tertiary Period and beginning of the Quaternary, left the trees and descended to the ground. This produced in them an upright posture, a prehensile hand with a usable thumb, a more vertical position of the skull in which the brain could further develop, and so on. The australopithecoids apparently used animal bones as weapons to kill their prey and lived on the meat obtained. Yet in spite of these activities, contemporary Soviet science does not regard these creatures as an immediate ancestor of man.[7]

Man's true precursor came on the scene with the transition to the second stage wherein there emerged from the *Australopithecus,* the *Pithecanthropus.* The australopithecoids merely used ready-made objects such as bones, sticks, and stones for their instruments; they were not yet able to fashion tools for themselves. This was in the power of the pithecanthropus group composed of the stages of *Pithecanthropus, Sinanthropus* and the *Neanderthal* man. It is because of this ability to fashion simple tools that this second stage of primitive man is of great importance and serves as a major landmark in the dialectical process of development from a herd of monkeys to primitive human society.[8] Even though anthropologists outside of the communist world have a tendency to consider the Neanderthal man as subsequent to *Homo sapiens,* the communist anthropologist takes as a fact that progressive science has demonstrated that the Neanderthalers, in a broad sense, were the immediate forebears of present man. With the advent of *Homo sapiens* the law of biological selection ceased. Since the Ice Age, man has maintained himself virtually unaltered biologically. Whatever development has occurred is in the area of social behavior and according to dialectical social laws unknown in the animal kingdom.[9]

As has been seen, production of man's needs has a decisive influence on the process of change in man's nature. It is not unusual therefore, for Engels to conclude that labor activity was responsible for the evolution of man from his primitive ancestors.[10] His labor was responsible for man becoming a social animal. It furnished the occasion for closer and more organized interrelations among prehistoric men, and so the socialization process began. Labor also brought about the further development of the hand and with it, the development of the brain. With the increase of cooperation among men and the increased power of the brain, came the advent of human language.[11] Primeval man developed in such a way that it became necessary that the primitive clan society come into existence. The beginnings of tribal order are even to be found in the Neanderthal phase, where evidence is to be found that this vertebrate began providing for others besides himself and his immediate family. Finally, tribal life with its division of labor became the characteristic life of man, and primitive human history began.[12]

Pavlovian Psychology

As was mentioned above, the evolution of man and his activities was accompanied by the development and enlargement of his mental capacity. This development, for the Marxist, represents a qualitative "leap" in the dialectical process of nature. Correspondingly, the mental capacities of humans are of a qualitatively different order than those of the animal kingdom. Human thought represents the evolution of matter in its highest form. This "leap" in nature sets man apart from the brute as surely as the organic world is distinguished from the inorganic. Man is not only a superior animal, but he is also superior to the animal. The qualitative distinction between man and the higher animals is explained by the contemporary Marxist, or at least by the Soviets, in the terms of the renowned psychologist Ivan Pavlov, who worked in close cooperation with the Soviet government in his last years.[13] This adherence to Pavlov persists despite the tendency of Pavlov's theories to be more mechanistic than dialectical.

For Pavlov, an organism constitutes a system in relatively stable equilibrium with its environment. Through their nervous system, men and animals are joined to their environment. In the lower animals, substances necessary for existence are extracted from the surroundings by direct contact between the food and the organism. In higher animals and man this contact comes about by means of a system of what Pavlov called "conditioned" *(ooslovny)* reflexes in distinction to the simple, more constant "unconditioned" reflexes — those fundamental nervous reactions or instincts by which the organism maintains equilibrium with the forces external to it.[14]

An example of an unconditioned reflex is the occurrence following the placing of food in the mouth of a dog. Saliva flows in the quantity and quality necessitated by the particular substance placed on the tongue. This is simply the reaction of the organism to the external world effected through the nervous system. An external stimulus is transformed into a nervous process and transmitted from peripheral endings along nerve fibers to the brain and then out to one or more organs of the body which is excited to activity.[15]

But we know that the action of the salivary glands to external influences is not restricted to these ordinary reflex actions. A similar reflex secretion is evoked when food is placed at a distance from the dog and only the visual and olfactory sense-organs (analyzers) are affected. Even the dish from which the food has been given, or the sight or the sound of the footsteps of the person who brings the food is oftentimes enough to evoke a reflex.[16] These phenomena represent *conditioned* reflexes. Such reflexes are quite transitory in character and sensitive to change in the environment; they are located in the cortex of the cerebral hemispheres. Physiologically, they act as "signals" for the unconditioned reflexes enabling the organism to better adapt itself to the environment by seeking out favorable situations and avoiding the unfavorable.[17]

It is the totality of the conditioned reflexes within the organism that constitutes the entire higher nervous activities in the higher animals as well as man.[18] Much human activity is attributed to the identical signaling system that is found in the brute. Man, as has been mentioned, does differ categorically from the higher animal, however. Man's exclusive quality consists in his "second" signaling system as represented in audible or visual words. It is speech that sets man above the animal, for it is speech that is the signal of the first signals. It has arisen on the structure of the primary signal as the effect of the socialization process wherein closer cooperation and idea-exchanges are required.[19] Although this second signaling is activity of the same nervous tissue as the first system, it allows man to engage in activities completely beyond the scope of the most highly developed animal.

Speech, of course, can act as a stimulus of the signaling system in animals. The difference between the reflex caused in the animal by speech and that in man is the fact that the sound impinging on the auditory analyzer in the animal operates exactly like any other influence stimulating the ear. A reflex may quite possibly follow upon this stimulus as from any other. Thus a trained dog may sit down as a response to the verbal command, "Sit!" In man, speech emerges as a signal of signals. Whereas the dog's muscles react to the direct signal of the sound, "Sit!" the reaction is different in a fully alert man. When man is asked to sit down, the stimulus impinging upon the auditory analyzer does not signal the direct response of his muscles to place the body in a sitting position but, rather, it is the signal to bring forward a generalized reflection of reality — in this case a generalized notion of "sitting" or "what it means to sit down." It is this generalized notion of sitting that then signals the muscles to react and place his body in a sitting position. Accordingly, the word "sit" or any other meaningful expression reflects a universalized notion of reality behind which is concealed a system of immediate influences on the part of objects and phenomena in the outside world. It is through this influence that man adjusts to his ever-changing environment.[20]

Because Pavlov's explanation of human mental processes is strictly physiological and has a tendency to be mechanistic, there have been animated discussions among Soviet theoreticians, beginning with the Pavlov Conference of 1950, as to whether the mental process is to be completely identified with higher nervous activity or whether there is a true subject matter of the science of psychology beyond pure physiology.[21] At present, there are two conflicting schools of thought on the matter. Those who hold that higher nervous activity and the subjective consciousness are two aspects of the same biological process are accused of vulgar materialism by the opposing group. Those of the second group look upon nervous activity and mental activities as two distinct, although inseparable, interconnected processes. Consciousness is the subjective reflection of the objective world in the human brain in a mode of existence that transcends all other material existences but somehow remains the product of material organs. This group is accused by their opponents of maintaining a position that inevitably leads to the admission of non-material motion and the position of a "spiritual substratum" or "soul" to account for this motion. The question remains unresolved. Hence, the contemporary Soviet Marxists are agreed that the mental activities of man qualitatively transcend those of the animal kingdom, but they cannot agree as to the explanation of the relation of this transcendence to the biological and neural activities of the human organism.

Since for Pavlov the second signaling system is not only the foundation for human thought but also the regulator of conscious purposeful activity,[22] man is completely determined by his instincts, conditioned reflexes and language. As such he has no indeterminate principle of choice, no free will in the traditional sense. Yet the Marxist often talks about the freedom of man, liberty from exploitation, and so on. What then does he mean by freedom?

Freedom of Man

For the Marxist as for Hegel, freedom means "the appreciation of necessity."[23] As Engels remarks:

> Freedom does not consist in the dream of independence of natural laws, but in the knowledge of these laws, and in the possibility this gives of systematically making them work towards definite ends. . . . Freedom of the will therefore means nothing but the capacity to make decisions with real knowledge of the subject. Therefore the freer a man's judgment is in relation to a definite question, with so much the greater necessity is the content of this judgment determined; while the uncertainty founded on ignorance, which seems to make an

arbitrary choice among different and conflicting possible decisions, shows by this precisely that it is not free, that it is controlled by the very object it should itself control. Freedom therefore consists in the control over ourselves and over external nature which is founded on knowledge of natural necessity.[24]

G. V. Plekhanov, who in spite of certain menshevist tendencies was considered by Lenin to be the best theoretician in the entire Marxian movement,[25] has perhaps left us the most detailed commentary on that notion of freedom adhered to by Marx and Engels. He looks to their definitions of freedom as a brilliant discovery of philosophic thought, but one that can be grasped only by those who have cast off the dualistic notion of concomitant spiritual and material powers in man, and who realize that there is an ontological unity existing between the object chosen and the subject choosing. This unity allows for the conclusion by Plekhanov that in human consciousness, necessity and freedom coincide. When one comes to this realization, then knowledge of the lack of "freewill" does not appear as a lack of freedom. Instead it is simply the conviction of the subjective and objective impossibility of acting differently from the way one is acting. When one's actions also appear as the most desirable of all other possible actions, then necessity becomes *consciously* identified with freedom and freedom with necessity. One sees that he is unfree only in the sense that he cannot disturb the identity between freedom and necessity nor feel the restraint of necessity. Yet this very lack of freedom is, at the same time, its fullest manifestation.[26]

For Plekhanov, history has shown that people imbued with theories which hold human conduct to be wholly governed by necessity are those that have been most energetic in practical life. One has only to look to Mohammed and his followers, to Napoleon who considered himself chosen by ineluctable destiny, to Calvin, and so on. Rather than being a hindrance to activity, deterministic doctrines have been shown to be a psychologically sound basis for energetic action in the course of history. This also holds true with the Marxist concept of freedom. Because historical materialism predicts that capitalism, like feudalism before it, must in time inevitably give way to socialism, this in no way places a psychological road-block in the way of conscious, voluntary participation in the process. The very opposite is true. The communist considers himself to be the instrument of historical necessity and "freely" puts himself at its service. Because of his place in history, his education, character and other aspects of his life conditioned by the economic mode of production, he cannot help but do so. He considers the lack of free-will as being tantamount to a complete incapacity for inaction.[27]

Such a concept of freedom leads to a liberation from the moral restraint which diminishes the energy of those still enmeshed in dualism of body and spirit and who, not being able to overcome the disparity between their ideals and actions, do not fully belong to themselves. Their lives and mental tortures represent a tribute paid to the external necessity that stands in opposition to them and their desires. But as soon as an individual throws off the yoke of this painful and degrading restriction, he is reborn to a new, more complete life and "his *free* actions become the *conscious and free* expression of *necessity.*"[28]

This free activity of the historical individual represents a necessary link in the chain of necessary events. To the extent that an individual is conscious of this fact, to that extent is he resolute in his actions to bring about the inevitable. If, in the view of Plekhanov, particular individuals through weakness fail to do their share in bringing about the necessary, others, perhaps aroused by the apathy of the former, will take their place determined to do what necessity demands.[29]

It is knowledge of the true nature of freedom that brings freedom to man. Necessity is blind only to the extent that it is not understood. Man is oppressed by nature and the laws of nature. By scientific inquiry revealing the laws of nature, man can change himself and his world. He, thereby, begins to rule nature rather than being ruled by it, and to that extent he "frees" himself from natural forces.[30] For man is the highest product of nature and must therefore rule nature by his higher mental processes.

Knowledge, however, is not sufficient. There is another force oppressing man and limiting his freedom. Man is oppressed by other men by reason of the relations between the social classes.

Only by destroying classes can man obtain that freedom of "spirit" denied him by the present economic order.

And there is *only one* way of breaking the resistance of those classes, and that is to find, in the very society which surrounds us, and to enlighten and organise for the struggle, the forces which can and, by their social position, *must* form the power capable of sweeping away the old and of establishing the new.

Only the philosophic materialism of Marx showed the proletariat the way out of spiritual slavery in which all oppressed classes have languished up to the present.[31]

As man's "essence" is developing, so also is his freedom. The overall tendencies of history however, transcend the influence of historical accidents and the cooperation or non-cooperation of particular individuals. They are determined by the force of class activities and the ensuing struggle resulting from economic relationships. If this be true, then the question may be rightly asked: What is the importance of the individual and what is his role in history?

Role of the Individual in History

The importance of the individual in the historical process appears to be presented in a somewhat ambiguous manner in the Marxist classics. At times, Marx and Engels refer to certain individuals and groups as "great men,"[32] whose influence has been "epoch-making."[33] On the other hand, there seems to be a greater abundance of belittling expressions concerning the importance of an individual in history. Those whom others consider as great and celebrated figures Marx considers, for the most part, men of weakness and worthy of ridicule.[34] The individual has little influence, for although it is man that weaves the fabric of history, he does not make "the whole cloth." Man does not make history out of conditions chosen by himself but out of the conditions he finds at hand.[35] Revolutions are not the work of single individuals; they are spontaneous and necessary manifestations of national social needs. Their success or failure is not to be attributed to the heroism or betrayal of individual participants.[36]

This ambiguity concerning the part played by the individual makes it difficult to arrive at a definite conclusion as to the position of Marx and Engels on this question. Yet it is clear that no single individual is of such importance as to successfully oppose the conditions brought forth by the prevailing mode of production, or alter the general course of history. Problems arise and the heroes who are to solve them emerge only as the conditions of history require. Man still proposes, but it is the mode of production that disposes.[37]

Yet the individual does have some importance. Outstanding minds and personalities, as historical accidents, can accelerate or retard the progress of history.[38] The extent of personal influence is determined, it is true, by the talents of the individual; but the individual can display his talents only when he occupies a position in a society that demands this talent, and this demand is not wholly an historical accident. The role of individuals is determined by the form of organization of the society. The exercise of social influence opens the door to historical accident. Yet historical accidents are something relative and appear only at the point of intersection of inevitable processes.

> A great man is great not because his personal qualities give individual features to great historical events, but because he possesses qualities which make him most capable of serving the great social needs of his time, needs which arose as a result of general and particular causes.[39]

Every age needs its heroes and leaders. "If it does not find them, it invents them."[40] No one individual is ever indispensable. That certain great men appear in certain countries at a given moment is pure accident. Suppress them and substitutes will arise. If Napoleon had been killed in battle at an early age or if Hitler had remained a paper-hanger, other personalities like them would have appeared. This has been proved by history itself, claims the Marxist. Whenever the conditions of society demanded a particular type of leader, a man has always been found to supply that need.[41]

Although the historical act is, in a sense, the result of human desires and will — for it is men's desires that are the immediate cause of their acting — nonetheless, the actual historical event rarely culminates in that which is willed or desired by the historical figures. For history, with its innumerable conflicts of individual wills and individual agents, reaches a conclusion which is analogous to nature with its interplay of chance causes. While on the surface accident holds sway, history is actually governed by those inner, hidden laws discovered by Marx and Engels — just as nature is governed by its dialectical laws.[42]

Hence the role of the individual in the shaping of human destiny is of negligible significance. The task of weaving human history in every historical epoch is not assigned to great individuals but to the classes and their struggles.[43] Talented people can change only the individual features of events, not the general trend, for they themselves are the products of that trend.[44]

From these philosophical notions of man and his world, the Marxist arrives at some interesting ethical conclusions.

Suggested Readings

CHAPTER IV

Primary Sources

*Engels, F., *The Dialectics of Nature,* Chapter IX.
*——, *Herr Eugen Dühring's Revolution in Science (Anti-Dühring),* Part I, Chapter XI.
——, *The Origin of the Family, Private Property and the State.*
Marx, K., *Economic and Philosophic Manuscripts of 1844.*
Pavlov, I. P., *Conditioned Reflexes: An Investigation of the Physiological Activities of the Cerebral Cortex,* trans. G. V. Anrep, New York, Dover Publications, Inc., 1960.
——, *Experimental Psychology and Other Essays,* New York, The Philosophical Library, 1957.

Secondary Sources

*Bober, M. M., *Karl Marx's Interpretation of History,* Chapter IV.
Chambre, Henri, *From Karl Marx to Mao Tse-tung,* Chapter II.
*Fromm, Erich, *Marx's Concept of Man,* New York, Frederick Ungar Publishing Co., 1961.
Laqueur, Walter Z. and Lichtheim, George (eds.), *The Soviet Cultural Scene, 1956-1957,* New York, Frederick A. Praeger, 1958, Chapters 19 and 20.
McFadden, Chas. J., *The Philosophy of Communism,* pp. 239-246.
Nesturkh, Mikhail, *The Origin of Man,* Moscow, Foreign Languages Publishing House, 1959.
*Plekhanov, G. V., *The Role of the Individual in History,* New York, International Publishers, 1940.
*Venable, Vernon, *Human Nature: The Marxian View,* especially Chapter VI.
Wells, Harry K., *Ivan P. Pavlov: Toward a Scientific Psychology and Psychiatry,* New York, International Publishers, 1961.
*Wetter, Gustav, *Dialectical Materialism,* pp. *385-391, *469-487, 490-506.

FOOTNOTES TO CHAPTER IV

1. K. Marx, and F. Engels, *Die deutsche Ideologie*, in *Historisch-Kritische Gesamtausgabe*, ed. V. Adoratskij and D. Rjazanov (Frankfort [etc.], 1927-1933), Abt. I. Bd. 5, p. 10.
2. Engels, *Dialectics of Nature* (New York, 1940), p. 13.
3. Cf. Engels, *Ludwig Feuerbach and the Outcome of Classical German Philosophy*, in *Karl Marx Selected Works*, 2 vols. (Moscow-Leningrad, 1935-36), I, p. 435. Hereafter cited as *KMSW*.
4. Marx, "Letter to Engels, Dec. 19, 1860," *Gesamtausgabe*, Abt. 3, Bd. 2, p. 533.
5. Cf. Gustav A. Wetter, *Dialectical Materialism*, trans. Peter Heath, revised ed. (New York, 1958), pp. 469-473. Hereafter cited as Wetter, *D.M.*
6. V. I. Lenin, *The State and Revolution* in *Lenin Selected Works*, 2 vols. in 4 (Moscow, 1952), II, Part I, p. 207.
7. V. G. Vlastovsky, "Sovremennye predstavleniya o proiskhozhdenii cheloveka," in *Estestvoznanie i religiya* (Moscow, 1956), pp. 122ff., as cited in Wetter *D.M.*, p. 470.
8. A. P. Okladnikov, "Vozniknovenie chelovecheskogo obshchestva. Ranniy drevnekamenniy vek (nizhniy paleolit)," in *Vsemirnaya istoriya*, 10 vols., I, p. 21, as cited in Wetter, *D. M.*, p. 471.
9. Okladnikov, "Razvitie pervobytno-obshchinnogo stroya. Pozdniy drevnekamenniy vek (verkhniy paleolit)," in *Vsemirnaya istoriya*, I, pp. 51-53, as cited in Wetter *D.M.*, p. 471.
10. Cf. Engels, *Dialectics of Nature*, p. 281.
11. *Ibid.*, p. 283.
12. Cf. Engels, *The Origin of the Family, Private Property and the State*, trans. Ernest Untermann (Chicago, 1909), Chapter I.
13. Cf. Wetter, *D.M.*, pp. 473-477.
14. I. P. Pavlov, *Conditioned Reflexes: An Investigation of the Physiological Activity of the Cerebral Cortex*, trans. G. V. Anrep (New York, 1960), pp. 7-15. Hereafter cited as Pavlov, *Conditioned Reflexes*.
15. Pavlov, *Lectures on Conditioned Reflexes*, trans. W. Horsley Gantt (New York, 1928), p. 83. Hereafter cited as Pavlov, *LCR*.
16. *Ibid.*, Pavlov, *Conditioned Reflexes*, p. 13.
17. Pavlov, *LCR*, pp. 63, 79, 84.

18. Cf. Pavlov, *Conditioned Reflexes*, p. 11.
19. *Ibid.*, p. 407. Pavlov, *Experimental Psychology and Other Essays* (New York, 1957), pp. 285 and 591.
20. Cf. Y. V. Shorokhova, in *Uchenie I. P. Pavlova i filosofskie voprosy psikhologii*, ed. S. A. Petrushevsky, *et al.* (Moscow, 1952), as cited in Wetter, *D.M.*, p. 475.
21. Cf. Wetter, *D.M.*, pp. 478-486.
22. Pavlov, *LCR*, Chapter XXVII, and *Experimental Psychology*, pp. 306-310.
23. Cf. G. W. F. Hegel, *Lectures on the History of Philosophy*, trans. E. S. Haldane, 3 vols. (New York, 1955), I, p. 26.
24. Engels, *Herr Eugen Dühring's Revolution in Science (Anti-Dühring)* (London, 1940), p. 128. Hereafter cited as Engels, *Anti-Dühring*.
25. Lenin, *Once Again on the Trade Unions*, in *Selected Works*, 12 vols. (New York, 1943), IX, p. 66.
26. G. V. Plekhanov, *The Role of the Individual in History* (New York, 1940), p. 16. Hereafter cited as Plekhanov, *RIH*. See Wetter, *D.M.*, pp. 386-396. A critique of the Marxist view of freedom is found in Chas. J. McFadden, *The Philosophy of Communism* (New York, 1939), pp. 239-246.
27. Plekhanov, *RIH*, pp. 15-17.
28. *Ibid.*, p. 18
29. *Ibid.*, pp. 19-21.
30. Engels, *Anti-Dühring*, pp. 128-129.
31. Lenin, *The Three Sources and Three Component Parts of Marxism*, *KMSW*, I, p. 59.
32. Cf. Engels, *Socialism: Utopian and Scientific*, *KMSW*, I, p. 141.
33. Cf. Marx, appendix to *Poverty of Philosophy* (New York, 1963), p. 194; Engels, *Anti-Dühring*, p. 30.
34. Cf. Marx, *Capital*, 3 vols. (Chicago, 1909), I, pp. 300n, 354, 556n, 654n, 668, 788n, 833n; appendix to *Poverty of Philosophy*, pp. 194, 198, 202, etc. See M. M. Bober, *Karl Marx's Interpretation of History*, 2d. ed. rev. (Cambridge, Mass., 1948), pp. 81-87.
35. Marx, *The Eighteenth Brumaire of Louis Bonaparte*, *KMSW*, II, p. 315.
36. Cf. Marx and Engels, *Germany: Revolution and Counter-Revolution*, *KMSW*, II, 41.
37. Engels, *Anti-Dühring*, p. 347.
38. Cf. Marx, "Letter to Dr. Kugelmann, April 17, 1871," *KMSW*, II, p. 531.
39. Plekhanov, *RIH*, p. 59. See also pp. 41-43. Cf. Engels, *Anti-Dühring*, p. 25.
40. Marx, *Class Struggles in France*, *KMSW*, II, p. 257.

41. Cf. Engels, "Letter to Heinz Starkenburg, January 25, 1894," *KMSW*, I, pp. 392-393; Plekhanov, *RIH*, pp. 46-51.
42. Cf. Engels, *Ludwig Feuerbach and the Outcome of Classical German Philosophy*, *KMSW*, I, pp. 456-459.
43. *Ibid.*, p. 459. Cf. Marx and Engels, *Manifesto of the Communist Party*, Part I, *KMSW*, I, pp. 204-218.
44. Cf. Plekhanov, *RIH*, p. 52.

CHAPTER V

MARXIAN ETHICS

Ultimate Values: Marxist Economics and the Labor Theory of Value

If, as has been seen, economics is for Marx the ultimate determinant of history — and, therefore, of human nature — then the ultimate value for man in life is labor, through which human nature is both transformed and fulfilled. Human labor thus appears as the principal efficient cause of man's happiness. For Marx, all other values in life are, in the last analysis, dependent on the human labor factor of production and its relationship to the other factors, *i.e.*, dependent on the prevailing mode of production.[1] Hence, these other values — whether they be ethical, religious or aesthetic — flow from, and are conditioned by, man's relationship to his labor.[2]

Marx's economic theory has been judged scientifically erroneous by the vast majority of economists outside the Marxist orbit. In spite of this, his theory still exercises a powerful influence on men, and thereby, on history. Because of this fact, a knowledge of its basic tenets is imperative for the objective student of communism, if for no other reason than that brought out by the eminent political scientist Harold Laski when he wisely insisted that a widely-accepted error must be investigated, as such an investigation always leads to a better understanding of the true needs of mankind.[3]

As Lenin points out, Marx derived his ideological theories in the main from three sources — German philosophy, French social theory and the British school of economic theory.[4] The British economists, best represented by Adam Smith and David Ricardo, adopted as their theory of value the one set forth by John Locke. Locke had defended private property on the principle that man has the right to possess that which had received its value through his labor,[5] and the classical economists had concluded that the value of a commodity depended somehow on the relative quantity of labor required to produce it.[6] Marx readily accepted this conclusion and used it as the starting point for his own economic theory — the outcome of which produced results that the British economists would not have dreamed.[7]

For Marx, the capitalist world revolves about the production of commodities. These commodities are produced because they are wanted. They are wanted because they are somehow useful to humans. They have, therefore, a kind of value Marx, following Smith and Ricardo, will call use-value. Capitalist production is constructed entirely upon use-values. A product is manufactured because it is useful to all or some of the people — otherwise it cannot be sold. Between the process of actual production and that of consumption by the human person there is carried on a complex series of exchanges. The commodity has not only use-value for the consumer but also an exchange-value for those who take part in its delivery into the hands of the consumer. While the consumer is interested only in use-value, the manufacturer, the jobber, the wholesaler and retailer are interested in the exchange-value *i.e.*, the amount of other commodities for which a product in question could be exchanged. This, in modern language, is termed "price" and is stated in terms of money. But Marx does not wish to convey that value is necessarily related to normal market price. What he does point out by numerous examples is that two commodities embodying the same amount of labor would possess the same exchange-value, the same price, that could be measured in terms of money.[8]

That a commodity possess value, Marx insists that it possess two characteristics.[9] The first is that it has utility — someone must want to possess or consume it. Secondly, it must have come about through man's social labor. Although all commodities must have these two characteristics, utility is not of the essence of value. For though all commodities possess usefulness, not all useful objects possess value, or are, in the strict sense, commodities. The only note Marx is prepared to admit as common to all commodities is that they are products of human labor. Thus, the atmospheric conditions are extremely useful to man but they lack value and are not commodities because they embody no human labor. Human labor alone is the source of value.

The classical economists had taught the value of the commodity, and its actual price could be determined by a measurement of the number of hours of labor needed to produce it. Marx points out, however, that under the capitalist mode of production the employer, through his superior economic power, is able to make contracts with his workers that are not based on the number of hours worked. Thus, wages need not correspond to the value of the commodity produced. It is not in fact labor hours that the employer bargains and pays for, but rather *labor power*.[10] The value of labor power is not the value of the labor expended but rather the value of the average number of labor hours required by a worker to enable him to support his life, to reproduce himself and to continue to work. The value of his labor power constitutes his *wages*. The wage system for the Marxist is thus, basically, unjust. The full value of labor can never be given in such a system, for as will be pointed out, *profit* must come from the value increment of the product resulting from labor.

> The cry for an *equality of wages* rests, therefore, upon a mistake, is an inane wish never to be fulfilled. . . . To clamour for *equal or even equitable retribution* on the basis of the wages system is the same as to clamour for *freedom* on the basis of the slavery system.[11]

It is on the conviction that human labor alone produces value that Marx was able to put forward his *theory of surplus value*. This theory was not an original insight for Marx, as Engels points out.[12] It is to be found in classical economic theory where there was a recognition that the value added to the materials of production by labor resolved itself into wages and profit. Further, the utopian socialists recognized the injustice of this division, but offered only flippant solutions to the problem through suggestions of mere reform within the existing system. It was Marx who made the surplus value theory meaningful. Marx is to the theory of surplus value, claims Engels, as Lavoisier is to the development of chemistry.[13]

The central thesis of the surplus-value theory is this. The objective factors of production, the raw materials, land, buildings, machinery and tools—called by Marx, "constant capital"[14]—produce nothing. True productivity comes about through the expenditure of an amount of labor power—called "variable capital"[15]—upon these objective factors. Thus, in the production of any commodity, all who do not contribute manual or mental labor power do not contribute value to that commodity. Anyone, therefore, receiving part of the fruits of production without making a labor contribution, takes on the role of a social parasite and robs the workers of a part of their return. Those whose only role in the production process is providing constant capital and/or lending money, as well as those who act as mere brokers in the process of exchange, are not responsible for any value increment in the finished product and, consequently, are not entitled in justice to any return, or *profit*. To Marx, profit, then, is always obtained by depriving the worker of some of the increased value of a commodity resulting from his labor.

The value of the laboring power is determined by the amount of labor necessary to maintain or reproduce it, but the *use* of that laboring power is only limited by the energies and physical stamina of the worker. By paying the laborer the daily *value* of his labor power, the employer secures the "right" of using that labor power for the *whole day*. If, says Marx, a worker is paid the daily value of his laboring power of three shillings, he must daily reproduce this laboring power. This he may be able to do in six hours. But this does not physically prevent him from working ten or twelve hours. By paying the daily value of the labor power, the capitalist can require him to work twelve hours. Beyond the six hours required to replace his wages, the worker is forced to work six additional hours which Marx designated as hours of *surplus labor*. This surplus labor will realize itself in a *surplus value* and a *surplus produce*. In the twelve-hour day, the laborer produces not the three shillings of value needed to pay his wages, but six shillings worth of the product. Because he has sold his laboring power to the capitalist, the whole value or produce created by him belongs to the employer. By advancing three shillings in wages, the capitalist will realize a value of six shillings; by advancing a value in which six hours of labor are crystallized, he will receive in return a value in which twelve hours of labor are crystallized. It is this continuous sort of transaction between the owners of constant capital and the sellers of labor power upon which production under capitalism and the wage system is based. Under such a system the worker always remains a worker, and the capitalist, the reaper of surplus value.[16] As such, only one part of the workman's daily labor is paid to him. The unpaid portion or surplus labor constitutes the fund out of which *surplus value* or *profit* is formed.

For Marx, profit and capital—for capital is merely that portion of profits which has been plowed back into the production process[17]—represent the fruits of the exploitation of man by man. They are always derived through withholding from the worker value earned. Capitalistic production and its offspring, the wage system are, therefore, fundamentally unjust. Capitalism in the eyes of the Marxist, is, at root, institutionalized thievery.[18] Economic justice and, consequently, all other species of justice can only begin to be realized in society when those who produce economic value receive from the productive process returns that are in proportion to the value contributed. This, in the Marxian viewpoint, comes to be only when it is the workers who own the means of production, and they who create the additional means for expanding production. This, of course, is *socialism,* wherein the state—acting as trustee for the working people—holds the productive property belonging to all. It proportions the fruits of production in such fashion that both the required expansion of productive facilities is provided, and the consumer needs of the workers are fulfilled in relation to the individual contribution of each worker. From this system there will arise, in time, an even higher economic justice—when due to a change in human motivation, men will contribute to society according to their talents, and find their greatest dignity and happiness in receiving from society according to their needs.

If capitalism is basically unjust, its continuance only serves to multiply the injustice. This multiplication of injustice historically has proceeded through the following three stages. First, competition requires the capitalist to accumulate capital. This means he must make the existing labor power produce more by introducing labor-saving machinery. However, this increase in the ratio of constant capital to variable capital, often results in a decline of profits.

Secondly, the competition forces the centralization of capital. The weaker are vanquished. One strong capitalist lays low a number of his fellow capitalists. Only monopolies, trusts, cartels and similar combinations are able to survive the ever-recurring business depressions. These monopolies soon transcend national borders and all the peoples of the world become enmeshed in the net of the world market.

Thirdly, as a result of the concentration of capital, there occurs a corresponding increase in the mass of poverty, oppression, economic enslavement and exploitation. The replacement of workers by machinery forces more workers into the "industrial reserve army" of the unemployed. Meanwhile, the workers still employed are required to work longer hours with the new machinery to make up for the decline in profits resulting from the increased use of machinery. The wrath of the working class is intensified by these conditions. Meanwhile, as they grow more numerous, they become more disciplined, unified and organized by the very mechanism of the capitalist method of production itself. Finally, the injustice becomes unbearable, the fetters are burst asunder, the knell of capitalism sounds and the expropriators are expropriated.[19]

Capitalism, in spite of its evils, represents for the Marxist an improvement and necessary advance over feudalism, with its individual private property based upon individual labor. Nevertheless, in its advanced stages, capitalism is no longer suitable for man and must give way as did feudalism before it.

Marx wrote in an era that prevented him from seeing all the potentialities of capitalism. There was a higher stage of capitalism, *imperialism,* which Marx did not live to see developed. He hinted at it in the last pages of volume I of *Capital* — as did Engels in *Socialism: Utopian and Scientific* — but he failed to realize its significance. It fell upon the shoulders of Lenin to complete the Marxist outline of history. This theoretical evolution is certainly in keeping with the mind of Marx and Engels who abhorred the idea that their theories might become stabilized dogma,[20] and who looked on their discoveries merely as guides to future studies.[21]

To Lenin, imperialism was the highest and final stage of capitalism. Whereas the old capitalism, as known to Marx, was basically a capitalism of free competition, imperiaiism is basically monopolistic.[22] Not only is the control of economic power in the hands of relatively few, but there is likewise a merging or coalescence of banking with industry — a finance capitalism, and a financial oligarchy. Under a holding system, banks become the executive directors of monopolistic industries. By controlling the parent company they, in turn, control still other subsidiaries. The "holding system" not only serves to increase the power of the monopolists enormously by allowing control of individual corporations through ownership of relatively small percentages of stock, but it also enables them to resort with impunity to cheating the public. The directors of the bank or of the parent company, are not legally responsible for the actions of "independent" subsidiaries.[23]

Moreover, under the finance capitalism, it is no longer commodities that are exported, but capital itself. Capital is exported primarily to backward countries because the profits are usually quite high. Capital is scarce, the price of land is relatively low, wages are low and raw materials cheap.[24] The cartels and monopolies then begin to divide the world between themselves.[25] Because of their tremendous influence, it is the welfare of the monopolies that sets the political course of the Great Powers. This results in the world being divided into vast spheres of political influence and actual political control.[26] In the year 1900 Lenin informs us, over 90% of Africa, over 98% of Polynesia, over 56% of Asia, 100% of Australia and over 27% of the Western Hemisphere were in the hands of the Colonial Powers.[27] What began as an amicable parsing of the world market, disintegrated into quarrelling, envy and hatred among the Colonial Powers. Instead of cooperative effort, nations now wanted only to seize land, to conquer foreign nations, to ruin competing nations and pillage their wealth, to divert the attention of the masses from their internal crises, to disunite the workers and fool them with nationalism and to weaken the revolutionary movement. This frame of mind naturally led, in time, to the outbreak of World War I and a redistribution of the world influence.[28]

Monopolies, oligarchy, the striving for domination instead of liberty, the exploitation of small, weak nations by an extremely small group of the richest and most powerful nations, are the distinctive features of imperialism. This allows Lenin to describe it as parasitic or decaying capitalism.[29] The bourgeoisie at this stage, tend more and more to reduce their contribution to production to that of "clipping coupons" while delegating any managerial duties to the "labor aristocracy," a small section of the working class which has been bribed by very high wages into renouncing its revolutionary role as proletarians in favor of defending the interests of the bourgeoisie. The decaying aspect of capitalism does not preclude, however, its rapid growth concomitantly. In its imperialistic stage, capitalism on the whole develops much more rapidly than in its previous stages. However, the rate of growth among the nations becomes much more uneven.[30] Under finance capitalism, any country which can acquire new markets in undeveloped regions, can progress at the expense of those nations not having these opportunities. This intensifies the rivalry and further destroys the stability in the distribution of the world market. Consequently, the irreconcilability between the opportunism of the bourgeoisie and the vital interests of the working class movement create conditions favorable to a proletarian revolution and, in fact, make it inevitable.[31] The death knell of capitalism rings much more loudly in the imperialistic stage than it did at the time Marx heard it.

Because capitalism represents the fruit of egoism, selfishness, social-chauvinism and institutionalized injustice, the proletarians must learn to be guided by another ethic — one that conforms to their higher interests and which is more in keeping with the dignity of the "new man" who is to live in the communistic world of the future. What, then, are the principles of this new ethic?

Moral Principles

To the Marxist, every moral code is simply a derivation of the mode of economic production proper to a particular time or age.[32]

Men are born to find themselves living in a society with a definite mode of production by which they are to procure for themselves and their families the material necessities of life. Obtaining these necessities is the most commanding motive for activity, for without them, life ceases. So long as men feel that the current mode of production is supplying them with their needs, they are not only content with this mode, but they are determined, moreover, to defend it. Thus, men consciously or unconsciously create a moral code whose purpose is to protect the current mode of economic production. The principal defenders of these moral laws would be those who profit most by them, namely, those who own the means of production. In the moral code these owners see one of the best defenses and supports of their dominance. The moral code of each historical period is a class morality, a system of morality whose purpose it is to protect the position of the then ruling and exploiting class. In brief, the Marxist conception of the nature and function of every moral code is to act as a defense and a justification of the currently prevailing mode of production.

> We maintain . . . that all former moral theories are the product, in the last analysis of the economic stage which society has reached at that particular epoch. And as society has hitherto moved in class antagonisms, morality was always a class morality; it has either justified the domination and the interests of the ruling class, or, as soon as the oppressed class has become powerful enough, it has represented the revolt against this domination and the future interests of the oppressed.[33]

It is this class morality that the Marxist absolutely rejects. He refuses to accept as eternal truths moral standards which are the creations of an exploiting system of economic production, based upon private ownership and used as a weapon of oppression to preserve the system and to entrench the exploiting class deeper in the position of power.

He considers it an historical fact that all codes of morality have been intimately bound up with religious beliefs. Instead of realizing the true basis of moral standards — economics — men have invariably placed the basis of their moral code in religion. All moral codes, it is believed, are derived from religious "truths" such as the existence of God, a future life, a future reward or punishment. The Marxist, on the other hand, with his superior knowledge, realizes that the true basis of this "bourgeois morality" is only an ideology created by the economic system of private ownership and, therefore, casts aside all such morality. It is only this false "bourgeois morality" which the Marxists reject. They must not be regarded as rejecting all ethics and morality. Lenin is explicit on this point.

In what sense do we repudiate ethics and morality?
In the sense in which it is preached by the bourgeoisie, who derived ethics from God's commandments. We, of course, say that we do not believe in God, and that we know perfectly well that the clergy, the landlords and the bourgeoisie spoke in the name of God in pursuit of their own interests as exploiters. . . .

We repudiate all morality taken apart from human society and classes. We say that it is a deception, a fraud, a befogging of the minds of the workers and peasants in the interests of the landlords and capitalists.[34]

If it is only "bourgeois morality" that is rejected, what then are the moral laws acceptable within the world of Marxism? In answer, the Marxian philosopher would call attention to the fact that he does not regard *all* current moral norms as products of religious superstition and the prevailing mode of production. He would acknowledge a science of morality which proposes numerous moral norms, some few of which are objectively valid for all times.[35] However, he too, would freely admit that it would be extremely difficult and, perhaps, impossible to single out any particular moral standard which men have, and always will accept as true. The Marxist believes that there are a few such standards mingled in the mass of moral laws which mankind now holds in reverence but, at present, it is implausible that anyone discover which these might be. But certainly the moral concepts which at the present time do *de facto* represent the hidden desires of man to overthrow the present social system are those most likely to possess the element of durability. For these are at least destined to endure beyond the present capitalist system. Hence, whatever eternal moral truths there are, we may expect to find them in the proletarian moral code of the present time.

This concept of morality is more easily comprehended if one recalls the Marxian doctrine professing the relative character of all truth. In the perpetual dynamism of both Marx's ontology and social philosophy, relativity is the *sine qua non* of progress; yet progress gives to the fruits of relativity a permanence and a universality. Thus, the criterion of morality can be said to be relativistic to a given epoch or class-controlled society, yet, nonetheless, there is found in humanity in some measure a common approach to the "good." This follows from the nature of the Hegelian dialectic itself. The synthesis, it is to be remembered, transcends the truth contained in the thesis and antithesis; it in no way destroys or discards it. The moral truth and goodness of the primitive and capitalistic societies are not foreign to true society. In the dialectical progression of man and his economic environment, nothing is lost, save error, evil and ugliness.[36]

Of all the sciences there is none which possesses so few of these stable truths as the science of morality. Precisely because ethics contains so few durable truths, it is extremely difficult to point out any moral standard which will remain valid for all time. The ethics of the Judaeo-Christian tradition and the moral codes of capitalism will die with those systems, whereas it is held that much of the proletarian morality has found its way into the socialist society now prevailing in the U.S.S.R. and the other countries of the Communist bloc. Some will endure even after the final stage of perfect, classless communism is reached. Since both the Judaeo-Christian and capitalistic moral codes have almost reached the term of their existence, whatever eternal moral truths there are, will most likely be found in the moral norms of the socialist society.

What, then, is the present socialist code of morality? What is the criterion which determines the moral goodness or badness of human activity? The answers to these questions are to be found in the works of Lenin. He tells us that the needs of the class-struggle determine the norms of morality. Whatever fosters the revolutionary task of the proletariat in its fight for economic emancipation, whatever aids in the struggle to overthrow the remnants of capitalism and feudalism, is a morally good act. Whatever hinders the revolutionary work of the proletariat, whatever serves to perpetuate the continuation of the reactionary aspects of society, is a morally evil act. Morality is wholly subordinated to the interest of the class-struggle.

We say that our morality is entirely subordinated to the interests of the class struggle of the proletariat. Our morality is derived from the interests of the class struggle of the proletariat. . . . That is why we say that for us there is no such thing as morality apart from human society; it is a fraud. Morality for us is subordinated to the interests of the class struggle of the proletariat.[37]

The struggle of the proletariat is not destined to go on indefinitely. Eventually, the proletariat will succeed in its class conflict. What, then, will be the norm of morality? In essence, it will be the same as it is at present. The reason can be grasped if the norm of morality is stated in more generic terms than those of Lenin above. *An act is morally good which by its very nature is conducive to the material betterment of mankind, to the economic development of society, to the inevitable state of future communism.*[38]

This material betterment and economic development for the Marxist lies in the class struggle and the perfection of the socialist state. The world-wide success of Marxist socialism will, in turn, be followed by true communism. Class struggles will have ceased, and the material betterment of mankind is no longer to be found at this level. It is rather to be found in greater social consciousness and in the unselfishness in one's own labor as contributing to the common need. It is such acts that would then be considered morally good. But in each period the basic norm of morality — material betterment and economic development — remains the same. One can readily understand why the Marxist feels that even socialist moral standards have, in general, only a transitory validity. The moral norms of today may not be valid

115

tomorrow precisely because that which now aids the proletariat may not help but, instead, hinder it in the future.[39]

Marxism offers a morality which is stripped of all superhuman elements and their alleged sedation — a morality which it represents as a truly "human morality" destined at all times to eradicate exploitation from man's life and to aid continually in the material prosperity of his life in society.

Attitude Towards Religion

The problem of religion has caused considerable difficulty and confusion to interpreters, both sympathetic and otherwise, of the theories of Marx and Engels. At times we hear protestations that freedom of religion is part of communist tactics, on other occasions, it is said that one cannot be a good communist without being an atheist, and so on.

About the origin of religion, however, there is no controversy within Marxism. Religion, unlike other phenomena of the social superstructure, in its earliest forms, was not derived from an economic basis. This was so simply because of the historical fact that religious practices arose previous to the system of private ownership. Primitive religion, consequently, did not serve as an institution to defend the economic supremacy of the dominant class, but arose from the ignorance and fear of natural forces.[40] From a naïve analysis of his dreaming, early man concluded that his thinking abilities were not activities of his body, but of a distinct soul which inhabits the body and leaves it after death. If in death there was a separation of the soul from the body, there was no reason to invent another death for it. Thus arose the idea of immortality.[41] In much the same manner, the first gods arose through the personification of natural forces. Gradually, in the course of man's intellectual development, these gods took on less of a physical form. Eventually, the many more or less limited and mutually limiting gods gave way to the idea in men's minds of the one exclusive God of the monotheistic religions, such as that of the vulgarized philosophy of the later Greeks and the national God of the Jews, *Jehovah*.[42]

The powerful forces of nature were the most important powers in the life of the primitive man. He depended upon the favorable operation of these natural forces for his very existence. Under such circumstances it was most fitting that he stand in awe and fear of these natural forces. From this wonder and fear there followed a desire to propitiate and influence these powers. With this end in mind, primitive man naturally began to believe that these mighty forces were actions of gods. Fire and lightning were thus the action of an angry deity; rain was the result of a deity looking favorably on man and providing the needed moisture for the crops. If displeased, this same god would but sweep away the lives and possessions of men by raging floods.

The next progression in the primitive's thought was to come to the realization or hope that if the forces of nature were the actions of the gods, then it might be possible to influence or control them to some extent. In this hope is found the origin of prayer and sacrifice to heavenly beings. The personification of the varied natural forces was the cause of polytheism. Later this was in many cases refined into a monotheistic religion among more advanced cultures.

With the birth of private property, however, a new function of religion was introduced. It is no longer needed merely to furnish men with a psychologically effective method — even if not objectively effective — of dealing with natural forces. With the coming of private property came also social exploitation. The advent of exploitation resulting from private property necessitated the creation of an entire social superstructure, which included religion, to protect and serve the ruling and exploiting class. Religion now became the psychological shield of the oppressed classes against the new terrors and tragedies which the social and economic forces create. And this is the present characteristic function of religion.

> It is not long before, side by side with the forces of nature, social forces begin to be active, forces which present themselves to man as equally extraneous, and at first equally inexplicable, dominating them with the same apparent necessity as the forces of nature themselves.[43]

The deepest root of religion is the socially downtrodden condition of the working masses and their apparently complete helplessness in the face of the blind forces of capitalism, which every day and every hour inflicts upon ordinary working people the most horrible suffering and the most savage torment, a thousand times more severe than those inflicted by extraordinary events, such as wars, earthquakes, etc. "Fear made the gods." Fear of the blind force of capital — blind because it cannot be foreseen by the masses of the people — a force which at every step in the life of the proletarian and small proprietor threatens to inflict, and does inflict "sudden," "unexpected," "accidental" ruin, destruction, pauperism, prostitution, death from starvation — such is the root of modern religion which the materialist must bear in mind first and foremost, if he does not want to remain an infant-school materialist.[44]

Religion, for the Marxist, arose as a superstitious means of subduing the effects of natural forces. It still exists as a sedative to relieve a similar fear of the action of social and economic forces. Modern man does not excessively worry about the action of natural forces because science and human ingenuity have provided him with sufficient protection against the ordinary destructiveness of nature. But now it is the uncontrollable economic forces that confront man. As long as these forces remain hidden and unpredictable — as such they must under capitalism[45] — religion will offer man an explanation of the tragedies which befall him as a result of these forces, and will help him psychologically bear up under the injustice of economic, political and moral exploitation. Religion helps soothe the anger which naturally exists between the opposing classes of society. It teaches the poor the blessings of poverty, and teaches the rich the necessity of giving alms that they may justify their exploitation and parasitical existence.[46]

Religion, however, is thereby justifying the present economic mode of production and rendering it permanent. It causes the continuation of the exploitation of the masses. Hence, religion is the opium of the people.[47] It intoxicates the minds of men and prevents them from knowing life and the material universe scientifically, *i.e.,* knowing them as they actually are.[48]

Religion is sort of a spiritual booze, in which the slaves of capital drown their human image, their demand for a life more or less worthy of man.[49] Those who toil and live in want all their lives are taught by religion to be submissive and patient while here on earth, and to take comfort in the hope of a heavenly reward.[50]

Since for the Marxist, religion is a natural reaction in man arising from the exploitation of the subservient class, it is to be expected that religion will spontaneously continue to exist in society as long as the exploitation exists. As long as man is the victim of exploitation, he will need the sedative effects of religion. If happiness is not to be found in this world, man will live in anticipation of finding it in a future one. Since exploitation continues because capitalism continues, religion will still appeal to man until that mode of production which breeds oppression is replaced by a higher form of society. Even during the transition period of socialism, remnants of the religious reflex will remain among certain of the workers. This is to be expected, since remnants of capitalism and its utilitarian approach to life will likewise be present. Until all such relics of the past be overcome by scientific economic development, toleration must be exercised and "freedom of conscience" respected.[51] Eventually, with the advent of perfect communism, religion will become extinct.

When society, by taking possession of all means of production and using them on a planned basis, has freed itself and all its members from the bondage in which they are now held by these means of production which they themselves have produced but which now confront them as an irresistible extraneous force; when therefore man no longer merely proposes, but also disposes — only then will the last extraneous force which is still reflected in religion vanish; and with it will also vanish the religious reflection itself, for the simple reason that there will be nothing left to reflect.[52]

The problem of destroying religion is not to take on any great importance for the Marxist. Lenin continually warns that the religious question must not be pushed into the foreground where it does not belong. Religious beliefs are rapidly losing all political significance and are only of third-rate importance. They are steadily being relegated to the rubbish heap in the normal course of economic development.[53] Any attempt to prohibit religion in socialist society or to declare open war on religion, as Engels had pointed out previously, would be to repeat the stupidity of Bismarck in the struggle against clericalism — the *Kulturkampf*. By this struggle Bismarck only strengthened the militant clericalism of the Catholics and injured the work of real culture by bringing religious conflicts instead of political ones to the forefront, and thus diverted the attention of some of the working class from the revolutionary struggle to that of bourgeois anti-clericalism. The Communist Party is not to repeat this absurdity.[54]

Rather, the workers party should labor patiently at those tasks of organizing and educating the proletariat, which will lead to the death of religion, and not rush into a political war *against* religion.[55]

Lenin, however, cautions that even this policy has been distorted by some into a form of "opportunism."[56] In their zeal to ingratiate themselves with religious workers and lead them into the Party, some have been willing to soft-pedal atheism — lest the godless aspects of communism frighten off those workers. These opportunists hold that Party considers religion a *private matter,* and the Party and the Party members do not have to accept atheism unless they see fit. This is not true, claims Lenin. What *is* true is that the socialist *state* should not take any definite position toward religion, but remain strictly neutral. The Communist Party members, however, must be confirmed atheists, if they are not to make Marxism an absurdity. This is the correct interpretation of the statements of Marx and Engels. To superficial interpreters of Marxism this may appear as contradictory or as mere wavering, but to those who take Marxism seriously this attitude toward religion represents a profound consistency and is inseparable from the philosophical principles of Marx. But let us permit Lenin to speak for himself:

> Engels . . . deliberately underlined that Social-Democrats regard religion as a private matter *in relation to the state,* but not in relation to themselves, not in relation to Marxism, and

not in relation to the workers' party. . . . To people with a slapdash attitude towards Marxism, to people who cannot or will not think, this history is a skein of meaningless Marxist contradictions and waverings, a hodge-podge of "consistent" atheism and "sops" to religion, "unprincipled" wavering between a r-r-revolutiónary war on God and a cowardly desire to "play up to" religious workers, a fear of scaring them away, etc. etc. . . .

But anyone who is able to treat Marxism at all seriously, to ponder over its philosophical principles and the experience of international Social-Democracy, will readily see that the Marxist tactics in regard to religion are thoroughly consistent, and were carefully thought out by Marx and Engels; and that what dilettantes or ignoramuses regard as wavering is but a direct and inevitable deduction from dialectical materialism. It would be a profound mistake to think that the seeming "moderation" of Marxism in regard to religion is due to supposed "tactical" considerations, the desire "not to scare away" anybody, and so forth. On the contrary, in this question, too, the political line of Marxism is inseparably bound up with its philosophical principles.[57]

Marxism is basically a materialistic philosophy. As such, it is as hostile to religion as were the Encyclopaedists, the followers of Feuerbach, or any other materialists. But Marxism differs from other materialist philosophies in that it *knows how* to combat religion. The struggle against religion must not be reduced to abstract propaganda that insists on the higher sophistication of an atheistic position, but it must be linked up with the concrete work of the class movement. Its aim must be to eliminate the social roots of religion. This means that the propagation of atheism by the Communist Party must be *subordinated* to its basic task — the development of the class struggle of the exploited masses with the exploiters.[58] The actual progress of the class struggle will convert religious workers to communism and to atheism a hundred times more effectively than any abstract atheistic arguments.[59]

A Marxist must be a materialist, i.e. an enemy of religion, but a dialectical materialist, i.e., one who treats the struggle against religion not in an abstract way, not on the basis of remote, purely theoretical, never varying preaching, but in a concrete way, on the basis of the class struggle which is going on *in practice* and is educating the masses more and better than anything else could.[60]

Whether modern communism is living up to these teachings of its patriarchs is certainly a moot question. Such a doctrine can possibly explain the survival of the Orthodox Church in the Soviet Union after nearly half a century of communist rule,[61] as well as the creation of national churches to replace Roman Catholicism in certain satellite countries. But can it explain the existence of untold numbers of modern martyrs who, apparently, have suffered and died for the sake of religion alone?[62]

Suggested Readings

CHAPTER V

Primary Sources

*Engels, F., *Anti-Dühring*, Chapters IX, X, XI.
———, *Ludwig Feuerbach and the Outcome of Classical German Philosophy*, Part III.
Lenin, V. I., *Imperialism, the Highest Stage of Capitalism*.
*———, *Socialism and Religion*.
*———, *Attitude of the Workers' Party to Religion*.
Marx, K., *Capital*, Volume I.
———, *A Contribution to the Critique of Political Economy*.
*———, *Toward the Critique of Hegel's Philosophy of Right*.
*———, *Value, Price and Profit*.
Smith, Adam, *The Wealth of Nations*, Chapter V.

Secondary Sources

Böhm-Bawerk, Eugen v., *Karl Marx and the Close of His System*, trans. Alice M. MacDonald, New York, The Macmillan Co., 1898.
Chambre, Henri, *From Karl Marx to Mao Tse-tung*, Chapters I, II, and X.
Freedman, Robt. (ed.), *Marx on Economics*, New York, Harcourt, Brace and World, 1961.
*Hunt, R. N. Carew, *The Theory and Practice of Communism*, Chapters V and VII.
Kamenka, Eugene, "Marx, Marxism and Ethics," *Soviet Survey*, No. 35, pp. 106-113; No. 39, pp. 49-60.
Kline, George L., "Current Soviet Morality," *Encyclopedia of Morals*, ed. Vergilius Ferm, New York, The Philosophical Library, 1956.
Kolarz, Walter, *Religion in the Soviet Union*, New York, St. Martin's Press, 1961.

———, "The Soviet Attitude Towards Religion," *Soviet Survey*, No. 13.

*Laski, Harold J., *Communism*, Chapter III.

Mac Eoin, Gary, *The Communist War on Religion*, New York, Devin-Adair, 1951.

*McFadden, Chas. J., *The Philosophy of Communism*, *Chapters VI, VII and Chapters XIV, XV.

Mayo, Henry, *Introduction to Marxist Theory*, New York, Oxford University Press, 1961, Chapter VII.

Meyer, Alfred G., *Leninism*, New York, Frederick A. Praeger, Inc., 1962, Chapter XI.

*Popper, Karl R., *The Open Society and Its Enemies*, 2 vols., New York, Harper and Row, 1963, Vol. II, Chapter 22.

Robinson, Joan, *An Essay on Marxian Economics*, London, Macmillan and Co., Ltd., 1947.

Selsam, Howard, *Socialism and Ethics*, New York, International Publishers, 1943.

FOOTNOTES TO CHAPTER V

1. K. Marx and F. Engels, *The German Ideology*, ed. R. Pascal (New York, 1947), p. 7.
2. Marx, *Preface to A Contribution to the Critique of Political Economy*, in *Karl Marx Selected Works*, 2 vols. (Moscow-Leningrad, 1935-36), I, p. 356. Hereafter cited as *KMSW*. Cf. Engels, "Letter to Heinz Starkenburg, January 25, 1894," *KMSW*, I, pp. 391-392.
3. Harold J. Laski, *Communism* (New York, 1927), p. 92.
4. V. I. Lenin, *The Three Sources and Three Component Parts of Marxism, KMSW*, I, p. 55.
5. John Locke, *Second Treatise on Civil Government*, Chapter V.
6. Adam Smith, *The Wealth of Nations*, Chapter V; David Ricardo, *On the Principles of Political Economy, and Taxation*, Chapter I.
7. Marx, *A Contribution to the Critique of Political Economy*, trans. N. I. Stone (Chicago, 1904), pp. 73-91. Hereafter cited as *Critique of Political Economy*. Cf. Laski, *Communism*, Chapter III.
8. See, for example, *Critique of Political Economy*.
9. *Value, Price and Profit, KMSW*, I, pp. 304-312.
10. *Ibid.*, pp. 312-315. Cf. R. N. Carew Hunt, *The Theory and Practice of Communism*, 5th rev. ed. (New York, 1961), Chapter V. Hereafter cited as Hunt, *TPC*.
11. Marx, *Value, Price and Profit, KMSW*, I, p. 314.
12. Preface to *Capital*, Volume II, *KMSW*, I, pp. 347-349.
13. *Ibid.*
14. Marx, *Capital*, 3 vols. (Chicago, 1909), I, p. 323.
15. *Ibid.*, p. 233.
16. Cf. Marx, *Value, Price and Profit*, Chapter VIII, *KMSW*, I, pp. 315-317.
17. Cf. Marx, *Capital*, I, p. 648.
18. Marx, of course, denies that profit results from the lending of money, the rent of land, or from the activities of the trader who conducts the exchange process. If this is true, it would follow that the higher the proportion of labor or variable capital is to constant capital in a business, the higher must be the surplus value, profit and price — and vice versa! But, as Marx himself realized, this contradicts all practical experience in the economic world. Marx insisted that the contradiction was only apparent and promised a solution. The solution did not appear in his lifetime, but

only many years after his death when Engels was finally able to publish Volume Three of *Das Kapital*. The solution offered therein by Marx is considered by a great consensus of economists to be unsatisfactory. Marx argued that although the price of a product in any particular instance might not be the sum of the value of labor power and surplus value, this did hold true when the total prices of all commodities were examined. Thus, his surplus value theory remained valid when capitalistic production as a whole was considered. For a critique of Marx's argument see, for example, Eugen v. Böhm-Bawerk, *Karl Marx and the Close of His System*, trans. Alice M. MacDonald (New York, 1898), especially Chapter III.

19. Cf. Marx, *Capital*, I, pp. 671-703, and 834-837. See also Hunt, *TPC*, pp. 63-65, and Laski, *Communism*, pp. 103-105.

20. Cf. Engels, "Letter to Conrad Schmidt, August 5, 1890," *Marx and Engels, Selected Correspondence*, trans. Dona Torr (New York, 1942), pp. 472-474.

21. *Ibid.*, p. 380. Cf. Engels, *The Communists and Karl Heinzen, KMSW*, I, xv.

22. Cf. Lenin, *Imperialism, The Highest Stage of Capitalism*, in *Selected Works*, 12 vols. (New York, 1943), V, 14-26. On the point of imperialism also see Hunt, *TPC*, pp. 181-188, and Alfred G. Meyer, *Leninism* (New York, 1962), Chapter XI.

23. Lenin, *Imperialism, The Highest Stage of Capitalism*, pp. 42-55.

24. *Ibid.*, pp. 56-60.

25. *Ibid.*, pp. 61-68.

26. *Ibid.*, pp. 69-79.

27. *Ibid.*, p. 69.

28. Cf. Lenin, *The War and Russian Social-Democracy*, in *Selected Works*, V, p. 123.

29. *Imperialism, the Highest Stage of Capitalism*, pp. 91-99.

30. *Ibid.*, p. 116.

31. *Ibid.*, p. 99. Cf. Hunt, *TPC*, p. 187.

32. The following section appeared in a slightly altered form as part of my article entitled "Marxist Jurisprudence in the Soviet Union: A Preliminary Survey," in *Notre Dame Lawyer*, Vol. XXXV (1960), No. 4. Reprinted with permission.

33. Engels, *Herr Eugen Dühring's Revolution in Science (Anti-Dühring)* (London, 1940), p. 105. Hereafter cited as Engels, *Anti-Dühring*.

34. Lenin, Speech to 3rd Congress of Communist Youth League, October 2, 1920, *Lenin Selected Works*, 2 vols. in 4 (Moscow, 1952), II, Part II, p. 483.

35. For a concise analysis of communist ethics, see Chas. J. McFadden, *The Philosophy of Communism* (New York, 1939), Chapters VII, XV,

and George L. Kline, "Current Soviet Morality," in *Encyclopedia of Morals,* ed. Vergilius Ferm (New York, 1956).

36. When the relativistic morals of Marxism are seen in the light of the dialectic, it does not necessarily follow for the Marxist that there is an "obvious contradiction" as Professor George A. Guins asserts (*Soviet Law and Soviet Society* [The Hague, 1954], p. 385, note 28), between the class character of morals, on the one hand, and the moral principles common to mankind for thousands of years, which Lenin admits of in *The State and Revolution* (*Selected Works,* VII, p. 81).

37. *Lenin Selected Works,* II, Part II, pp. 483-484. This quotation is most often taken to mean that the Marxist becomes committed thereby to the moral axiom: "the end justifies the means." This conclusion, however, is strongly denied by the Marxist, Professor Mihailo Markovic of Belgrade University (Address to the Society for the Study of Dialectical Materialism, American Philosophical Association, Detroit, May, 1962). Although he admits that, in the recent past, moral commitments have been sacrificed to political goals by both socialist and capitalist countries, he rejects both the principle and practice of this subordination of morals to politics. While it is true, he argues, that morality as an expression of the interests of a particular class is politically colored, nonetheless, the Communist Party, which claims to speak in the interests of all humanity, must follow moral values in its political struggle. Nor must it overlook the close connection between the moral values of goals and those of the means. Noble goals can only be realized by noble men. The use of bad, degrading means morally degrades those who employ them. Since man's practical activity is the most important factor that determines the evolution of his consciousness, the continued use of immoral means would eventually change the concept of the goals to be obtained. What then comes into existence is likely to be something vastly different, and mostly morally inferior to the initial idea.

However, claims Markovic, it does not follow from this that friendly persuasion remains the only legitimate means of political change, or that force cannot be allowed from a moral point of view, for often the only good alternative is the use of force against those who abuse the weak and helpless. Thus, there must be a unity among goals and means, in that the same moral standards must be used in both cases. It is in this sense that Lenin's insistence on the subordination of morality to the interests of the class-struggle is to be taken.

This interpretation should be compared with that of Howard Selsam, "The Ethics of the Communist Manifesto," in *Science and Society,* XII (1948), No. 1, pp. 22-32.

38. McFadden, *The Philosophy of Communism,* pp. 141-142.

39. Lenin, "Left-Wing" Communism, An Infantile Disorder, in Selected Works, VII, p. 111.
40. Cf. Engels, Anti-Dühring, p. 353.
41. Cf. Engels, Ludwig Feuerbach and the Outcome of Classical German Philosophy, KMSW, I, p. 430. Hereafter cited as Engels, Ludwig Feuerbach.
42. Ibid.; Anti-Dühring, pp. 353-354. See also, McFadden, The Philosophy of Communism, Chapter VI.
43. Engels, Anti-Dühring, pp. 353-354.
44. Lenin, Attitude of the Workers' Party to Religion, Collected Works (Moscow, 1960-63), XV, pp. 405-406. Hereafter cited as Lenin, AWPR.
45. Cf. Engels, Anti-Dühring, p. 354.
46. Cf. Marx, "The Communism of the Paper Rheinischer Beobachter," Deutsche-Brüsseler-Zeitung, No. 73, September 12, 1847, in Marx and Engels, Basic Writings on Politics and Philosophy, ed. Lewis S. Feuer (Garden City, N. Y., 1959), pp. 268-269. Hereafter cited as Feuer, BWPP. See also Lenin, Socialism and Religion, Collected Works, X, p. 83.
47. Marx, Toward the Critique of Hegel's Philosophy of Right, in Feuer, BWPP, p. 263. Cf. Lenin, AWPR, p. 402.
48. Marx, Toward the Critique of Hegel's Philosophy of Right, in Feuer, BWPP, pp. 262-263.
49. Lenin, Socialism and Religion, pp. 83-84.
50. Ibid., p. 84.
51. Cf. Article 124, The Constitution of the Union of Soviet Socialist Republics, in John N. Hazard, The Soviet System of Government, 2d. ed. (Chicago, 1961), appendix, pp. 207-230.
52. Engels, Anti-Dühring, p. 355.
53. Lenin, Socialism and Religion, p. 87.
54. Lenin, AWPR, pp. 403-404.
55. Ibid., p. 404.
56. Ibid.
57. Ibid., pp. 404-405.
58. Ibid., p. 405.
59. Ibid., pp. 407-408.
60. Ibid., See also Lenin, Socialism and Religion, pp. 86-87.
61. On this point see, for example, Constantin de Grunwald, The Churches and the Soviet Union (New York, 1962), and Walter Kolarz, Religion in the Soviet Union (New York, 1961).
62. On the subject of religious persecution and suppression, see, for example, Boleslaw Szczesniak, The Russian Revolution and Religion (Notre Dame, Ind., 1955), and Gary Mac Eoin, The Communist War on Religion (New York, 1951).

Part II

SOME PRINCIPLES APPLIED

CHAPTER VI

COMMUNIST PHILOSOPHY OF THE STATE AND LAW

The Theory of the State and Law

V. I. Lenin,[1] following in the dogmatic footsteps of Marx and Engels,[2] asserts that the state is essentially "a machine for upholding the dominance of one class over another."[3] When, historically speaking, man existed in a state of primitive communism, there were no classes in society — no special group set apart for exercising dominion over all the rest of society. Class conflict arose only with the appearance of slavery which came about when a certain portion of the people by crude agricultural toil were able to produce a surplus over and above what was essential for life. This strengthened the existence of one class over the others who became its debtors and slaves. In order that this new slaveholding class might remain in power and strengthen its position, it was essential that the state appear. And it did appear — a mechanism giving over into the hands of the slave owner the power and possibility of governing all the slaves. For without a permanent mechanism of control, one part of society cannot be forced to work systematically for another and smaller part.

Historically it was noted that as the form of exploitation changed, so also did the governmental form. Out of slavery came serfdom, which closely resembled slavery but opened the gate to greater emancipation of the oppressed. The development of trade led to the segregation of a new class — the capitalist. With its rise and with the decline of the squire, the fief, the vassal and the guild system, society was reorganized in such a way that while in theory all citizens were considered equal, in practice they were not. The right to property was universal, but the control of property was not. The property rights of the few allowed them, once again, to encroach economically on the many; classes were created, with one class in control of the state machinery while the other became subservient. Thus arose the bourgeoisie and proletariat.

The Marxist notion of law follows directly from the concept of the state as the organ of authority of the dominant class. In its activity, the state realizes the *will* of the dominant class. It guarantees and protects the interests of that class. To achieve this, it is necessary that the mandates of the will of the governing class be binding on society. All the citizens of the state must be subject to, and observe them. In a socialist state, it is the will of the working class — which has abolished exploitation and which thereby expresses true human values — that is binding upon all citizens.

The realization of the will of the dominant class for the purpose of establishing and strengthening social conditions advantageous to this class is attained with the aid of law. Norms of conduct and their sanctions are derived ordinarily through legislation.[4] To the Marxist, the nature of bourgeois law is the key to understanding the nature of all law. Law is merely the will of the dominant class elevated into governmental regulation. As bourgeois law expresses the will of the exploiter class, the law of socialist society likewise expresses the will of the now dominant working class. Socialist law is the will of the workers elevated into legislation. It is the will of the people who have built socialist society under the guidance of the working class headed by the Bolshevik Party.

It is the teaching of Marxism-Leninism that neither the state nor the law takes precedence over the other. As we have seen, law emerged jointly with the state in consequence of the disintegration of the primordial-communal social order, the appearance of private property and the division of society into classes. In class society the antagonistic classes struggle among themselves, and the dominant class, aided by the instrument of social control, the *state,* holds the oppressed classes obedient, and aided by *law* dictates its will to them.

> Law and state are not two distinct phenomena — one preceding the other — but are two sides of one and the same

phenomenon: class dominance, which is manifested (a) in the fact that the dominant class creates its apparatus of constraint (the state), and (b) in the fact that it expresses its will in the shape of rules of conduct which it formulates (law) and which — with the aid of its state apparatus — it compels people to observe.[5]

The law of the socialist state, like the socialist state itself, passes through an evolutionary process, in the course of which it becomes stronger. When, and only when, both the state and law have reached their maximum strength in the preceding stages of their historical development will they "wither away." The dictatorship of the proletariat and its law will exert maximum control as long as remains of the old order exist within the socialist state, or while this state is in danger from foreign imperialist powers. The "withering away" of the state and its laws cannot be abortive without disaster.

The state will wither away, not as a result of a relaxation of the state power, but as a result of its utmost consolidation, which is necessary for the purpose of finally crushing the remnants of the dying classes and of organizing defense against the capitalist encirclement, which is far from having been done away with as yet, and will not soon be done away with.[6]

The state and the law in Soviet thought are historical phenomena, emerging under the specific conditions mentioned above. The law and the state will disappear only with the disappearance of the causes that evoked them. With their "withering" will come the higher form of society — perfect communism.

From the foregoing principles we can now define law as seen in the light of Marxist-Leninist legal philosophy. Law is defined as *the aggregate of the rules of conduct expressing the will of the dominant class and established by legislation, as well as of customs and rules of community life confirmed by state authority, the application whereof is guaranteed by the coercive force of state to the end of safeguarding, making secure and developing social relationships and arrangements advantageous and agreeable to the dominant class.*[7]

Not all norms of conduct existing and operative in society belong to the category of law. Norms of morality and rules of community living are not always governmentally regulated. A norm of conduct is characterized as legal by the fact that state authority is the source of its force and binding power. It is state authority which compels compliance with the norm and imposes effective sanctions upon offenders. This does not mean that for the Marxist it is only by direct constraint that the vitality and effectualness of law is realized. Legal norms are for the most part effected without the state's intervention. Thus, from the Marxist viewpoint it would be incorrect to assert that a legal norm is *put into operation* coercively by direct constraint on the part of the state. Rather, the coercive power of the state *guarantees* that legal norms are put into operation.[8]

The regulation of human conduct by legislation means, according to the Marxist, that by legal norms definite rights are not merely secured but actually *granted;* obligations are not only enforced but also *imposed*. In virtue of these legal rights one can require that others carry out or refrain from definite actions indicated by the legal norm. Those so obligated must fulfill this duty or the state will compel them to do so. The legal order then, for the Marxist, always "creates" correlative rights and obligations. It is on the strength of the rights and obligations which the legal norm creates that this norm becomes a "living reality" among the people. In this connection the term "law" takes on two meanings signifying:

> (1) the rules of conduct themselves — the norms — expressed in statutes and other legislative measures of state authority, and (2) that a citizen or an organization can require definite acts on the part of other persons and of organs of authority.
>
> When we say that soviet socialist law (pravo) establishes the method and measure of wages payable to workers and clerks, we have in mind law (pravo) as an aggregate of norms. But when one declares: "the law (zakon) grants me the right (pravo) to demand payment for work," this means that out of the norms of law (pravo) — definite rights which he can utilize are created in his behalf.[9]

This two-fold distinction of law must not be taken to mean that the Marxist subdivides law into the concepts of "law in the objective sense" and "law in the subjective sense," as found in some civil law systems, or into the "law" vs. "rights" dichotomy as found in common law countries. Such distinctions often found in bourgeois jurisprudence are attributed by Marxists to the desire of the exploiters to conceal the class essence of law. For the same reason some bourgeois jurists insist on contrasting law with civil rights. This, claims the Marxist, leads logically to the idea that law exists objectively, it somehow expresses principles eternal and independent of the reality of a peculiar social phenomenon existing in definite social conditions. In an attempt to cover up the exploitative character of the bourgeois state some bourgeois jurists regard *rights* as isolated from the operative norms of the state. This gives to these rights an independent nature in the eyes of the people; they become attributes innate to the person and prior to both the legal norms reflecting the will of the dominant class and to the social relationships which they regulate.

In contrast, the Marxist looks upon law in a single sense — as the expression of social class relationships. Rules of conduct expressed in the legislative acts of state authority *grant* to the citizens definite rights and *impose* definite obligations. Civil rights, therefore, are *established* by law. Because of them, citizens may require other citizens or authorities to respect their interests to the extent determined by the legal norms.

The class relationships which the law expresses are, of course, human relationships existing in society. As we know from Marx's basic doctrine of "economic determinism," this social life is founded on production relationships — mutual relationships into which people enter during the production process. These economic relations are the foundation or the basis on which law and politics (as well as religion, art, literature, philosophy, etc.) develop. Based as they are on the methods used by any given society to produce, buy and sell its commodities, these relations are historically determined and arise independently of human volition. Independent of the class will, they also arise independently of law.

In the social production which men carry on they enter into definite relations that are indispensable and independent of their will. These relations of production correspond to a definite stage of development of their material powers of production. The sum total of these relations of production constitutes the economic structure of society — the real foundation, on which rise legal and political superstructures and to which correspond definite forms of social consciousness. The mode of production in material life determines the general character of the social, political and spiritual processes of life.[10]

Law, then, for Marx, is the product of economic relations, but unlike these relations it emerges out of conscious human activity. As such, it has its repercussions on the economic foundation. Economics is never to be looked upon as the sole cause of activity in society, with law and the other ideologies passively changing as economics directs. To do so is to seriously misunderstand the Marxist concept of development in society. Progress comes about through human activity. "Political, juridicial . . . development is based on economic development. But . . . these react . . . also upon the economic base. It is not that the economic position is the *cause and alone active,* while everything else only has a passive effect."[11]

Yet for Marx, significant changes in juridical theory do not come about by mere criticism of prevailing legal thought or the current status of society. A revolutionary change in the material basis of society, the mode of production, is the only force strong enough to bring about the evolvement of the true nature of law — or of any reality. For example, the *content* of the constitution and statutory law of the U.S.S.R. is quite similar to that of the United States and Western Europe, but the Soviets insist that the *form* is essentially different. The law of a socialist state and that in a capitalist society differ in *principle* regardless of their extrinsic similarity.[12] This essential difference follows necessarily, in the Marxist viewpoint, from the more perfect status of the economic and social relationships found in the socialist society of the Soviet Union. As the socialist society changes to the higher form of communism, both the state and law will "wither away." The rules of life will be observed without constraint, but solely in virtue of the conscious discipline of the communist social order based as it is on the most perfect mode of production — "from each according to his capacities, to each according to his needs."

Relationship of Law and Morality

As to be expected, the bond between the law and morality is very close within Marxist ideology. Law has been defined by the Marxist as the aggregate of the rules of human conduct; yet for him, moral norms too, regulate human conduct and are operative in society. Moral norms, then, are to be differentiated from legal norms by the fact that it is merely the influence of social opinion and not coercive power of the state that guarantees their observance.

Contrary to some bourgeois moralists, the Marxist holds that morality, like law, is a social phenomenon and not merely one of the inner activities of man's psychic life. As a tonic for social discipline moral norms have important social significance, and like legal norms they have a place in the social relationships of mankind. The application and observance of these ethical norms, therefore, cannot be relegated *ad forum internum*. External, social constraint must, in a certain measure, be called in as their guarantor. But this constraint is not the coercive mechanism of the state. It is, rather, the constraint exerted by social environment, social opinion, the attitude of persons living in society towards those who violate moral norms. Social condemnation of immorality, loss of respect, exclusion from membership in social groups, etc., unquestionably induce the observance of moral norms. Such constraint is essentially different from that of the state, being effectuated without use of the governmental organs of compulsion or without application of special techniques or procedures, as are needed in the domain of law. The force of moral influence rests on the conviction of any class in the society — on the social opinion expressing the views and ideas prevalent in the given society. Morality, then, for the Marxist, is identical with the notion of social "mores."

Both morality and law have a class nature and are delimited by the material conditions of the life of society. The norms of morality, however, according to the Marxist, lack the unity to be found in the law. The law of the state, insofar as it represents the will of the dominant class raised to the statutory level, is unified. Within a single state, moral norms, on the other hand, may vary in respect to the different classes to be found in that state. That which, from the viewpoint of the capitalist, may be perfectly moral conduct (*e.g.*, strike-breaking by individual workers), may, at the same time, be considered a serious moral violation in the eyes of the working class. In the Marxist outlook, only socialist morality, reflecting, as it does, true moral principles in the genuinely human sense of the word can realize in single class society a unity within itself and an integration with legal norms.

The interrelation of law and morality is of considerable interest to the communist legal philosopher and moralist. The issue involves difficulties whose solution is far from being self-evident even to those most well-versed in the classic postulates of Marxism. By their very content many socialist legal norms comprise moral norms. At the same time there are legal norms touching matters which are no concern of morality, such as norms of legal procedure, technical aspects of the law of contracts, and so on. What, then, is the relationship between the two spheres?

A better insight of the Marxian position can be had if their criticism of non-Marxist theories be briefly considered before we investigate their own standpoint. This is in keeping with Marxist dialectical method wherein truth is best discovered as emerging from contradiction.[13] Several different generic points of view on the matter of this relationship have been singled out for castigation by the Marxist. Perhaps the most widely held by non-Marxist students of the law is that in which the realms of law and ethics are strictly differentiated — both by internal content and by methods of effectuation. Morality, in this view, would belong to the province of man's inner spiritual life, and law, to that of external relationships. To the Marxist, this position is obviously incorrect. As we have seen, morality is also concerned with man's behavior in society, and it too regulates human conduct. This comes about chiefly through influence upon man's internal sensibilities rather than external force. At the same time, both civil law and criminal law to some extent consider the internal stimuli evoking external action, as well as the external actions in themselves. A patent example is found in the varying degrees of punishment inflicted under criminal law for the same external action in proportion to the perversity of intention and motive. Likewise, law attempts by positive influence to stimulate man internally towards voluntary fulfillment of its requirements as being reasonable and socially expedient. The two realms, claims the Marxist, must necessarily blend into one another.

Another "bourgeois" theory of law asserts with Jellinek that "law is the minimum of morality." This is interpreted rather simply by the Marxist to mean that from the entire ensemble of moral norms, some small number of them — those necessary for the well-ordering of society — is taken, and the character of law is attributed to them. Law, therefore, is a part of morality. As it relates to bourgeois morality such a theory is considered unsound. The Marxist adjudges it so because bourgeois laws are often immoral, even by bourgeois norms of morality (the legalization of prostitution, for example, in some countries). Basing their morality often on super-human concepts, these bourgeois jurists destroy the true human basis for law — economic relationships.

Going to the other extreme, some analytic jurists maintain that the requirements of morality have no significance whatever for law. Norms of law draw their force from within themselves, from their promulgation, or from their promulgators — not from morality. This is a less hypocritical standpoint for the bourgeois theorist to hold, considers the Marxist. Nonetheless, it makes a mockery of the elementary ideas of legal justice as entertained by the broad masses of the people.

The true relationship between bourgeois law and morality is seen, by the Marxist, in the fact that they are considered different means of confirming the exploitation and oppression of the masses — of misleading and deceiving the proletarian class. In some cases, the rules of human conduct expressing bourgeois interests are guaranteed by governmental coercion (law); while in other cases, ideological influence and psychological prompting (morality) are adequate to induce the desired rules of conduct. Bourgeois law and bourgeois morality aim at precisely the same purpose — the dominance of the class and the protection of its interests. But, since the moral norms of the opposing classes conflict in such a society, the bourgeoisie is forced to keep to a minimum the correlation of law to moral principle. Law, *i.e.,* rules whose sanctions are guaranteed by governmental agencies are, for the most part, consciously isolated from the domain of morality and considered completely extraneous to it.

The link between socialist law and morality rests on foundations completely different in principle. As we have seen, they have a common base and common principles. Also the tasks of socialist *law* — to eliminate capitalist remnants in human consciousness and to cooperate in the building of a classless communist society — are, at the same time, *moral* tasks in that they are moral norms also. As is to be expected, law and morality in many instances have a common content owing to their common foundation. The most basic norm, in the eyes of Lenin — "the struggle for the strengthening and consummation of communism" — is also guaranteed by the coercive force of the state under Article 130 of the U.S.S.R. constitution.[14] Yet, in becoming a legal norm it loses none of its moral content. Similarly, Article 12 states that labor in the U.S.S.R. is both an *obligation* and a matter of *honor;* Article 130 enjoins every citizen to perform public duties and to respect the rules of socialist behavior. Thus, in content and form they are at once legal and moral — not merely a coincidence of norm content.[15]

Since, for the Marxist, moral norms differ from legal norms insofar as they are not guaranteed by state sanction, many rules of conduct lie outside the scope of law in socialist society. On the other hand, law is partly made up of norms that pertain to legal technique and procedure only and often are of no concern of morality. The Russian jurists S. A. Golunskii and M. S. Strogovich have suggested that the interrelationship between the two realms *qua* content may be graphically portrayed by two intersecting circles which coincide in one part and are in different planes in all other parts.[16] The relation between these circles is contingent — they may come together, or they may draw apart, depending on whether the state authority enforces the given rules of conduct or relegates their observance to the social discipline of the citizens.

In arriving at a decision regarding what norms of social morality are to be elevated into law, the state considers several factors.

The moral norm would ordinarily be of some special importance from the state's point of view. However, not all such norms can be successfully guaranteed by state constraint. The moral norms requiring love among spouses and friendship among the workers, although vitally important to the state, are impossible to enforce by legislation.[17]

The Marxist jurists would here seem to be falling back into the conception of law as "the minimum of morality" in spite of their harangues about its meaninglessness. In fact they come very close to the position of Aquinas[18] and others — whose thought the Marxist is only too eager to characterize as an archaic remnant of feudalism — on the point of relegating the question of the demarcation of the two realms to the arena of prudence.

The bond between socialist law and morality does not presuppose that state coercion can be automatically transferred into the sphere of morality, for Golunskii and Strogovich. There always remains this line of demarcation between the spheres. Hence, any arbitrary application of state sanction for the violation of moral norms in the Soviet Union would of itself be unlawful by the constitution and contrary to the best interest of the proletariat.[19]

The bond between law and morality finds further expression in the fact that observance of law is the moral duty of the citizen of the socialist state, irrespective of the threat of constraint. Furthermore, socialist law becomes a salubrious factor in the development and confirmation of moral views in the community. By applying the law and compelling observance, the state strengthens the citizens' consciousness of their moral obligations with reference to the state and to each other.[20]

As the historical cycle is completed and man once again finds himself living in a classless communist society, the law and state constraint will have withered away. Only morality and social customs will then regulate the relationships of communal life, and in the words of Lenin:

> ... people will gradually *become accustomed* to observing the elementary rules of social intercourse that have been known for centuries and repeated for thousands of years in all copybook maxims; they will become accustomed to observing

them without force, without compulsion, without subordination, without the *special apparatus* for compulsion which is called the state.[21]

These rules observed from force of habit will be the moral norms and social customs of mankind in its perfection.

Suggested Readings

CHAPTER VI

Primary Sources

*Engels, F., *Anti-Dühring*, Part I, Chapters IX, X, XI; Part III, Chapter V.
———, *Origin of the Family, Private Property and the State.*
*Lenin, V. I., *The State and Revolution.*
Marx, K., *The Civil War in France.*
*———, *The Critique of the Gotha Programme.*

Secondary Sources

Aspaturian, Vernon V., "The Contemporary Doctrine of the Soviet State and Its Philosophical Foundation," *American Political Science Review*, XLVIII (1954), pp. 1031-1057.
*Berman, Harold J., *Justice in Russia: An Interpretation of Soviet Law*, Cambridge, Mass., Harvard University Press, 1950.
*Chambre, Henri, *From Karl Marx to Mao Tse-tung*, Chapter VI.
Chang, Sherman M., *The Marxian Theory of the State*, Philadelphia, Univ. of Penna. Press, 1931.
Gsovski, Vladimir, "The Soviet Concept of Law," *Fordham Law Review*, VII (1938), pp. 1-44.
*Hazard, John (ed.), *Soviet Legal Philosophy*, trans. Hugh W. Babb, Cambridge, Mass., Harvard University Press, 1951.
Hunt, R. N. Carew, *The Theory and Practice of Communism*, Chapter VI.
Kelsen, Hans, *The Communist Theory of Law*, New York, Frederick A. Praeger, 1955.
*Laski, Harold J., *Communism*, Chapter IV.
McFadden, Chas. J., *The Philosophy of Communism*, Chapter V, XIII.
Romashkin, P. S. (ed.), *Fundamentals of Soviet Law*, trans. Yuri Sdobnikov, Moscow, Foreign Languages Publishing House, 1960.

Sanderson, John, "Marx and Engels on the State," *The Western Political Quarterly*, XVI (1963), pp. 946-955.

Schlesinger, Rudolf, *Soviet Legal Theory*, New York, Oxford University Press, 1945.

Vyshinsky, Andrei, *The Law of the Soviet State*, trans. Hugh W. Babb, New York, The Macmillan Co., 1948.

FOOTNOTES TO CHAPTER VI

1. A portion of this chapter is drawn from my article, "Marxist Jurisprudence in the Soviet Union: A Preliminary Survey," *Notre Dame Lawyer*, XXXV, (1960), pp. 525-536. Reprinted with permission.
2. Cf. Karl Marx, *The Civil War in France* in *Karl Marx Selected Works*, ed. V. Adoratsky, 2 vols. (Moscow-Leningrad, 1935-36), II, pp. 495-496; Frederick Engels, *Ludwig Feuerbach and the Outcome of Classical German Philosophy, ibid.*, I, p. 463; Engels, *The Origin of the Family, Private Property and the State*, trans. Ernest Untermann (Chicago, 1909), pp. 130, 209, 214, etc.
3. Lenin, "The State," *Pravda* (No. 15), January 18, 1929. Reprinted in *Soviet Legal Philosophy*, ed. John N. Hazard, trans. Hugh W. Babb (Cambridge, Mass., 1951), p. 7. On this point, however, see the view of John Sanderson, "Marx and Engels on the State," *The Western Political Quarterly*, XVI (1963), pp. 946-955.
4. S. A. Golunskii and M. S. Strogovich, *The Theory of the State and Law* (Moscow, 1940), as reprinted in part in *Soviet Legal Philosophy*, p. 365. Hereafter cited as *GSTSL*.
5. *Ibid.*, p. 366. Cf. Hans Kelsen, *The Communist Theory of Law* (New York, 1955), p. 145.
6. Joseph Stalin, "The Result of the First Five-Year Plan," Report to the Central Committee of the C.P.S.U. (b), January 7, 1933, *Problems of Leninism* (Moscow, 1953), p. 538. Cf. Andrei Y. Vyshinsky, *The Law of the Soviet State*, trans. Hugh W. Babb (New York, 1948), pp. 40f.

N. S. Khrushchev insists that Stalin was incorrect both as to his intensification of state power and in his demand for a continuing emphasis on the class struggle. Khrushchev also declares that "the capitalist encirclement no longer exists." Cf. "Report to the 21st Congress of the C.P.S.U.," *Pravda*, January 28, 1959, reprinted in *Current Digest of the Soviet Press*, XI, No. 5 (March 11, 1959), pp. 13-17. Yet, even Khrushchev in this same report cautions that the state and its functions can wither away only with the "complete triumph of communism," which implies not merely that the Soviet Union must be able to repel any attack by an enemy, but also that all the socialist countries must be "guaranteed against the possibility of aggression by the imperialist states." Khrushchev seems at first to condemn Stalin and then to revert to an only slightly modified Stalinist position. Cf. P. S. Romashkin (ed.), *Fundamentals of Soviet Law,* trans. Yuri Sdobnikov (Moscow, 1960), p. 22. On this point also see, George A. Brinkley "The 'Withering' of the State Under Khrushchev," *The Review of Politics,* XXIII (1961), pp. 42-45.

7. A. Y. Vyshinsky, "The Fundamental Tasks of the Science of Soviet Socialist Law," Address at the First Congress on Problems of the Sciences of Soviet State and Law (Moscow, 1938), reprinted in *Soviet Legal Philosophy,* p. 336. Cf. Rudolf Schlesinger, *Soviet Legal Theory* (New York, 1945), p. 243, and W. Friedmann, *Legal Theory,* 3rd. ed. (London, 1953), p. 257.

8. *GSTSL,* p. 369. W. Friedmann maintains that there has recently been an attempt in the Soviet Union to restore law as an instrument of authority and the protector of individual rights. Under the previous phase of political dictatorship, however, legal issues were removed from the normal administration of justice and subjected to secret political and uncontrolled procedure behind closed doors. Even at present there are still many channels through which politics can be directly injected into the administration of the law. *Legal Theory,* pp. 257-259. Cf. J. Walter Jones, *Historical Introduction to the Theory of Law* (London, 1956), p. 275.

Harold J. Berman, however, insists that evidence points to an utmost respect for the legal system in the Soviet Union even in periods of extreme political and ideological repression. There was a surprising degree of official compartmentalization of the legal and the extralegal. Only one case can be recalled wherein the Communist Party attempted to interfere with the operation of the legal system. In that case the procurator went against the Party decision and, in effect, annulled it. *Justice in Russia* (Cambridge, Mass., 1950), preface, p. viii.

9. *GSTSL,* pp. 370-371. For a critique of Golunskii and Strogovich's theory of state and law, see Kelsen, *Communist Theory of Law,* Chapter 8.

10. Marx, *A Contribution to the Critique of Political Economy,* trans. N. I. Stone (Chicago, 1904), preface, p. 11.

11. Engels, "Letter to H. Starkenburg, January 25, 1894," *Marx and Engels, Selected Correspondence,* trans. Dona Torr (New York, 1942), p. 517. Cf. "Letters to Conrad Schmidt, August 5 and October 27, 1890," *ibid.,* pp. 472-475 and 477-484; "Letter to Joseph Bloch, September 21, 1890," *ibid.,* pp. 475-477; "Letter to Franz Mehring, July 14, 1893," *ibid.,* pp. 510-512.

Some hold that the theory of the interaction of the superstructure on the economic foundation is merely an interpretation of Engels forced upon him by a number of criticisms raised against Marx's unilaterality, and that no passage in Marx indicates he himself would have said this. It may be said in reply that there are several clear illusions to this point in Marx — the sum total of which indicate that Marx would be in agreement with the statements of Engels in the 1890's. In regard to the active causality of law in particular, see *Capital,* 3 vols. (Chicago, 1909), I, p. 552, and *A Contribution to the Critique of Political Economy,* appendix, p. 289. In regard to the interaction of economic foundation and superstructure in general, see *The German Ideology* (New York, 1947), pp. 28-29, and *Third Thesis on Feuerbach,* appendix, pp. 197-198. As Engels points out in his letter to Joseph Bloch, Marx's, *The Eighteenth Brumaire of Louis Bonaparte* is an excellent example of the application of the theory that individual wills contribute to the flow of history, *i. e.,* react on the economic mode of production in which they find themselves. Within bolshevik tradition, this interpretation of Engels has been considered as representing that of Marx. G. Plekhanov emphasized that ultimately economic conditions are decisive, but he recognized reciprocal action between the various social forces. Cf. *Fundamental Problems of Marxism,* ed. D. Riazanov (New York, 1929), pp. 57-58, and pp. 72f. It was strongly re-emphasized in the Soviet Union with the publication in 1950 of Stalin's letters on linguistics (*Marxism and the Problem of Linguistics* [Moscow, 1957]). At that time it was considered somewhat of an innovation on the part of Stalin. Cf. Gustav Wetter, *Dialectical Materialism,* trans. Peter Heath (New York, 1958), pp. 200-201. It is presently accepted in the Soviet Union as the proper interpretation of historical materialism. Cf. Romashkin, *Fundamentals of Soviet Law,* p. 20.

Outside the bolshevik tradition, the active causality of law and ideology is recognized. This is the position of the noted Austrian Marxist, Karl Renner in his *The Institutions of Private Law and their Social Functions.,* ed. by O. Kahn-Freund (London, 1949), especially pp. 55-60.

For a discussion of the active causality of law in Soviet legal theory see Kelsen, *Communist Theory of Law,* pp. 8f; Berman, *Justice in Russia,* p. 10; Vladimir Gsovski, "The Soviet Concept of Law," *Fordham Law Review,* Vol. VII, 7ff, and his *Soviet Civil Law,* 2 vols. (Ann Arbor, 1948-1949), I, pp. 165-166.

12. It was precisely the point of distinction between *form* and *content* of Soviet Law that led, above all else, to the "disappearance" of Evgenii Bronislavevich Pashukanis in 1937, at the height of the Stalinist purge. Pashukanis who was, perhaps, the outstanding and — prior to his retractions in the 1930's — the most "orthodox" of the Marxist legal

philosophers, held that law originated in the market place, when production for the purpose of exchange for other commodities appeared. Law reached its flowering under capitalism where economic life and culture was centered about the market place.

For Pashukanis, the link between legal forms and the forms of trade entered into by the bourgeoisie is so profound that law is, as to its form-content, strictly bourgeois. Hence, law is foreign to a socialist society and should begin "withering away" along with the state immediately upon the inception of the proletarian society. The Soviet regime, as well as the constitution and the civil and criminal codes flowing therefrom were obnoxious to Pashukanis because of their bourgeois *form* as represented in their *content*. Naturally, his thesis of the withering of the law and the state was in opposition to Stalin's thesis of the possibility of socialism existing in one country, where the law and the state must be ever strengthened to protect that country from enemies both inside and abroad.

For Pashukanis' theory of law, see his *The General Theory of Law and Marxism*, 3d. ed. (Moscow, 1927), as translated in *Soviet Legal Philosophy*, pp. 111-225, especially pp. 111-124. This work should be compared with his later work in which he made partial retractions of his ideas, "The Soviet State and the Revolution in Law," *Sovetskoye Gosudarstvo i Revolyutaiya Prava*, No. 11-12 (1930), pp. 17-49, ibid., pp. 237-280. In this work Pashukanis makes a distinction between the withering of the law and the withering of the state. He then concedes the possibility of state power becoming stronger with a concomitant weakening of the legal system. For law is only one of the possible means of social control, and ". . . the idea of absolute obedience to some norm-establishing body is in itself not synonymous with law." (pp. 278-280). Cf. Berman, *Justice in Russia*, pp. 34-35; Rudolf Schlesinger, "Recent Developments in Soviet Legal Theory," *Modern Law Review*, Vol. VI, p. 24; S. Dobrin, "Soviet Jurisprudence and Socialism," *Law Quarterly Review*, Vol. LII, p. 423.

A concise but excellent presentation of Pashukanis' legal theory is to be found in Lon. L. Fuller, "Pashukanis and Vyshinsky: A Study in the Development of Marxian Legal Theory," *Michigan Law Review*, XLVII, pp. 1157-1166. See also Kelsen, *The Communist Theory of Law*, Chapter 5; Berman, *Justice in Russia*, pp. 19-21; Schlesinger, *Soviet Legal Theory*, pp. 152ff; Gsovski, *Soviet Civil Law*, I, p. 166, and "The Soviet Concept of Law," pp. 9-13.

For the influence of Jellinek, Laband and German jurisprudence on Pashukanis' thought see Dobrin, "Soviet Jurisprudence and Socialism," pp. 405-424.

For a criticism of Pashukanis by a Stalinist, see Vyshinsky, *The Law of the Soviet State*, pp. 56-62.

13. Berman considers that the Marxist theory of law represents more a critique of law than a science of law. *Justice in Russia*, p. 12.

14. Vyshinsky, *The Law of the Soviet State*, p. 641. For the complete text of the Constitution of the Union of Soviet Socialist Republics as amended to December 22, 1960, see John N. Hazard, *The Soviet System of Government*, 2d. ed. (Chicago, 1961), appendix, pp. 207-230.

15. Cf. Friedmann, *Legal Theory*, p. 262.

16. *GSTSL*, pp. 379-380.

17. Even some of the basic civil rights granted by the Soviet constitution are not fully guaranteed by the state. The constitution provides no protection or method of enforcement of rights or duties through legal procedure, similar to that provided in Western constitutions. The guarantee is stated to be simply the "placing at the disposal of the working people and their organizations printing presses, stacks of paper, public buildings," etc. — Article 125. Cf. Berman, *Justice in Russia*, p. 286; Friedmann, *Legal Theory*, p. 265; Jones, *Historical Introduction to the Theory of Law*, pp. 277-278.

18. St. Thomas Aquinas, *Summa Theologica*, Piana ed., 5 vols. (Ottawa, 1941), II (*Prima Secundae*, Q. 96, art. 2), pp. 1236-1237; III (*Secunda Secundae*, Q. 77, art. 1, ad. 1), p. 1812, and (*Secunda Secundae*, Q. 50, art. 2), p. 1688.

The notion that law is an "ethical minimum" is to be found in the works of Christian Thomasius, Julius Stahl, Friedrich von Savigny, Georg Lasson and Georg Jellinek. Gustav Schmoller refers to law as the "maximum of enforceable morality." Immanuel Kant looked upon legal duties as belonging to the domain of morals despite the fact that some of the original norms from which certain of these duties arise, are not always moral norms in the strict meaning of the term.

19. Cf. Schlesinger, *Soviet Legal Theory*, p. 13.

20. Cf. Romashkin, *Fundamentals of Soviet Law*, p. 11 and p. 24.

21. *The State and Revolution*, Lenin Selected Works, 2 vols. in 4 (Moscow, 1952), II, Part I, p. 292.

CHAPTER VII

COMMUNIST PHILOSOPHY OF EDUCATION

Education: A Superstructure and Weapon

The communist cannot accept the proposition held by many Western educators that education can change the world. Marxism denies that man is a passive product of his environment and education, or that he is changed passively as the result of new modes of education. The Marxist claims to have discovered a new relationship between environment and education on the one hand and man on the other. In a sense, men are the result of education, yet education is also shaped by men. As Maurice Shore puts it:

> The changing man changes the changing environment and the educational process that change him, and thereby becomes the changed man — a process *ad infinitum*. Man reacts consciously to the conditioning forces of environment and education, and he continuously changes them by his action which is revolutionary in character.[1]

These changes in man which seem to come about with changes in men's circumstances Marx explains in terms of dialectical revolution. "The coincidence of the changing of circumstances and of human activity or self-changing can only be comprehended and rationally understood as *revolutionary practice.*"[2]

Marxism insists that man's ideas and consciousness are interwoven with productive activity. As has been noted, culture as expressed in language, politics, laws, morals and religion is the result of the social relationships of production of the particular society. Ideas are produced by real human activity, conditioned by definite material productive forces. "Life is not determined by consciousness, but consciousness by life."[3] Hence fundamental changes in the course of historical development cannot come about through the mere propagation of ideas. Such changes can be effected only by class conflict and revolutionary tactics.[4] Ideas then are simply reflections of the basic productive practice *(praxis)* in which men must engage in order to subsist and "make history."[5] Ideas are mere "superstructures" on the economic foundation.[6]

Likewise, changes in education are not brought about by mere criticism of prevalent educational theories. It is revolution only that affects the basic historical conditions. A revolutionary change in the material basis of human society is the only force potent enough to bring changes in theories of education.

In the social production which men carry on they enter into definite relations that are indispensable and independent of their will; these relations of production correspond to a definite stage of development of their material powers of production. The sum total of these relations of production constitutes the economic structure of society — the real foundation, on which rise legal and political superstructures and to which correspond definite forms of social consciousness. The mode of production in material life determines the general character of the social, political and intellectual life processes in general.[7]

Marx believed that he had discovered the basic driving force of man in the definite material limitations and conditions surrounding human life. All men are dependent upon nature for their means of subsistence. Continuance in existence is the first law of man's nature. In addition to this basic condition however, Marx considered two more conditions as all important: the appearance of new human needs and consequently new tools, and secondly, the institution of the family with the subsequent creation of new social relations.[8] These three sides of social activity have conditioned historical development and therefore educational development as well.

Primitive education was not systematic. It probably came about by accident. In any event, utility was its motivation. It always resulted from man's actual attempts to gain a livelihood.

Primitive education was a participation in the accumulated experience of previous generations. It was an imitation of and an improvement on the knowledge and skills of the older generations, motivated by the desire to gain the material necessities of life.

Primitive education was bound up with every phase of human activity in man's struggle for existence. The more educated man became, the better fitted he was for the struggle of survival. Success in this life struggle depended on the satisfaction of certain needs requiring production. For the satisfaction of needs and for the tools and techniques needed to produce them, education was helpful and necessary.

Man's gradually increasing "educational store" brought about new needs to be satisfied. The institution of the family — required because of man's prolonged infancy — likewise caused new needs to arise. Hence production also required new social adjustments and relationships, which in turn, often resulted in improved education.

Finally, education in primitive society did not depend upon politics. In other words, purposive education through labor, forced by the struggle for survival, made its appearance in advance of the political, legal and even religious institutions.[9]

The appearance of private property and the concentration and monopolization of the means of production caused a break in the peaceful and simple social relationships. Class conflict and exploitation appeared. To justify economic oppression, political and religious institutions were created by the ruling class. Education then became the servant of politics. Every change in the economic mode of production brought forth a change in the political conditions. This, in turn, had its effect on education. The educational process began to be directly dependent on the economic and political conditions of each phase of history.[10]

The intellectual content of the educational process became dependent on the ruling ideas of the dominant class. "The class which is the ruling material force of society, is at the same time its ruling intellectual force." The dominant class, in control of the means of production, was also in position to control the thoughts of the ruled class.

The class which has the means of material production at its disposal, has control at the same time over the means of intellectual production, so that thereby, speaking generally, the ideas of those who lack the means of mental production are subject to it. The ruling ideas are nothing more than the ideal expression of the ruling material relationships, the ruling material relationships grasped as ideas; hence of the relationships which make the one class the dominant one, therefore the ideas of its dominance.[11]

According to Marx, all prevailing ideas in a given historical period are the expression of those relations set up by the dominant class. For the ruling class is required to represent its interest as though it serves the common interest of all the members of the society. It must give to its ideas a universality; it must represent them as the only ones that are rational and scientifically valid.[12] Such are the ideas taught in the class-controlled schools. The ruling class, through intervention in the educational process, consciously or unconsciously indoctrinates the young of all classes with its class ideas.

Under socialism, the proletarian class appropriates the means of material production and changes the social relations. The young are then indoctrinated with new ideas, those favorable to the proletariat. With the gradual transition to classless society, the social relations produced by the new mode of production become devoid of any class character. Hence the ideas which permeate the school gradually lose their class character. The socialist school purports to rear the younger generation in the spirit of the most progressive, the most scientifically accurate ideas. These of course are the ideas of communism.

It forms in the youth a materialistic world outlook — the foundation of a truly scientific conception of the world. Socialism has opened unlimited vistas for the growth of the material and spiritual riches of society, for an all-around development of personality. Under socialism all the achievement of world culture becomes the property of the masses.[13]

To Marx, economics is the basis from which man's ideas spring. Economic factors condition every historical development. Marxism insists that all works of philosophy, politics, law, religion, literature, art and education have as their cause, economics. They are, in reality, simply expressions of the basic conflicts between social classes.[14]

Without a change in the mode of production and social relations, education, it would seem, is impotent to change society. Yet it is important to note that the Marxist conception of history does not maintain that productive forces are the only determining factor in human society. It acknowledges that religion, art, philosophy and the other ideological forces do play an important part in directing the course of history.

> Political, juridical, philosophical, religious, literary, artistic, etc., development is based on economic development. But all these react upon one another and also upon the economic base.[15]

These ideological forces form, however, only the superstructure of society. Each is directly or indirectly the resultant of the productive forces of its age. Consequently, each of these factors does partially determine the course of history, but it does so only as a proximate cause. Engels states:

> According to the materialist conception of history the determining element in history is *ultimately* production and reproduction in real life. More than this neither Marx nor I have ever asserted. If, therefore, somebody twists this into the statement that the economic element is the *only* determining one, he transforms it into a meaningless, abstract and absurd phrase. The economic situation is the basis, but the various elements of the superstructure — political forms of the class struggle and its consequences, constitutions established by the victorious class after a successful battle, etc. — forms of law — and then even the reflexes of all these actual struggles in the brains of the combatants: political, legal, philosophical theories, religious ideas and their further development into systems of dogma — also exercise their influence upon the

course of the historical struggles and in many cases preponderate in determining their *form*.[16]

Engels does not imply that social changes occur at the mere will of reformers or of the society at large. Yet Marx and Engels are far from discounting the role of human desires as an immediate cause of change. To have change, society has to be made ready for it through the mode of production. This comes about by a conflict between productive forces and the lagging property relationships. The conflict expresses itself in the form of a social revolution.

However, human desires are of importance as the immediate cause of revolutionary change. The conflict between the forces of production may be considered the ultimate cause, but this conflict shows forth experientially as a conflict of human interests, *i.e.*, as the class conflict.[17] At a certain point in the historical development the necessity of change becomes obvious. Human needs, created and limited by the objective mode of production, bring about the social revolution.[18] Human volition then, is the proximate cause of social change.

From the viewpoint of education, the consideration of human volition as a factor of social progress takes on great importance. When facts and theories are made known and fully understood, there is a better chance for intelligent decisions. Education by affecting the human will can become not only a vital force for revolutionary change, but can also serve to hasten it.[19]

While Marxism does not consider education as the ultimate cause of social progress, it nevertheless attributes to it a role of great importance. If social changes occurred only because of objective economic forces independent of the human will, education would have to bow out from any social planning or reform. Education would have to remain entirely passive under the influence of each phase of history. But such a fatalistic interpretation of *economic determinism* is contrary to the whole spirit of Marxism,[20] and especially is it opposed to its dialectical theory of knowledge. Marx's doctrine of the inseparable unity of thought and action culminating in objective practice makes Marxism a philosophy of progress. In fact, one of the most vitalizing factors in Marxism is its firm conviction that progress is effected by conscious human activity.[21]

The role of education in society is obvious. Not only is it an ideological reflection of productive relations, but it becomes, of itself, an active force, reacting on the basic economic mode of production, and within limits, even modifying it.[22] If education can to some extent change the economic foundation of a society and so contribute to the evolution of a new society, then education is a force of significance — important enough to change the nature and character of the historical struggle.[23]

Education becomes a principal weapon in the class struggle. The dominant class maintains itself in position by the indoctrination of ideas, and consequently by control of the schools.[24] In socialist society, education serves to permeate the student's mind with the spirit of the class struggle, the overthrow of the bourgeoisie, the eventual elimination of classes and the abolition of exploitation of man by man. In short, the purpose of communist education is to imbue the young with communist ethics.[25] To do this, free and universal public education is required[26] whereby every youth can receive the all-round training necessary to actively participate in creating the conditions for a socialist, and eventually, a communist society.[27] When the class struggle has been completed and all mankind lives under the socialist mode of production, education becomes a tool for the unlimited improvement of the classless society, for the abolishment of the division of labor and the integral development of the individual.[28]

The first basic principles of the communist philosophy of education can be summed up as follows:

Education can never become the ultimate cause of revolutionary change or progress. However, it may, within certain limits set by the material forces and relations of production, become by its effect on human volition, the immediate and catalytic cause of revolutionary development in the class struggle. In the classless society of the future it will serve as the immediate cause of gradual, but unlimited, progressive development within that society.

Polytechnism: Link Between Education and Production

Marxism holds that labor is the very touchstone for man's self-realization. Labor is the medium for creating the world of his desires; it is labor which should make him happy. Man labors to transform his world, to put his mark on it, to make himself at home in it and to master its forces. This is what differentiates him from the brute.[29] But man has yet to fully accomplish this. It is the future that is to bring about man's complete realization.

The normal existence of animals is given by the conditions in which they live and to which they adapt themselves — those of man, as soon as he differentiates himself from the animal in the narrower sense, have as yet never been present, and are only to be elaborated by the ensuing historical development. Man is the sole animal capable of working his way out of the merely animal state — his normal state is one appropriate to his consciousness, *one to be created by himself.*[30]

By the historical development of the different modes of production, by the consequent specializing effect of the new divisions of labor, and by the technological knowledge stimulated from age to age, man's labor has produced a thousandfold greater output than formerly. Man has to a limited degree mastered the forces of nature as he knows them. But he has lost himself in the process. He has become dehumanized, divided from his labor, himself and his neighbor — "alienated" *(entfremdet).*[31]

The worker therefore only feels himself outside his work, and in his work feels outside himself. He is at home when he is not working, and when he is working he is not at home. His labour is therefore not voluntary, but coerced; it is *forced labour.* It is therefore not the satisfaction of a need; it is merely a *means* to satisfy needs external to it.
. . . man (the worker) no longer feels himself to be freely active in any but his animal functions — eating, drinking, procreating . . . and in his human functions he no longer feels himself to be anything but an animal. What is animal becomes human, and what is human becomes animal.[32]

Under capitalism most of all, the worker is alienated from his work. He is considered as a unit of labor costs, a factor in the cost of production, a saleable commodity. Hence, in his social relations he becomes a *thing*.[33] In this unnatural situation, that which can be exchanged for things receives the highest respect. Money has value, human labor a price. Men become a means, not an end. The effect of this degradation of human labor is the abstract concept of an *economic man,* and the concealment of the human relations in the economic order. Human values are then derived from economics. Acquisition, work, thrift and sobriety become the highest virtues. Moral laws become the expression of the laws of political economy.[34] The individual comes in contact with his fellow man only under conditions created by commodity exchange. His needs are to be satisfied by somehow enticing from the other person his very being, *i.e.,* his money. The need for money is the only need created by capitalistic production. General exploitation of communal human nature under the guise of amiability becomes the basic social custom.[35] Commodities become a fetish. To man in this final stage of specialized labor, the capitalist factory system, "the relations connecting the labour of one individual with that of the rest appears, not as direct social relations between individuals at work, but as what they really are, material relations between persons and social relations between things."[36]

There are many effects of the alienation of man from himself and his society. The division of labor separates the interests of the individual from the interests of the community. It splits the several human functions from one another; happiness vs. work, intellectualism vs. manual labor, production vs. consumption, etc. It transforms the worth of the human person into material value, the money value of his labor. The division of labor gives the social relationships among men an independent, uncontrolled existence in which men are victims. The economic crises of the market direct the decisions and lives of men. The division of labor intensifies with the years, forcing the specialization of function to such a narrow and monotonous degree that man is reduced to exercising a mere fragment of his potential ability. He comes to serve as a mere appendage to the machine.[37]

To the Marxist, the change can be attained by actively socializing the social relations to match the productive relations. But the process cannot remain there. The people must become socially conscious. Self-government must be realized by a full and conscious mass participation in community democracy. Men and women must freely recognize the desirability of their labor. The achievements of science must finally eliminate the drudgery of life, as well as the anarchy of production with its crises, unemployment and wars. By uncovering the laws of social development, it must offer man the means of consciously guiding his own development. Then man will finally be united with himself, his comrades and his world. Only then will he be truly human and free.

The seizure of the means of production by society puts an end to commodity production, and therewith to the domination of the product over the producer. Anarchy in social production is replaced by conscious organization on a planned basis. . . . And at this point, in a certain sense, man finally cuts himself off from the animal world, leaves the conditions of animal existence behind him and enters conditions which are really human. . . . The laws of his own social activity, which have hitherto confronted him as external, dominating laws of Nature, will then be applied by man with complete understanding, and hence will be dominated by man. . . . The objective external forces which have hitherto dominated history, will then pass under the control of men themselves. It is only from this point that men, with full consciousness, will fashion their own history. . . . It is humanity's leap from the realm of necessity into the realm of freedom.[38]

It must be emphasized once again, though, that for the Marxist this is no automatic or inevitable achievement, for such a fatalistic interpretation denies human creativeness and the power of human volition.

The outstanding characteristic of capitalist man is that objectively he has become a factory worker, but subjectively he has been emotionally divorced from what is essentially human — the use of labor to create a truly human world.

In order that education have a sound basis, claims the Marxist, it is first necessary that it have a psychologically sound social relation to the labor process. The educative value of labor must be reiterated. This, however, can come about only through the reconstruction of society. Only a society which is able to harmonize its productive forces and technology with the human, social relations involved, can bring about social harmony and happiness. Only in a genuinely classless and cooperative society can education become truly constructive, and can the full development of all individual talents and personalities be realized. Only then can the breach between mental and physical labor, theory and practice, ideals and reality be closed.[39]

In a society in which the workingman is honored and no one lives without labor, education must be linked with the actual mastery of the material environment. This, for Marx, must be the true basis of education for the industrial man.

From the Factory system budded, as Robert Owen has shown us in detail, the germ of education of the future, an education that will, in the case of a child over a given age, combine productive labour with instruction and gymnastics, not only as one of the methods of adding to the efficiency of production, but as the only method of producing fully developed human beings.

Modern industry . . . through its catastrophes imposes the necessity of recognizing, as the fundamental law of production, variations of work, consequently, fitness of the labourer for varied work, consequently the greatest possible development of his varied aptitudes. It becomes a question of life and death for society to adopt the mode of production to the normal functioning of this law. Modern industry, indeed, compels society under penalty of death, to replace the detail-worker of today, crippled by life-long repetition of one and the same trivial operation, and thus reduced to a mere fragment of a man, by the fully developed individual, fit for a variety of labours, ready to face any change of production, and to whom the different social functions he performs, are but so many modes of giving free scope to his own natural and acquired powers. . . . There can be no doubt that when the working class comes into power, as inevitably it must, technical instruction, both theoretical and practical, will take its proper place in the working-class schools.[40]

Education, if it is to be of real value to man and his society, must consist of a combination of productive labor, intellectual education, physical exercise and polytechnic instruction. Marx states:

> First, intellectual education; second, physical training, as given in the schools of gymnastics and in military training; third, polytechnic training, which gives instruction in the general scientific principles of all production processes and at the same time initiates the child and young person into the practical use and operation of the simpler tools in all occupations.[41]

Polytechnical education (polytechnism) is an essential part of the Marxist theory of education. Because labor is central to man's very being for Marx, there can be no separation of labor education from general education, in theory or practice.[42] Hence we understand why the Soviets stress, and should have always stressed the role of the workshop, the laboratory and other aspects of school life to the community, to the local factory, to the cooperative farms, to the regional and national industrialization and agricultural schemes. For the Marxist, there is no conflict between the understanding of the principles of science and an immersion in the problems of manufacturing at the local plant. On the contrary, such problems form the basis for the pupil's personal involvement in scientific understanding. In the process of his education, the Marxist student will become acquainted with the reality of social production and its scientific basis. Moreover, he will gain firsthand knowledge of the techniques and basic tools of this production over and above the mere theoretical understanding.[43] He will have teachers who have broken with all purely verbal methods of passive education. The twin evils of pure verbalism and pure vocationalism will no longer be allowed to atrophy the pupil's education. No more the isolated shop course, the purely vocational or secretarial schools. Equally to be proscribed is the college-preparatory but technologically illiterate secondary school or academy.[44] These evils must be avoided by denying neither the practical skills of technology nor the liberal arts and theoretical science.

The emphasis on polytechnism, the training in the central principles of industry is significant in that it assists the general, vocational, aesthetic, moral and political education without eliminating them. Polytechnism does not mean instruction in everything and every process. This would be an impossible goal and would, moreover, ignore the tremendous pace of scientific and technological change. What is needed, claims the Marxist, is the understanding of a complete set of technological principles, for such an understanding will make the worker into an intelligent man. To accomplish this the working day and the working week must be considerably shortened to allow the worker more free time in which to receive his all-around education with its universal compulsory polytechnical training.[45] Then labor will become a pleasure instead of a burden; then will labor be converted in the eyes of man from a nuisance into "the prime necessity of life." Then will it be possible to maintain the communist formula: "from each according to his ability, to each according to his needs."[46]

Thus the second basic principle of communist education may be summed up as follows:

Labor being the touchstone for man's self-realization and that of his society, true education must be linked to the mastery of the material environment. This is accomplished by universal polytechnical training — a training in the central and practical principles of social production, unified with the theoretical principles of science and the humanities.

The attempt of the Soviet to put the principle of polytechnic education into practice has produced some interesting history.[47]

There are three main stages in the development of Soviet primary and secondary education, and consequently, three stages in the evolution of polytechnical training. The first stage extended from the Revolution until about 1930; the second stage continued through the thirties and forties up to the publication of Joseph Stalin's *Economic Problems of Socialism in the U.S.S.R.*, in 1952. The third stage has continued from 1952 until the present, with much greater emphasis placed on polytechnism since 1958.[49]

During the first stage, polytechnical training was held in high regard in the Soviet Union. Under the guidance of Lenin and his wife, N. K. Krupskaya, free, universal, compulsory, general and polytechnical education was imposed on all youths up to age 16. Its purpose was to familiarize the student with all the major branches of production in both theory and practice, and to assure the close unity of education and socially productive work.[49] This period was characterized by experimental and pragmatic applications of Marxian educational principles as dictated by the changing needs of the infant society. Soviet educators likewise borrowed liberally from non-Marxist educators such as Montessori, Kerschensteiner, Dewey, Lay, Decroly, Thorndike, Kilpatrick and others, as well as pre-revolution Russian educational practices.[50]

The second stage of development in Soviet schools may be characterized as a "retreat from polytechnism toward traditional academic education."[51] With the launching of the First Five Year Plan in late 1928, the successful completion of the "Plan of Great Works" was proclaimed to be the primary role of the school. One group of educators led by Krupskaya, held that this role could be best accomplished by increased emphasis on theoretical acquaintance with various forms of labor, by conscious participation of pupils in communal affairs and by training students in practical labor experience.[52] Another group sought to ban further experimentation in education, to end all tendencies toward "progressive" methods of education and to return to more traditional methods of instruction. In the opinion of this latter group, the student could best help the cause of socialism by "the mastery of knowledge." The pupil's first responsibility was not to engage in "socially useful work," but to acquire a general liberal education by the study of language, history, science and mathematics. It was this second group that gained official support of the Party and consequently prevailed. Through a series of decrees of the Central Committee of the CPSU promulgated in the early thirties, educational practices were greatly transformed. The end result more resembled the academic schools of Western Europe than the Soviet schools of the 1920's.[53] This new approach marked the beginning of a prolonged period in which polytechnical training was not greatly discussed. What remained of polytechnism took the form of classroom instruction in the fundamentals of science, supplemented by some practical application of this scientific knowledge in the formation of work habits.[54]

The third phase of Soviet educational development is best characterized as a return to the principle that polytechnism forms an essential part of a well-rounded academic education. Hence, this third period seems to constitute something of a synthesis of the strong points of the previous periods. From the first period came the emphasis on polytechnic instruction, socially useful work and the unity of theory and practice. But from the second came the insistence on a well-rounded general education, with special emphasis on mathematics, the several fields of science, foreign languages, as well as the study of the humanities.[55] This general education serves as the basis for polytechnical instruction, by which every child is prepared for useful work and for active participation in the building of a communist society.[56] At the same time it provides for the full development of the talents of the individual.[57]

This third phase of educational development was begun by Stalin and the 19th Party Congress in 1952. Its principles were incorporated in the Fifth Five Year Plan (1951-1955). But, the return to polytechnism progressed slowly. At the 20th Party Congress in February, 1956, Khrushchev called for an end to mere verbal discussion of polytechnic reforms. A radical reshaping of the instruction programs of secondary schools in the direction of greater production specialization was what was needed.[58] Two years later, in April, 1958, Khrushchev re-emphasized this point in an address to the 13th Komsomol Congress.[59]

On September 21, 1958 there appeared in *Pravda* a statement by Khrushchev stating that the basic weakness of Soviet education was its "divorce from life." He suggested that secondary education might, in the future, consist of two phases. The first stage would consist of seven or eight years of instruction concentrating on the fundamentals of science, polytechnical instruction, teaching of work habits, moral, physical and aesthetic training; the second stage would consist of two or three years of specialized vocational training in industry or agriculture. Finally, he insisted that higher education too must be drawn closer to production, and in fact, link up with production directly.[60]

In November, 1958, Khrushchev issued the celebrated forty-eight "theses" in his report to the forthcoming 21st Congress of Communist Party. These theses, which were later adopted by the Central Committee of the Communist Party and the Council of Ministers of the U.S.S.R., had as their fundamental theme the radical improvement of the entire system of public education through strengthening the relationship of the school with life. Provision was made to increase universal, compulsory education from seven to eight years and to insure the combining of polytechnic labor instruction with socially useful work in future education. These theses likewise sought both to improve the training of teachers of polytechnics and to improve ideological indoctrination at all levels of education. These contemplated reforms will thus:

> . . . enhance the role of the school in the education and rearing of youth, will raise considerably their general educational level and their practical qualifications, will serve as a better guaranty of training highly qualified personnel for all branches of the national economy, science, and culture, and will contribute in even greater degree to the growing might of the Soviet Union which marches with a firm step on the road to the building of Communism.[61]

These reforms were enacted into law by the Supreme Soviet of the U.S.S.R. on December 24, 1958. They will go into effect gradually over a period of five years. By 1965 the new law is expected to form the basic framework of the Soviet school system.[62] Only then will the Soviet school fully conform to the scientific prevision of Marx, Engels and Lenin. Then, claims the Marxist, will the reconstructed Soviet school, as an integral part of the Seven-Year Plan, be ". . . of decisive importance in the triumph in peaceful competition of the socialist over the capitalist system."[63]

Suggested Readings

CHAPTER VII

Primary Sources

*Central Committee of the Communist Party and the Council of Ministers of the U.S.S.R., *On Strengthening the Relationship of the School with Life and On the Further Development of the System of Public Education in the Country.*
Khrushchev, N. S., *Address to the 13th Komsomol Congress,* April, 1958.
*Lenin, V. I., *The Tasks of the Youth Leagues,* Speech to the Third Congress of the Russian Young Communist League, 1920.
*Marx, K., *Economic and Philosophic Manuscripts of 1844, I (Estranged Labour).*
Marx, K. and Engels, F., *The German Ideology,* Part I, Chapter I.
Stalin, Joseph, *Economic Problems of Socialism in the U.S.S.R.,* Part IV.

Secondary Sources

*Bereday, G. Z. F., Brickman, W. W. and Read, G. H. (eds.), *The Changing Soviet School,* Boston, Houghton Mifflin Co., 1960, Chapter X.
Bowen, James, *Soviet Education: Anton Makarenko and the Years of Experiment,* Madison, Wisc., Univ. of Wisconsin Press, 1962.
Chambre, Henri, *From Karl Marx to Mao Tse-tung,* Chapter II.
*Cohen, Robert S., "On the Marxist Philosophy of Education," *Modern Philosophies and Education,* ed. Nelson B. Henry, 54th Yearbook of NSSE, Part I, Chicago, University of Chicago Press, 1955, pp. 175-214.
Counts, George S., *The Challenge of Soviet Education,* New York, McGraw-Hill Book Co., 1957, Chapter III.
*――――, *Khrushchev and the Central Committee Speak on Education,* Pittsburgh, University of Pittsburgh Press, 1959.
*De Witt, Nicholas, *Education and Professional Employment in the U.S.S.R.,* Washington, D. C., National Science Foundation, 1961, pp. 3-17, *78-90.

———, *Soviet Professional Manpower*, Washington, D. C., National Science Foundation, 1955.
*Fromm, Erich, *Marx's Concept of Man*, Chapter V.
Hechinger, Fred M., *The Big Red Schoolhouse*, New York, Doubleday and Co., 1959.
King, Beatrice, *Changing Man: The Education System of the U.S.S.R.*, New York, The Viking Press, 1937.
Kline, George L. (ed.), *Soviet Education*, New York, Columbia University Press, 1957.
Korol, Alexander G., *Soviet Education for Science and Technology*, New York, John Wiley and Sons, Inc., 1957.
*Krupskaya, N. K., *On Education*, trans. G. P. Ivanov-Mumjiev, Moscow, Foreign Languages Publishing House, 1957, pp. 164-173 and 185-209.
Makarenko, A. S., *The Road to Life*, 3 vols., trans. I. and T. Litvinov, Moscow, Foreign Languages Publishing House, 1955.
*Medlin, W. K., Lindquist, C. B. and Schmitt, M. L., *Soviet Education Programs*, Bulletin No. 1960-17, Washington, D. C., U. S. Dept. of Health, Education and Welfare, 1960, Chapters I and III.
Pinkevitch, Albert P., *New Education in the Soviet Republic*, ed. George S. Counts, New York, The John Day Co., 1929.
Prokofiev, M. A., Chilikin, M. G. and Tulpanov, S. I., *Higher Education in the U.S.S.R.*, Educational Studies and Documents No. 39, Paris, UNESCO Publications, 1960.
Rapacz, Richard V., "Polytechnical Education and the New Soviet School Reforms," in *The Politics of Soviet Education*, ed. George Z. F. Bereday and Jaan Pennar, New York, Frederick A. Praeger, 1960, pp. 28-44.
*Shore, Maurice J., *Soviet Education: Its Psychology and Philosophy*, New York, Philosophical Library, 1947, Chapters II, IV, XI, XIV and XVII.
Soviet Education, (Translations of Soviet Educational Journals), New York, International Arts and Sciences Press.
Tucker, Robert C., *Philosophy and Myth in Karl Marx*, New York, Cambridge Univ. Press, 1961, Part III.
Utechin, S. V., "Educating the New Man," *Survey* No. 38, pp. 126-136.
Wittig, Horst, "Marx on Education: Philosophical Origin of Communist Pedagogy," *Soviet Survey*, No. 30, pp. 77-81.

FOOTNOTES TO CHAPTER VII

1. Maurice J. Shore, *Soviet Education: Its Psychology and Philosophy* (New York, 1947), p. 25.
2. K. Marx, *Theses on Feuerbach,* III, in K. Marx and F. Engels, *The German Ideology,* ed. R. Pascal (New York, 1947), appendix, pp. 197-198.
3. Cf. Marx and Engels, *The German Ideology,* pp. 14-15.
4. *Ibid.,* pp. 28-29.
5. *Ibid.,* p. 16.
6. Cf. Engels, "Letter to Joseph Bloch, September 21, 1890," in *Karl Marx Selected Works,* ed. V. Adoratsky, 2 vols. (Moscow-Leningrad, 1935-36), I, pp. 381-382. Hereafter cited as *KMSW*.
7. Marx, *A Contribution to the Critique of Political Economy,* preface, in *KMSW,* I, p. 356.
8. Marx and Engels, *The German Ideology,* pp. 16-17.
9. Cf. Shore, *Soviet Education,* pp. 26-28.
10. *Ibid.,* p. 28.
11. Marx and Engels, *Die deutsche Ideologie, Historisch-Kritische Gesamtausgabe* (Frankfort [etc.], 1927-33), Abt. I, Bd. 5, 35. Cf. *Manifesto of the Communist Party, KMSW,* I, pp. 209-210, 223-224.
12. Marx and Engels, *The German Ideology,* pp. 40-41. Cf. V. I. Lenin, Speech to Third All-Russian Congress of the Russian Young Communist League, Oct. 2, 1920, in *Selected Works,* 12 vols. (New York, 1943), IX, p. 469.
13. "On Strengthening the Relationship of the School with Life and On the Further Development of the System of Public Education in the Country," Theses of the Central Committee of the Communist Party and the Council of Ministers of the U.S.S.R., in George S. Counts, *Khrushchev and the Central Committee Speak on Education* (Pittsburgh, 1959), p. 34. Hereafter cited as *KCCSE*. Cf. Marx and Engels, *The Manifesto of the Communist Party, KMSW,* I, p. 224.
14. Engels, preface to English edition (1888) of the *Manifesto, KMSW,* I, p. 202; preface to German edition (1883), *ibid.,* pp. 192-193.
15. Engels, "Letter to H. Starkenburg, January 25, 1894," *KMSW,* I, p. 392. See Chapter VI, note No. 11, above.
16. Engels, "Letter to Joseph Bloch, September 21, 1890," *KMSW,* I, p. 381.

17. Cf. Marx and Engels, *Manifesto of the Communist Party, KMSW,* I, pp. 204-218.
18. Cf. Marx, "Letter to P. V. Annenkov, December 28, 1846," *KMSW,* I, pp. 372-377, and "Letter to Joseph Weydemeyer, March 5, 1852," *ibid.,* p. 377. See also, G. Plekhanov, *Fundamental Problems of Marxism,* ed. D. Riazanov (New York, 1929), pp. 57-58.
19. Cf. Engels, "Prefatory Notes to *The Peasant War in Germany,*" *KMSW,* II, pp. 548-549; Lenin, *What is to Be Done?, Selected Works,* II, pp. 47-48; N. S. Khrushchev, *Pravda,* Feb. 5, 1959, as cited in Nicholas DeWitt, *Education and Professional Employment in the U.S.S.R.* (Washington, D. C., 1961), p. xxxvii. Hereafter cited as DeWitt, *EPE.*
20. Cf. Marx, *Theses on Feuerbach, III,* in *The German Ideology,* appendix, pp. 197-198; Engels, "Letter to Joseph Bloch, September 21, 1890," *KMSW,* I, p. 381; Lenin, *Urgent Tasks of Our Movement, Selected Works,* II, p. 14.
21. Cf. Chas. J. McFadden, *The Philosophy of Communism* (New York, 1939), p. 97.
22. Cf. Engels, "Letter to Conrad Schmidt, October 27, 1890," *KMSW,* I, pp. 383-388.
23. Cf. William K. Medlin, Clarence B. Linquist and Marshall L. Schmitt, *Soviet Education Programs* (Washington, D. C., 1960), p. 7, and Shore, *Soviet Education,* pp. 32-33.
24. Cf. Marx and Engels, *The German Ideology,* p. 39.
25. Lenin, Speech to Third Congress of Young Communist League, *Selected Works,* IX, p. 474, and *Proletarian Culture, ibid.,* p. 484. Cf. Thesis III of the Central Committee of the Communist Party, *KCCSE,* p. 33, and Khrushchev, Speech to 21st Congress of the Communist Party of the Soviet Union, Jan. 27, 1959 as cited in *Soviet World Outlook,* 3rd. ed., Dept. of State Publication 6836 (Washington, D. C., 1959), p. 164.
26. Cf. Marx and Engels, *Manifesto of the Communist Party, KMSW,* I, p. 228; Marx, *The Civil War in France, KMSW,* II, p. 499; Engels, *Zwei Reden in Elberfeld, Gesamtausgabe,* Abt. I, Bd. 4, p. 380, and *Grundsätze des Kommunismus, ibid.,* Abt. I, Bd. 6, p. 515; Lenin, *Materials Relating to the Revision of the Party Programme, Selected Works,* VI, p. 118 (Hereafter cited as Lenin, *MRRPP*); Article 121 of the Constitution of the Union of Soviet Socialist Republics; Thesis VIII, *KCCSE,* p. 36.
27. Cf. Thesis II, *KCCSE,* pp. 31-32; I. A. Kairov (ed.), *Pedagogika* (Moscow, 1956), pp. 20-22, as cited in Medlin, *et al, Soviet Education Programs,* p. 11.
28. Cf. Marx, *Critique of the Gotha Programme,* ed. by C. P. Dutt (New York, 1938), p. 10; Lenin, *The State and Revolution,* in *Selected*

Works, VII, p. 87; G. Fedorov, "Bor'ba mezhdu novym i starym v usloviyakh sovetskogo obshchestva," *Bol'shevik*, 1947, 19, p. 48, as cited in Gustav A. Wetter, *Dialectical Materialism*, trans. Peter Heath (New York, 1958), p. 318.
29. Cf. Marx, *Economic and Philosophic Manuscripts of 1844*, trans. Martin Milligan (Moscow, 1961), pp. 75-76. Hereafter cited as Marx, *EPM*. Cf. Erich Fromm, *Marx's Concept of Man* (New York, 1961), p. 47, and Henri Chambre, *From Karl Marx to Mao Tse-tung*, trans. Robt. J. Olsen (New York, 1963), p. 46.
30. Engels, *Dialectics of Nature* (New York, 1940), p. 187.
31. Marx, *EPM*, pp. 67ff. On Marx's notion of alienation, see Fromm, *Marx's Concept of Man*, especially Chapter V; Chambre, *From Karl Marx to Mao Tse-tung*, Chapter II; and Robert C. Tucker, *Philosophy and Myth in Karl Marx* (New York, 1961), especially Part III.
32. Marx, *EPM*, pp. 72-73.
33. *Ibid.*, pp 84-86.
34. *Ibid.*, pp. 120-121. Cf. Robert S. Cohen, "On the Marxist Philosophy of Education," *Modern Philosophies and Education*, ed. Nelson B. Henry, 54th Yearbook, NSSE, Part I (Chicago, 1955), pp. 190-192. Hereafter cited as Cohen, *OMPE*.
35. Marx, *EPM*, p. 116.
36. Cf. Marx, *Capital*, 3 vols. (Chicago, 1909), I, p. 84.
37. *Ibid.*, p. 708; Marx, *EPM*, pp. 117-118. Cf. Marx and Engels, *The German Ideology*, pp. 20ff.
38. Engels, *Herr Eugen Dühring's Revolution in Science (Anti-Dühring)* (London, 1940), pp. 311-312. Cf. Wetter, *Dialectical Materialism*, p. 388.
39. Marx, *Critique of the Gotha Programme*, p. 10. Cf. Cohen, *OMPE*, pp. 198-199; DeWitt, *EPE*, p. 79.
40. Marx, *Capital*, I, pp. 529-530, 534.
41. Marx, "Instructions to the German Delegation of the International Workingmen's Association in Geneva, 1886," *Der Vorbote* (Geneva), 1866, No. 10, p. 151, as cited in Horst Wittig, "Marx On Education: Philosophical Origins of Communist Pedagogy," *Soviet Survey*, No. 30 (1959), p. 79. Also cited in Shore, *Soviet Education*, p. 53. Cf. Lenin, *MRRPP*, p. 118; N. K. Krupskaya, *On Education*, trans. G. P. Ivanov-Munjiev (Moscow, 1957), pp. 193-198; Thesis XV, *KCCSE*, p. 42; N. K. Goncharov, "Sovetskaia pedagogicheskaia nauka," *Narodnoe obrazovanie*, No. 11, 1957, as cited in DeWitt, *EPE*, p. 78.
42. Cf. DeWitt, *EPE*, p. 79.
43. Theses V, VI and VII, *KCCSE*, p. 34-36. Cf. Cohen, *OMPE*, pp. 200-201.
44. Cf. Khrushchev, "Memorandum," *Pravda*, September 21, 1958, pp.

1-2, as cited in George Z. F. Bereday, William W. Brickman and Gerald H. Read (eds.), *The Changing Soviet School* (Boston, 1960), p. 247. Cf. *Soviet World Outlook*, p. 165. See also statement of the Academy of Pedagogical Sciences, in Bereday, *et al, The Changing Soviet School*, pp. 253-254.
45. Cf. Joseph Stalin, *Economic Problems of Socialism in the U.S.S.R.*, in *Current Soviet Policies* (New York, 1953), p. 14 (hereafter cited as Stalin, *EPS*); Thesis V, *KCCSE*, p. 34. See also, Cohen, *OMPE*, pp. 203-204.
46. Marx, *The Critique of the Gotha Programme*, p. 10; Stalin, *EPS*, p. 14; Thesis V, *KCCSE*, p. 34.
47. The best recent histories of polytechnism in the U.S.S.R. are Counts, "The Reconstruction of Soviet Education," *KCCSE*, pp. 1-23; R. V. Rapacz, "Polytechnical Education and the New Soviet School Reforms," in G. Bereday and J. Pennar (eds.), *The Politics of Soviet Education* (New York, 1960) (hereafter cited as Rapacz, *PENSSR*); DeWitt, *EPE*, pp. 78ff; Medlin, *et. al., Soviet Education Programs*, pp. 94ff; Bereday, *et al, The Changing Soviet School*, pp. 240ff. The most complete treatment up to 1947 is found in Shore, *Soviet Education*, pp. 146-150, 164-169, 189-196 and 227-240.
48. Cf. DeWitt, *EPE*, pp. 78ff. G. S. Counts divides the development of Soviet education into two periods. The first ended in the early thirties, the second in 1956-58. See *KCCSE*, pp. 5-6. W. W. Brickman places educational development in the U.S.S.R. into several periods. Cf. Bereday, *et al, The Changing Soviet School*, pp. 50-105.
49. Lenin, *MRRPP*, p. 118; Krupskaya, *On Education*, pp. 164-165, 192-198. Cf. DeWitt, *EPE*, p. 80; Shore, *Soviet Education*, pp. 146ff.; Bereday, *et al, The Changing Soviet School*, pp. 52ff.
50. Cf. Albert P. Pinkevitch. *The New Education in the Soviet Republic*, ed. G. S. Counts (New York, 1929), *passim;* Bereday, *et al, The Changing Soviet School*, p. 55; Counts, *The Challenge of Soviet Education* (New York, 1957), pp. 10-11.
51. DeWitt, *EPE*, p. 82.
52. Krupskaya, *On Education*, pp. 197-198. Cf. Shore, *Soviet Education*, p. 166. Krupskaya, however, realized that overemphasis on practice while ignoring theory could stand in the path of knowledge. She denounced the extremists and aligned herself with the moderate center. Cf. Shore, *Soviet Education*, p. 172.
53. See, for example, the provisions contained in the decree of the Narcompros of the R.S.F.S.R. of March 4, 1937, as given in Shore, *Soviet Education*, p. 193. Cf. Counts, *KCCSE*, pp. 10-12; DeWitt, *EPE*, pp. 82-83.

54. M. N. Skatkin, *O politekhnicheskom obrazovanii v obshcheobrazovatel' noi shkole* (Moscow, 1953), p. 13, as cited in DeWitt, *EPE*, p. 83.
55. Cf. Theses XVII and XVIII, *KCCSE*, pp. 44-45. See also Counts, *ibid.*, p. 12; Rapacz, *PENSSR*, p. 31.
56. Stalin, *EPS*, p. 14; Thesis IX, *KCCSE*, pp. 39-40. Cf. Medlin, *et al, Soviet Education Programs*, p. 128.
57. Thesis V, *KCCSE*, p. 34. Cf. Statement of the Director of the Institute of Theory and History of Pedagogy to Marshall L. Schmitt, as quoted in Medlin, *et al, Soviet Education Programs*, p. 128.
58. Khrushchev, Address to 20th Communist Party Congress, *Pravda*, February 15, 1956, in *Current Soviet Policies-II* (New York, 1957), p. 50. Cf. DeWitt *EPE*, pp. 84-85; Rapacz, *PENSSR*, pp. 32-33.
59. Khrushchev, "Educating Active and Conscious Builders of a Communist Society," trans. by Ina Schlesinger, *School and Society*, Vol. 87 (Feb. 14, 1959), p. 66. Cf. Bereday, *et al, The Changing Soviet School*, p. 91; Rapacz, *PENSSR*, p. 34.
60. Khrushchev, "Memorandum," *Pravda*, Sept, 21, 1958, in *Soviet World Outlook*, pp. 164-165, 167. Cf. Theses XXXVI-XLVIII, *KCCSE*, pp. 54-65; Bereday, *et al., The Changing Soviet School*, p. 92; V. Yelyutin, "Adapting Higher Schools to Contemporary Demands," *School and Society*, Vol. 87 (1959), pp. 67-72.
61. *KCCSE*, p. 66. N. DeWitt holds that these reforms of Khrushchev actually constitute a deviation from Marxist-Leninist concepts of polytechnical education. Khrushchev is primarily motivated by the need to equip factories and farms with qualified laborers and to provide graduates. Cf. *EPE*, pp. 85-87. G. S. Counts, however, insists that the central object of the reforms is the cultivation of the elements of communist morality in the young in order that the "New Soviet Man," dedicated to the creation of classless society, may more quickly appear. Cf. *KCCSE*, p. 12.
62. Cf. Bereday, *et al, The Changing Soviet School*, pp. 97-98; Counts, *KCCSE*, pp. 2-3; Rapacz, *PENSSR*, p. 39. See Thesis XXV, *KCCSE*, p. 49.
63. Thesis I, *KCCSE*, p. 31.

CHAPTER VIII

COMMUNIST AESTHETICS

An attempt to discover the theoretical principles of art under Marxism leads one to the realization that neither Marx, Engels nor Lenin has left to communism anything approaching a complete aesthetics. There is a dearth of explicit consideration of this matter in their writings. Whatever they have written on aesthetics must be gleaned bit by bit from their principal writings and correspondence. These statements must then be patched together in an attempt to fashion their true position on this significant aspect of life.[1]

Role of Art

As has been noted, economic conditions ultimately determine historical development for the Marxist. These conditions are the factors and methods used in any society to produce and exchange products. Economic development is the base on which all the ideological superstructures of society develop. Among these ideological superstructures are of course literature and other forms of artistic expression.[2]

These ideological factors react upon one another and upon the economic base itself. Economics is not looked upon as the sole cause of activity in society with ideologies passively changing as economics direct. To do so would be a serious misunderstanding of the Marxist concept of development in society.

Political, juridical, philosophical, religious, literary, artistic, etc. development is based on economic development. But all these react upon one another and also upon the economic base. It is not that the economic position is the *cause and alone active*, while everything else only has a passive effect. There is, rather, interaction on the basis of economic necessity.[3]

Historical development however, shows forth as a history of class conflicts. Just as changes in productive relationships determine the domination of one class by another, so does the class conflict provide the basis for a class ideology. The political, philosophical, ethical and religious ideologies, both reflect and serve the interests of the social class which adhere to them.

Art, like ethics, religion, philosophy and science is an ideology. As such, art necessarily serves the purpose of creating and spreading some particular system of thought. It is consequently a tool of the class struggle. It has a special function to perform in this struggle — a function that scientific knowledge, for example, cannot perform. Science does not act on the feelings and emotions; science does not please the senses; this is the function of art.[4]

Artistic endeavor also serves the aggrandizement of a given social class.[5] In other words, every class seeks to represent itself to its growing generation and to posterity as an exemplar, as a reasonable class whose ideas are the light of the world.[6] By means of art and literature the dominant class, consciously or unconsciously, molds the thought of another class and holds it in servitude. Insofar as art serves the bourgeoisie in an attempt to make the life and condition of man meaningful, it ordinarily plays a negative role; it serves to perpetuate the exploitation of man by perpetuating the values found within the capitalistic mode of production.[7]

Because art is a weapon in the class struggle, it follows that the role of art in Marxist society is vastly important. The proletariat, while they still remain a class, will use all artistic forms to bring about the victory of the socialist revolution.[8] In proletarian literature, as in the art gallery, architecture, the concert hall, the ballet, art must hold a message — a social message, which if but listened to, will bring the world closer to a classless and perfect society.

Criterion of Beauty

The problem then arises concerning the criterion of beauty within Marxism. What is it that distinguishes the artistic from the ugly? By what norm shall man judge beauty? It would seem at first glance that there can be no absolute criteria of beauty for the Marxist. For art is an ideology; thus a people's conception of beauty unquestionably changes in the course of the historical process. Can one speak about the beautiful in general, or rather, must one speak about what is aesthetic for a given epoch, a given society, and a given social class? The answer is not simple.

There is a close parallel between the problem of aesthetic criteria and that of moral standards, as envisaged by Marx. Morality, as has been pointed out,[9] is certainly relative to the society in which it exists. For Marx, it has been formulated by the exploiting class according to the necessary modes of economic production. And yet, Marx recognizes a science of morality, having within itself some few universal moral laws, valid for all times.[10] So also in the field of aesthetics, the conception of society will depend upon the maturity of the society, the goals of the exploiting class and, of course, ultimately upon the prevailing mode of production. And yet there are common elements in the conception of the beautiful recognized by the most diverse peoples and cultures.[11] Certainly the Marxist will continue to delight in the sculpture of ancient Greece, Gothic architecture, the works of the Italian Renaissance, the Flemish painters and Shakespearean drama.[12] Even today he may still value the literary creations of artists who wrote for other classes, at other times, and in foreign lands. He has only to look to Marx himself for his example. Marx's favorite authors were Shakespeare, Aeschylus, Goethe, Heine, Diderot; his favorite heroes, Spartacus and Kepler.[13]

This "lack of relativity," Marx explains, is due to a disproportion between material development and artistic production. History shows the highest development of art has at times taken place in societies of primeval modes of production. This was due to the fact that certain important artistic forms were possible only at a low stage of artistic development. If this is true of the mutual relationships in the realm of art itself, how much more so in the relation of art taken as a whole to the general development of society.

It is well known that certain periods of highest development of art stand in no direct connection with the general development of society, nor with the material basis and the skeleton structure of its organization. . . . As regards certain forms of art, as *e.g.,* the epos, it is admitted that they can never be produced in the world-epoch-making form as soon as art as such comes into existence; in other words, that in the domain of art certain important forms of it are possible only at a low stage of its development.[14]

Greek art, for example, could have arisen only because of Greek mythology; yet mythology, because of its necessary relationship to man's view of nature and society would never have been part of the ideological superstructure of a society advanced in the material modes of production.

It is a well known fact that Greek mythology was not only the arsenal of Greek art, but also the very ground from which it had sprung. Is the view of nature and of social relations which shaped Greek imagination and Greek [art] possible in the age of automatic machinery, and railways, and locomotives, and electric telegraphs? . . . All mythology masters and dominates and shapes the forces of nature in and through the imagination; hence it disappears as soon as man gains mastery over the forces of nature. . . . In no event [could Greek art originate] in a society which excludes any mythological explanation of nature, any mythological attitude towards it and which requires from the artist an imagination free from mythology.[15]

But the main difficulty, says Marx, is not in understanding how certain types of art may come from economically underdeveloped societies. It lies rather in understanding why the art of a productively immature society still affords an advanced society a source of aesthetic enjoyment; and why, in some respects, such art prevails as the aesthetic norm and model beyond attainment. In the answer to this difficulty is to be found the reason for the apparent universal criteria of beauty common to all men, which Marx admits.

The answer to this problem lies in the nature of the dialectic itself. The synthesis, it is to be remembered, *transcends* the truth, goodness and beauty contained in the thesis and antithesis; they are not annihilated.[16] The truth, the goodness and beauty of less mature societies are not rejected by advanced society — they are transcended. Hence, in the dialectical progression of man and his economic environment there remains a residue of the past incorporating on a transcendent level everything that was worthwhile. Nothing is discarded except error, evil and ugliness. Marx explains the process as relating to art in the following way:

A man cannot become a child again unless he becomes childish. But does he not enjoy the artless ways of the child and must he not strive to reproduce its truth on a higher plane? Is not the character of every epoch revived perfectly true to nature in child nature? Why should the social childhood of mankind, where it had obtained its most beautiful development, not exert an eternal charm as an age that will never return?[17]

The criterion of beauty like the criterion of morality can be said to be relative to the given epoch or class-controlled society. Nevertheless, Marx insists that we find in all ages some common measure of approach to the beautiful. G. V. Plekhanov seems then to be correctly interpreting Marx's thought when he views artistic criticism as a two-stage process. The first stage consists of a judgment of the art creation according to the correctness of its description of the social relations at any given time.[18] The literary critic, for example, must "translate the idea of the . . . work from the language of art into the language of sociology, to find what might be called the sociological equivalent of a given literary phenomenon."[19]

But when this judgment is made as to the truthfulness or "realism" of the art, the critique is not complete; for not all that is realistic or socially significant is artistic or beautiful. Consequently, a second stage is involved by which the merely useful is distinguished from the aesthetically useful; where there is an "evaluation of the esthetic merits of the work under analysis."[20]

Neither Marx nor Engels has left us an adequate definition of the aesthetic experience. But from their notions of human nature which deny all spirituality,[21] it is possible to conclude that such an experience cannot transcend the material level. Yet, this is not to say that the perception of the beautiful, or the production of art is common to both man and animal. Marx is very clear on this point. Man is the only species that produces according to the laws of beauty, for man is the only species that can produce independently of his physical needs. He is the only species that can produce according to the measure of every species and supply the inherent measure of the object.

> Admittedly animals also produce. . . . But an animal only produces what it immediately needs for itself or its young. It produces one-sidedly, whilst man produces universally. It produces only under the dominion of immediate physical need, whilst man produces even when he is free from physical need and only truly produces in freedom therefrom. An animal produces only itself, whilst man reproduces the whole of nature. . . . An animal forms things in accordance with the standard and need of the species to which it belongs, whilst man knows how to produce in accordance with the standard of every species, and knows how to apply everywhere the inherent standard to the object. Man, therefore, also forms things in accordance with the laws of beauty.[22]

If for Marx art consists in man producing according to the inherent measure of the object, there is little doubt that the former Soviet Commissar of Education, A. V. Lunacharsky, was correctly surmising Marx's thought when he defined the beautiful as "the object whose form contains a regularity or symmetry which makes its contemplation pleasurable and which is made as if to the measure of the human eye, ear and brain."[23] Nor is there any reason to doubt the Marxian orthodoxy of Plekhanov when he sees the perception of the beautiful to be a matter of "intention" rather than "reason," "instinct" rather than "calculation."[24] It is the ability of man to produce art in accordance with the "inherent standard" and to perceive art instinctively according to that standard that allows Marx and the Marxist to speak of objectivity in aesthetics, and an appreciation of the beautiful, common to all ages and all classes.

Only man is capable of producing art, for man alone among the animals has the ability to produce tools. Hence, labor played an important role in the origin of art. Only because man evolved to the point where he was physically able to labor could he by means of labor further develop until he was able to produce art. But for labor there would be no art. Engels, writing on the evolutionary stages of man states:

> *The hand became free* and could henceforth attain even greater dexterity and skill and the greater flexibility thus acquired was inherited and increased from generation to generation.
>
> Thus the hand is not only the organ of labor, *it is also the product of labor.* Only by labor, by adaptation to ever new operations, by inheritance of the resulting special development of muscles, ligaments, and, over longer periods of time, bones as well, and by the ever-renewed employment of these inherited improvements in new, more and more complicated operations, has the human hand attained the high degree of perfection that has enabled it to conjure into being the pictures of Raphael, the statues of Thorwaldsen, the music of Paganini.[25]

Up to this point, we have derived the following aesthetic principles of Marxism:

Art is a product of man's labor directed towards the creation of form according to the inherent measure of the object. The beautiful is that object whose form contains a regularity or symmetry which makes its contemplation pleasurable and which is made as if to the measure of the human eye, ear or brain.

Art is an ideological superstructure based on the economic mode of production. As such it is a powerful weapon in the class struggle, having a specialized role to play. Hence, the criterion of beauty may be expected to change in accordance with the historical process. Yet there are common elements of beauty recognized by all classes and in all stages of the process.

Socialist Realism

For the Marxist, artistic endeavor, like all intellectual activity, serves an end that is greater than, and external to, the activity itself. Marxist aesthetical principles require that art disseminate certain information and inculcate certain behavior patterns, for art is an instrument to be used to further the historical process and bring about the success of the proletarian cause. The practical application of these principles takes the form of what has come to be known in the communist world as "socialist realism." Socialist realism stated in very general terms is merely the insistence that art performs its proper function in socialist society only by depicting reality[26] and inculcating moral and political values according to their dialectical development.[27] The "realism" of socialist realism means the artistic recognition of an external reality, whereas "socialist" signifies the artistic representation of reality in its "revolutionary development."[28]

Socialist realism starts from a somewhat ideal image to which it adapts the living reality. To discover "truth" in "reality" one must see and represent life in the light of its ideal; to represent reality not as it is found but as it ought to be, and as it will inevitably become.[29]

> Our demand "to represent life truthfully in its revolutionary development" is really nothing but a summons to view truth in the light of the ideal, to give an ideal interpretation of reality, to present what should be as what is. For we interpret "revolutionary development" as the inevitable movement toward Communism, toward our ideal, in the light of which we see reality. We represent life as we would like it to be and as it is bound to become, when it bows to the logic of Marxism.[30]

Socialist realism resembles more a species of "romanticism" than the literary method of the 19th century known as "realism." Yet it is not to be considered as an embellishment of life, or pure fantasy. It is truth presented in its revolutionary development.

We are against illusions and against idealizations; we write only the truth and at the same time present life in its revolutionary development. Why should we embellish life? It is quite beautiful as it is, we are not out to embellish it, we just want to show the seeds of the future it contains. Romanticism is legitimate provided it does not conflict with realism. Revolutionary romanticism, like "revolutionary development" and "seeds of the future," is inherent in life, which, as inveterate romantics, we depict truthfully.[31]

The discovery of reality and its truthful representation require the appreciation of two additional principles. The first is *"narodnost"* which insists that literature and the arts are for the people and must be comprehensible to them. The second is the principle of *"partiinost"* which means "partymindedness," that is, obedience to the official party line.

The principle of *narodnost* stems from writings of Marx himself. Marx insisted that truth must be discovered through practice. There is always a unity of theory and practice. Truth is to be found not only in the contemplation of the universe, but more surely in the struggle to change it. Speculative truth is worthless unless it can be brought to bear on the problems of human needs and their satisfaction. Truth must appear as ideology.[32]

But this is not the whole story, insists Lenin. This ideology must be discovered in proletarian class consciousness, for it is class consciousness, not individual consciousness, wherein truth is to be most surely sought. All ideology, including capitalism, serves the interests of the class supporting it — even if that class seeks to hide this fact under the mask of objectivity.[33] But of all class ideologies, it is that of the proletariat which reflects in its *subjectivism (narodnost)* the *objective laws (ideinost)* of reality. The more the interests of the masses find expression, the more completely and profoundly will the objective laws of man and nature be exposed, for the Marxist theory of history insists that the class interests of the proletariat are those most in keeping with the objective laws of social development. Armed with this principle Lenin could logically conclude that:

> Materialism includes, so to speak, partisanship, which enjoins the direct and open adoption of the standpoint of a definite social group in any judgment of events.[34]

Hence, only art that is meaningful to the masses and loved by them can be considered capable of representing socialist reality. Only such art is aesthetically acceptable in socialist society. To Lenin:

> Art belongs to the people. It must penetrate with its deepest roots into the very midst of the laboring masses. It must be intelligible to these masses and be loved by them. It must unite the feeling, thought, and will of these masses; it must elevate them.[35]

The citizen under a communist regime must base his concepts of art on these foundations if art is to play its proper role in his life. He has but to look around him to see this aesthetical theory in practice. The demand of Lenin that all art be realistic in order that it be understood by the worker is taken quite literally. Although some modern abstract art has recently been produced in the Soviet Union, it has always been met with official disapproval.[36]

In the field of architecture, construction necessitated by war damage in Russia, while showing evidence of new style, conspicuously lacks any show of "modernism" — Constructionism, New Functionalism or any other manifestations of the Western "Technocratic" movement so foreign to the Marxist aesthetic ideal.[37]

Perhaps the Moscow Metro (subway) offers the best illustration of the difference between the communist and the Western approach to the role of architecture. In the West, structures such as subways are built primarily along functional lines. The spaciousness and airiness of the Moscow stations, the costly marbles, mosaics, monumental frescoes, bas-reliefs and sculpture have understandably caused much astonishment in the Western visitor. But it must be remembered that for the Marxist, architecture, even though utilitarian, is an instrument of education — aesthetical, political and social. This is why the Metro, like the towers, locks and stations of the Moskva-Volga and the Volga-Don canals, has been conceived not only as a means of transportation but also as a source of inspiration, as a symbol of a higher culture and a promise of a happier and more abundant life in the future.[38]

As in architecture, so also in painting, sculpture, music, theatre, literature and all the fine arts, the worker sees the Marxist concept of true art. This concept implies that the substance of art demands the thematic, and demands too that it be a part of the socialist dynamic. The artist is not to dwell on the negative, static characteristics of society, but must bring forth the positive, progressive aspect of socialism.[39] His art is to represent the inner longings and deeds of the outstanding workers and leaders in a "deliberately magnified" image, for this is "the essence of a given social-historical phenomenon."[40] It is to be realistic enough to be comprehensible to the workers without being a mere copy of external reality — an art socially useful and educational.

The classic example of this socialist realism was the sculptured stainless steel group entitled "Workers and Woman Collective Farmer" surmounting the Russian pavilion at the Paris World's Fair in 1937. It was intended to reflect the new society on the move through the unification of the interests of the industrial worker and peasant. Typical historical themes are found in the colored glass panels of the Novoslobodskaia Station of the Moscow Metro and in the mosaics of the Komsomol'skaia Station. The glorification of labor theme can be found in the concourse of the Botanical Gardens Station; the vitality and potential of youth is depicted in the bronze statues in front of Moscow University,[41] and so on.

Everywhere in his everyday life, the Soviet citizen finds the communist theory confirmed. Here, he feels, must be the true philosophy of aesthetics — in it is found the meaningfulness of art for man.

Partisan Control of the Arts

It has been pointed out that for the Marxist the truthful representation of reality in the arts, as well as the achievement of truth in general, is more closely approached as the proletariat, the most advanced class, achieves its rightful position in society. As the proletariat becomes dominant, its interests more surely find expression, and the evolutionary progression of truth and beauty continue.

But it is only the Communist Party, the avant-garde of the working class, its most progressive segment, that can interpret *de facto* the interests of the proletariat, properly apply Marxism to the practical aspects of everyday life and guide the evolutionary development of the Marxist-Leninist ideology.[42] The resolutions of the Party must therefore be regarded as ". . . classical examples, not merely of the application of Marxist-Leninist theory to life . . . but also of the creative advancement of Marxist-Leninist theory."[43]

The Party's point of view *(partiinost)* must define the purposes of literature and direct the production of all art. Literature and art must become party literature and art. Literary affairs must become a part of organized party work. Lenin, writing about literature in particular, states:

> It amounts to the fact that for the socialist proletariat, literary endeavor cannot be an instrument of individual or group profit . . . independent of common proletarian aims. Down with non-party litterateurs! Down with the literature of supermen! . . . Literary work, must be established as part of organized, systematic, united, social-democratic work.[44]

In spite of his demand for party control of literature, Lenin was equally insistent that there be freedom for individual initiative, thought, form and content — lest the artistic aspects of the work be injured.

> There is no disputing that literary work lends itself less than anything else to a mechanical equalizing, to a leveling, to the rule of the majority over the minority. Nor is there any disputing that in this kind of endeavor it is absolutely necessary to guarantee the largest measure of personal initiative, individual tastes, thought and fantasy, form and content.[45]

Marxist theory here seems to be balanced on a thin line between apparently conflicting aims of control and freedom in the realm of literature, and by extension, the rest of the arts. Much of the apparent inconsistency of the position is cleared away — at least in Marxist eyes — by a return to a brief consideration of the Marxist notion of freedom.

It has been pointed out earlier that for the communist, freedom means "the appreciation of necessity."[46] It is knowledge of the necessary laws of nature and the historical struggle of the classes that brings freedom to man.[47] It is only by means of socialist victory, a victory of the proletariat, that the spiritual slavery of the oppressed classes ends and man can fulfill his true nature. In practice, this means that free activity becomes synonymous with activity by which the inevitable success of socialism is advanced. For the artist who faithfully serves his people "the question of whether he is free in his creativity does not exist."

> For such an artist the question of the approach to reality is clear: he does not have to adapt himself, to constrain himself; the correct picturing of life from the position of the Communist party-mindedness (partiinost) is the demand of his soul; he persistently stands on such a position, maintains and defends it in his work.[48]

Freedom in the arts means freedom from the influence of capital, freedom from careerism and bourgeois anarchistic individualism, freedom to develop socialism, to fertilize the revolutionary thoughts of humanity, to begin human history anew.[49] Hence, a modern Soviet writer boldly states:

> It is with ... joyous felicity that this artist accepts the directives of the Party and the government, from the Central Committee and its First Secretary. For who, if not the Party and its leader, knows best what kind of art we need? It is, after all, the Party that leads us to the Purpose in accordance with all the rules of Marxism-Leninism, the Party that lives and works in constant contact with God [*i.e.,* historical destiny]. And so we have in it and in its leader the wisest and most experienced guide, who is competent in all questions of industry, linguistics, music, philosophy, painting, biology, etc. He is our Commander, our Ruler, our High Priest. To doubt his word is as sinful as to doubt the will of God.[50]

The application of the principle of *partiinost* to the arts has a varied history in the Soviet Union.[51] It was so interpreted in the early 1920's that a great deal of freedom was allowed artists. Fear of persecution was nonexistent. Gradually, however, the Party began taking more and more interest in and subsequent control over artistic endeavors. At first, it acted merely as a referee amongst proletarian groups opposed as to the amount of influence the state and Party should have over the arts. Systematically, however, the Party became a dictator, with complete command over publication of literature and the performance and exhibition of the arts, as well as power to specify their form and content. This power of the Party reached its zenith under Stalin and Andrei Zhdanov in the years 1946-1952.[52]

Control of the arts, of course, is not a unique feature of communism. The history of art is more a history of control than one of freedom. This control has taken the form of political and ecclesiastical censorship, as well as that of conservatism and clichés among artists themselves. Often the finest art was produced in periods devoid of individuality. Great beauty is found in Egyptian art although it is stereotyped, as are the Russian icons and folklore. It was not until the Renaissance, that art lost its teleological character and freed itself from the service of religion and morality. Even so, rulers such as Catherine the Great, Napoleon and Dr. Goebbels still attempted to use the arts in the service of the state.[53] Since rigid measures of social control were prevalent throughout even pre-revolutionary Russian culture it is not surprising that the Marxist principle of *partiinost* received such a rigid totalitarian interpretation during a recent period of Soviet history.

Since the death of Stalin, however, there has been an evident "thaw" in the intensity of Party control of artistic endeavor. In general, there has been a spirit of moderation in the cultural policies of Khrushchev's regime. Whatever rebuffs have been given to writers and artists have for the most part lacked the coercive aspects and defamation that characterized the Zhdanovist methods of the past.[54] The application of the principle of *partiinost* has followed rather closely the Council of People's Commissars' *Decree on the Press* promulgated in the first days following the

Revolution (November 13, 1917).[55] Restrictions and censorship seem to apply only to those authors and artists guilty of perversion of facts and erroneous interpretation of ideology, to those guilty of offering excessive negative criticism of government or Party activity without offering any corresponding constructive advice or insight, or to those who call for open resistance to the government.

The lessening of restrictive measures under Khrushchev is not to be interpreted as a willingness of the Party to relinquish control of the arts. While it is true that the Party stresses its concern for the flowering of literature and the arts and for the unlimited development of creativity in the individual artist,[56] nonetheless the role of the Party in the life of the people must continually increase, claims Khrushchev. Ideology, and, therefore, Party control becomes increasingly important as Soviet society moves towards perfect communism. In matters of artistic creation, therefore, the Party will continue to demand from all — from the most honored and most popular personality to the mere novice — "the steadfast carrying out of the party line."[57]

Whether the future will see an interpretation of the principle of *partiinost* other than the one which currently prevails in the Soviet Union and the communist world, is a question whose answer must be based on mere speculation. It may be safely assumed, however, that the principle of *partiinost* itself will remain undisturbed.

Suggested Readings

CHAPTER VIII

Primary Sources

*Khrushchev, N. S., "For a Close Link Between Literature and Art with the Life of the People."
———, Speech to the 22nd CPSU Congress, 1961.
Lenin, V. I., "Party Organization and Party Literature."
Mao Tse-tung, *Problems of Art and Literature,* New York, International Publishers, 1950.
Marx, K. and Engels, F., *Literature and Art: Selections From Their Writings,* New York, International Publishers, 1947.

Secondary Sources

Counts, George S. and Lodge, Nucia, *The Country of the Blind: The Soviet System of Mind Control,* Boston, Houghton Mifflin Company, 1949, Chapters III, IV and V.
Dementiev, Alexander, "Truth and Falsehood About Soviet Literature," *Partisan Review,* Vol. XXIX (1962), pp. 303-308.
Ehrenburg, Ilya, "Literature in the Age of the Sputniks," *Atlantic Monthly,* Vol. 205 (June, 1960), pp. 45-47.
Ermolaev, Herman, *Soviet Literary Theories 1917-1934: The Genesis of Socialist Realism,* Berkeley and Los Angeles, University of California Press, 1963, Chaps. VII and VIII.
*Franklin, Mark, "Khrushchev Faces a Khrushchevian Dilemma," *New York Times Magazine,* May 12, 1963, pp. 21ff.
Hayward, Max, "Soviet Literature 1917-1961," *Partisan Review,* Vol. XXVIII (1961) pp. 333-362, and Vol. XXIX (1962), pp. 309-310.
Laqueur, Walter Z. and Lichtheim, George (eds.), *The Soviet Cultural Scene 1956-1957,* New York, Frederick A. Praeger, 1958, Part I.

McLanathan, Richard B. K., "Art in the Soviet Union," *Atlantic Monthly,* Vol. 205 (June, 1960), pp. 74-76.

*Pinkevitch, Albert P., *New Education in the Soviet Republic,* Chapter XII.

Plekhanov, G. V., *Art and Social Life,* edited by Andrew Rothstein, London, Lawrence and Wishart, Ltd., 1953.

Reavey, George, *Soviet Literature Today,* New Haven, Yale University Press, 1947, Chapters I and VII.

*Rubin, Burton, "Plekhanov and Soviet Literary Criticism," *American Slavic and East European Review,* Vol. XV (1956), pp. 527-542.

*Simmons, Ernest J., "The Origins of Literary Control," *Survey,* No. 36, pp. 78-84, No. 37, pp. 60-67.

―――― (ed.), *Through the Glass of Soviet Literature: View of Russian Society,* New York, Columbia University Press, 1953, pp. 3-26, 244-289.

Slusser, Robert M., "Soviet Music Since the Death of Stalin," *The Annals of the American Academy of Political and Social Science,* Vol. 303 (Jan. 1956), pp. 116-125.

Soviet Studies in Literature, (Articles from Soviet literary journals), International Arts and Science Press.

Struve, Gleb, *Soviet Russian Literature, 1917-1950,* Norman, University of Oklahoma Press, 1951.

*Swayze, Harold, *Political Control of Literature in the U.S.S.R., 1946-1959,* Cambridge, Mass., Harvard University Press, 1962, Chap. I.

*Tertz, Abram, *On Socialist Realism,* intro. by Czeslow Miloz, trans. by George Dennis, New York, Pantheon Books, 1960.

Trotsky, Leon, *Literature and Revolution,* trans. Rose Strunsky, Ann Arbor, University of Michigan Press, 1960.

Vickery, Walter N., *The Cult of Optimism: Political and Ideological Problems of Recent Soviet Literature,* Bloomington, Indiana University Press, 1963.

Voyce, Arthur, "Soviet Art and Architecture: Recent Developments," *The Annals of the American Academy of Political and Social Science,* Vol. 303 (Jan., 1956), pp. 104-115.

*Zetkin, Clara, "Lenin on Culture," *Reminiscences of Lenin,* New York, International Publishers, 1934.

FOOTNOTES TO CHAPTER VIII

1. Cf. Albert P. Pinkevitch, *New Education in the Soviet Republic,* ed. George S. Counts (New York, 1929), p. 318. Hereafter cited as Pinkevitch, *NESR.* See also Harold Swayze, *Political Control of Literature in the U.S.S.R., 1946-1959* (Cambridge, Mass., 1962), p. 2. Hereafter cited as Swayze, *PCL.*
2. Cf. Frederick Engels, "Letter to H. Starkenburg, January 25, 1894," in *Karl Marx Selected Works,* ed. V. Adoratsky, 2 vols. (Moscow-Leningrad, 1935-36), I, p. 392. Hereafter cited as *KMSW.* See also G. V. Plekhanov, *The Development of the Monist View of History,* trans. Andrew Rothstein (Moscow, 1956), pp. 219-221. Hereafter cited as Plekhanov, *DMVH.*
3. Engels, "Letter to H. Starkenburg, January 25, 1894," *KMSW,* I, p. 392. Cf. Plekhanov, *DMVH,* pp. 23-24. See above, Chapter VI, note No. 11.
4. Pinkevitch, *NESR,* p. 320. On this point see also the view of Swayze in *PCL,* pp. 12-13.
5. Pinkevitch, *NESR,* p. 320.
6. Karl Marx and F. Engels, *The German Ideology,* ed. R. Pascal (New York, 1947), p. 39. Cf. Pinkevitch, *NESR,* p. 320.
7. Cf. Plekhanov, *Art and Social Life,* ed. Andrew Rothstein (London, 1953), p. 196; Pinkevitch, *NESR,* p. 320; Swayze, *PCL,* p. 7; Barton Rubin, "Plekhanov and Soviet Literary Criticism," *American Slavic and East European Review,* Vol. XV (1956), 529n. Hereafter cited as Rubin, *PSLC.*
8. Cf. V. I. Lenin, "Proletarian Culture," *Selected Works,* 12 vols. (New York, 1943), IX, 484; N. S. Khrushchev, "For a Close Tie of Literature and Art with the Life of the People," *Kommunist,* Nov. 12, 1957 (hereafter cited as Khrushchev, *CTLA*), as quoted in *Soviet World Outlook,* 3rd ed., Dept. of State publication 6836 (Washington, D. C., 1959), p. 132; Mao Tse-tung, *Problems of Art and Literature* (New York, 1950), pp. 8, 32-33.
9. See Chapter V, above.
10. On this point see Charles J. McFadden, *The Philosophy of Communism* (New York, 1939), Chap. VII.
11. Cf. Marx, "Letter to Ferdinand Lassalle, July 22, 1861," in Marx and Engels, *Literature and Art: Selections From Their Writings* (New York, 1947), pp. 21-22.

12. Cf. Pinkevitch, *NESR*, pp. 319-320.
13. Marx, "Confessions," *Literature and Art*, appendix, p. 145; Franz Mehring, *Karl Marx: The Story of His Life*, trans. E. Fitzgerald (London, 1948), pp. 503-504.
14. Marx, *A Contribution to the Critique of Political Economy* (Chicago, 1904), appendix, pp. 309-310. Hereafter cited as *Appendix to the Critique of Political Economy*. Also in *Literature and Art*, p. 18.
15. Marx, *Appendix to the Critique of Political Economy*, pp. 310-311; *Literature and Art*, pp. 18-19.
16. See above, Chapter III.
17. Marx, *Appendix to the Critique of Political Economy*, p. 312; *Literature and Art*, p. 19. On this notion of a common norm of the beautiful also see Engels "Letter to Margaret Harkness, April, 1888," *Literature and Art*, pp. 41-43.
18. Plekhanov, *DMVH*, pp. 220ff. Cf. *Art and Social Life*, pp. 109, 164-165; Leon Trotsky, *Literature and Revolution*, trans. Rose Strunsky (Ann Arbor, 1960), p. 178; Pinkevitch, *NESR*, pp. 319, 324-325; Rubin, *PSLC*, p. 529.
19. G. V. Plekhanov, *iskusstvo i literatura*, ed. N. F. Bel'chikov (Moscow, 1948), p. 207, as cited in Rubin, *PSLC*, p. 530. Cf. Swayze, *PCL*, pp. 5-6.
20. Plekhanov, *iskusstvo i literatura*, p. 212, as cited in Rubin, *PSLC*, p. 530. Cf. Pinkevitch, *NESR*, pp. 319, 321-324; Swayze, *PCL*, p. 6.
21. See above, Chapter IV.
22. Marx, *Economic and Philosophic Manuscripts of 1844*, trans. Martin Milligan (Moscow, 1961), pp. 75-76. Also in *Literature and Art*, pp. 14-15.
23. A. V. Lunacharsky, as quoted by Pinkevitch, *NESR*, p. 320.
24. Plekhanov, *Sochineniya*, ed. D. Ryazanov (Moscow, 1923-1927), XIV, p. 119, as cited in Swayze, *PCL*, p. 6.

In view of the nature of the Marxist dialectic in general, and the insistence of Marx on man's ability to produce according to the "laws of beauty" in particular, it is difficult to concur with B. Rubin (*PSLC*, p. 531) when he holds that Plekhanov's notion (that an evaluation of the aesthetic merit of a work can be made independently of the social milieu) is not to be found in Marxist theory. Likewise it is difficult to concur with H. Swayze (*PCL*, pp. 7-8) when he states that there is an inconsistency involved in Plekhanov's demand for objectivity and his defense of relativism in aesthetics and art criticism. On this point see Mao Tse-tung, *Problems of Art and Literature*, pp. 36-38; Trotsky, *Literature and Revolution*, pp. 233-234.

25. Engels, *Dialectics of Nature* (New York, 1940), p. 281; *Literature and Art*, pp. 15-16. Cf. Plekhanov, *Art and Social Life*, pp. 45ff., 95.
26. Cf. Marx and Engels, "Book Review of A. Chenu: *Les Conspirateurs*

and Lucien de la Hodde: *La Naissance de la Republique en Fevrier 1848*," as translated in *Literature and Art*, p. 40; Engels, "Letter to Margaret Harkness, April, 1888," *ibid.*, pp. 41-43; Engels, "Letter to Ferdinand Lassalle, May 18, 1859," *ibid.*, pp. 50-56; Lenin, "Letter to M. Gorky, Feb. 7, 1908," in *Sochineniya*, 4th ed. (Moscow, 1947), XXXIV, pp. 330-332, as cited in Herman Ermolaev, *Soviet Literary Theories 1917-1934: The Genesis of Socialist Realism* (Berkeley and Los Angeles, 1963), p. 169 (hereafter cited as Ermolaev, *SLT*); Trotsky, *Literature and Revolution*, pp. 235-236; Khrushchev, Speech to Soviet Intellectuals, Feb., 1958, quoted in *Soviet World Outlook*, p. 132; Mao Tse-tung, *Problems of Art and Literature*, p. 23.

27. Cf. Engels, "Letter to Minna Kautsky, Nov. 26, 1885," in *Literature and Art*, pp. 44-46; Lenin, "Party Organization and Party Literature," *Sochineniya*, X, pp. 26-31 as quoted in Ernest J. Simmons, "The Origins of Literary Control," *Survey*, No. 36 (1961), p. 79 (hereafter cited as Simmons, *OLC*); Khrushchev, Interview with Henry Shapiro, *TASS*, Nov. 18, 1957, as cited in *Soviet World Outlook*, p. 133; Mao Tse-tung, *Problems of Art and Literature*, pp. 32-33. See also Ermolaev, *SLT*, pp. 169ff.

28. *First All-Union Congress of Soviet Writers*, 1934, p. 716, as quoted in Abram Tertz, *On Socialist Realism*, intro. by Czeslaw Milosz (New York, 1960), p. 24. Cf. Swayze, *PCL*, p. 16.

29. Cf. A. Fadeyev, "Zadachi literaturnoi kritiki," *Oktyabr*, No. 7, 1947, p. 150, as quoted in Swayze, *PCL*, p. 20.

30. Tertz, *On Socialist Realism*, pp. 76-77. Cf. Mao Tse-tung, *Problems of Art and Literature*, pp. 25-26. See also Swayze, *PCL*, pp. 20-21; Ernest J. Simmons (ed.), *Through the Glass of Soviet Literature: Views of Russian Society* (New York, 1953), introduction, pp. 22-23 (hereafter cited as Simmons, *TGSL*); Mark Franklin, "Khrushchev Faces a Khrushchevian Dilemma," *New York Times Magazine*, May 12, 1963, p. 80. Hereafter cited as Franklin, *KFKD*.

31. Tertz, *On Socialist Realism*, p. 77. Cf. Trotsky, *Literature and Revolution*, pp. 235-236; Lunacharsky, Speech to Soviet Writers, 1933, as quoted in Franklin, *KFKD*, p. 80; Ilya Ehrenburg, "O rabote pisatelya," *Znamya*, No. 10, 1953, trans. in *The Current Digest of the Soviet Press*, V, No. 52 (February 10, 1954), p. 12.

32. Cf. Marx, *Theses on Feuerbach*, XI, in *KMSW*, I, p. 473.

33. Lenin, *Materialism and Empirio-Criticism, Collected Works* (Moscow, 1960-63), XIV, pp. 342-343, 348, 358.

34. Lenin, *The Economic Content of Narodism and the Criticism of It in Mr. Struve's Book, Collected Works*, I, p. 401. Cf. Khrushchev, Interview with Henry Shapiro, *TASS*, Nov. 18, 1957, in *Soviet World Outlook*, p. 131; Mao Tse-tung, *On Problems of Art and Literature*, p. 32.

35. *Lenin o kulture i iskusstve,* ed. M. Lifshits (Moscow, 1938), p. 299, as trans. in Swayze, *PCL,* p. 10. Cf. Khrushchev, *CTLA, Soviet World Outlook,* p. 133; Mao Tse-tung, *Problems of Art and Literature,* pp. 18ff., and *passim.*
36. For Khrushchev's reaction to the abstract art exhibited in Moscow in November-December, 1962, see "The Connoisseur Speaks," *Time,* Vol. LXXX, No. 24 (Dec. 14, 1962), p. 26; Franklin, *KFKD,* pp. 21f.
37. Cf. Arthur Voyce, "Soviet Art and Architecture: Recent Developments," *The Annals of The American Academy of Political and Social Science,* Vol. 303 (January, 1956), p. 104. Hereafter cited as Voyce, *SAA.*
38. *Ibid.,* pp. 110-111. Cf. Trotsky, *Literature and Revolution,* pp. 249ff.
39. Voyce, *SAA,* pp. 113-114.
40. G. M. Malenkov, *Otchetnyi doklad XIX s'ezdu partii o rabote TSK VKP (b)* (Moscow, 1952), p. 73, as quoted in Voyce, *SAA,* p. 114.
41. Cf. Voyce, *SAA,* p. 114n.
42. Cf. Lenin, *Urgent Tasks of Our Movement, Selected Works,* II, p. 11; Joseph Stalin, *Problems of Leninism* (Moscow, 1953), pp. 164-188; Khrushchev, Speech at Kiev, April 26, 1958, as quoted in *Soviet World Outlook,* p. 35: Mao Tse-tung, *Problems of Art and Literature,* pp. 33-34.
43. "Edinstvo teorii i praktiki," *Voprosy filosofii,* 1954, No. 2, p. 5, as quoted in Gustav A. Wetter, *Dialectical Materialism,* trans. Peter Heath, revised ed. (New York, 1958), p. 273.
44. Lenin, "Party Organization and Party Literature" ("Partiinaya organizatsiya i partiinaya literatura") *Collected Works,* X, p. 45, (hereafter cited as Lenin, *POPL*), as quoted in Simmons, *OLC,* p. 79. Cf. Swayze, *PCL,* p. 8; Simmons, *TGSL,* pp. 4-5.
45. Lenin, *POPL,* p. 46, as quoted in Simmons *OLC,* p. 79. Cf. Swayze, *PCL,* p. 9.
46. See Chapter IV, above.
47. Cf. Engels, *Herr Eugen Dühring's Revolution in Science (Anti-Dühring)* (London, 1940), p. 128; Lenin, *The Three Sources and Three Component Parts of Marxism, KMSW,* I, p. 59.
48. Khrushchev, *CTLA,* in *Soviet World Outlook,* p. 131. Also in Tertz, *On Socialist Realism,* pp. 41-42.
49. Cf. Marx, "Debaten über Pressfreiheit," *Historisch-Kritische Gesamtausgabe* (Frankfort, [etc.], 1927-1933), Abt. 1, Bd. 1, pp. 222-223, in *Literature and Art.* p. 63; Lenin, *POPL,* pp. 48-49, in Simmons, *OLC,* pp. 80-81; Khrushchev, *CTLA,* in *Soviet World Outlook,* pp. 131-133; Mao Tse-tung, *Problems of Art and Literature,* pp. 44-45. See also Tertz, *On Socialist Realism,* pp. 40-42.
50. Tertz, *On Socialist Realism,* p. 42.

51. For detailed histories of literary control in the Soviet Union, see for example, Ermolaev, *SLT;* Swayze, *PCL;* Simmons, *TGSL,* introduction; Simmons, *OLC,* and *OLC-II, Survey,* No. 37 (1961), pp. 60-67; W. N. Vickery, *The Cult of Optimism* (Bloomington, 1963).

52. Zhdanov's views on the arts and the role of the Party and the state are found in his *Essays on Literature, Philosophy and Music* (New York, 1950).

53. On this point, see Tertz, *On Socialist Realism,* pp. 88-89; Simmons, *TGSL,* p. 5.

54. The attack on Boris Pasternak however constitutes a notable exception to this rule of moderation. Cf. Swayze, *PCL,* pp. 200-203, 286, note No. 50.

55. *O partiinoi i sovetskoi pechati* (Moscow, 1954), p. 173, cited in Simmons, *OLC,* p. 83.

56. Khrushchev, *CTLA,* in *Soviet World Outlook,* p. 133.

57. Khrushchev, Interview with Iverach McDonald, *TASS,* February 15, 1958, in *Soviet World Outlook,* p. 37; Speech of March 8, 1963, in Franklin, *KFKD,* p. 79.

Part III

SOME PRINCIPLES FOR THE FUTURE

CHAPTER IX

THE CLASSLESS SOCIETY AND POLITICAL ORDER

The "Withering" of the State

The Marxist concept of the classless society has been interpreted, by both those favorable and those unfavorable to the general ideology, as an attempt to envision and then transpose into existence by means of social activity a more perfect human society. One aspect of its perfection is seen to rest in the absence of a "state" within this community of men. This particular aspect of Marxism appears to be outside the arena of interpretive dispute. However, care must be taken to avoid any necessary inference that the absence of a "state" is somehow identifiable with the absence of a political order within such a classless society. Rather, with the aid of concepts developed and made explicit by recent social analysis, an examination of the idea of the classless society, as expressed in Marxist writings, will make evident that Marx and the Marxist do not seek the dissolution of the political order through such a society. The Marxist certainly is not to be classed as a political anarchist in the strict sense. Yet it must be admitted at the same time, that there is a persistent tendency in the Marxism of the past as well as the present — among the bolshevist, the menshevist and other interpreters of Marx — to reduce and equate the political order with governmental forms.[1] Yet by clearly identifying the political order, it can be shown that the concept of the perfect Marxist society, by the Marxist's own insistence, is to be a nonexploitative, altruistic, yet, at the same time, a well-defined political society.

The Soviet political theorist, G. Shaknozarov, in characterizing the socialist state as it now exists in the Soviet Union as one whose functions are primarily social as distinguished from exploitative, cites those activities of organizations by which the economic, educational and "cultural" institutions are maintained and advanced as the essential control function of the state. Yet these control functions will continue under perfect communism, for as he writes:

> . . . it would be impossible to conceive of a communistic society even after the state has withered away, continuing to exist without *organized* and rationally *centralized planning* of the national economy, *distribution* of resources and labor among its branches, *guidance* in science and other cultural spheres. In fact, under communism the demands of society for such organization will be much greater.[2]

Shaknozarov's views on this point are by no means unusual, but have a theoretical history reaching as far back in Marxism as Marx himself with his "future 'state' of communist society,"[3] and Engels with his forecast of "communal control over production";[4] through Lenin with his solution of the problem of distribution of goods by means of training all members of society "to independently administer social production, independently keep accounts and *exercise control* over idlers," which will, in turn, remove all need for state control or coercion;[5] to more recent pronouncements by such authorities as the Academician, S. G. Strumilin, who stresses "the need for people to *guide* production processes [under universally triumphant communism],"[6] and finally the attempts of N. S. Khrushchev at the 21st Party Congress to dispel the "vulgar" conception of communism "as a *formless, unorganized* and *anarchic* mass of people." Khrushchev holds that classless society will be "a highly *organized* and arranged cooperation of workers." Everyone will have to fulfill his functions of labor and his social duties "at a *determined* time and in an *established* order."[7]

Shaknozarov, completely in tune with his ideological elders, would want to imply that the degree of political control will be quite high in classless society. Yet, at times, he seemingly wishes to characterize such control as being almost spontaneous.[8] He writes:

> ... when we imagine communist self-government in its mature form we presuppose the organization of a harmonious system of bodies elected by the population — bodies which are no longer political organizations but which enjoy the natural authority commanded by the oldest and most experienced members of any collective.[9]

Nevertheless, when the "natural authority" is set forth in detail by Shaknozarov it is seen to be not spontaneous, but quite premeditated. The administration of economics, cultural development and educational supervision would be accomplished by councils of elected citizens whose activities cannot be characterized as other than functionally independent of the values sought through their existence. The very concept of an "elected council" carries with it the connotation of a group "set apart" by the people with power to be explicitly directed towards the maintenance of that order necessary for the obtaining of the values sought in communistic society.[10] This, as will be shown below, is to be called political power, or as seen in the abstract, political control.

Beyond economic control, cultural development and educational guidance there lies that vast arena which the Marxist has designated "the public order." The maintenance of this order in classless society would be brought about by the members of the society themselves habitually obeying the rules of social behavior known and observed for thousands of years.[11] Yet because of individual failings, indiscretions, over-zealousness, mistakes of judgment in general, citizen squads would be organized that they might step in at such times and carry out the necessary sanctions.[12] These citizen squads would be, in a sense, the residue of the "parapolice" and "parajudicial" groups which are now in operation in the Soviet Union, and whose functions for the present, in Khrushchev's words, "is to act alongside and parallel with such agencies as the militia and courts to perform the functions of safeguarding public order and security."[13]

Naturally, as the transition to the perfect order of communism progresses, the coercive aspects of social control as represented by Soviet law, the courts, the police and militia gradually will be weakened. The control functions and their corresponding roles will, at the same time and in the same proportion, be transferred to the "public" organizations whose mode of control will be principally "persuasive" rather than "coercive," as is the case of their present counterparts.[14] But because the Soviet society must have the foresight to make the transition orderly, Khrushchev has insisted that ". . . we now have to prepare for this and to teach people to develop habits for these functions."[15] Likewise, he deems an ideological necessity "the inclusion of the widest strata of the population in the management of the affairs of the country during transition to communism."[16]

Consequently, early in 1959, the people's militia *(druzhiny)* and its role was formalized in a joint decree of the Central Committee and the Council of Ministers, "On Participation of Workers in the Maintenance of Public Order." Within a month of the decree's issuance, it was announced that "voluntary" militia units had been formed in most large industrial and agricultural enterprises. By late in 1960, it was claimed that there were 80,000 units with more than 2.5 million members.[17]

In the decree governing their activity, the authority of the people's militia, for the present at least, was clearly restricted to warning offenders and to listing their names so that further misdemeanors on their part could be dealt with more severely by the regular police, or perhaps the comrades' courts. In practice, however, their actions have frequently involved transgressions of the Soviet law and invasions of personal privacy.[18]

These excesses have been attributed by the Soviet press, and perhaps with some partial justification, to the uniqueness of the experiment in social control.[19] Nonetheless, there is no apology made by the press for public inquiry and intervention into private life — and logically so — for as has been seen, the Marxist concept of morality does not limit the ethical realm to the internal forum of the individual. Rather, morality is a social phenomenon and, as such, the sanctioning aspect of this phenomenon has a place in the social relationships of man.[20]

When the judicial aspect of public order is considered, the problem becomes a bit more complex. The maintenance of public justice in classless society could, in the eyes of the Marxist, come about as the result of either of two forms of parajudicial activity present in the transitional stage of communism in the Soviet Union today, or perhaps, could ensue from an eclectic combination of both.

In the Soviet Union at the present time, there exists some confusion over the division of responsibility between the "public meetings" authorized under the "anti-parasite" laws which were presented for public approval in 1957-58,[21] and the "comrades' courts" which more recently have been favored as the chief means of support to be given the Soviet law and courts by the public organizations, and the chief instrument by which the people can be trained for their juridical functions in future society after the Constitution, the law and the Soviet court system have withered away.

The anti-parasite laws, as they now stand, authorize public organizations to hold open trials against "parasitical elements" without specifying to any great extent who is meant. The public meetings, at which a minimum of 100 persons must be present, can act by simple majority, even in the absence of the alleged offender, to impose sentences up to two to five years in exile with compulsory labor.[22] There is no appeal from the decision of these meetings, although sentences, at least in the Georgian republic, must be confirmed by the executive committee of local soviets.[23] Naturally, there is some concern about the "public meeting" and questions are being raised as to the prudence of making such an organization the instrument of public justice within the Soviet Union. It has been pointed out that there is the inherent possibility that such proceedings could be used by a community against any individual on artificially contrived pretexts and become thereby an instrument of pure terror within such a community along with all the bitter possibilities of unrestrained "mob rule" potentially contained therein.[24]

The apprehension over the anti-parasite laws has led to the recent revival of the "comrades' courts," a more formal institution than the "public meeting." They are set up wherever a collective exceeds fifty persons, whether it be industrial or agricultural, in educational institutions, apartment blocks, and so on.[25] They are to deal not only with questions of production but with questions of everyday life of a moral nature — cases of wrong behavior by members of collectives who have violated the standards of public order.[26]

In distinction to the "public meetings," the "comrades' courts" are restricted to expressing public reprimand or censure, imposing a fine up to 100 rubles on offenders and/or issuing regrets to victims, recommending transfer, demotion or dismissal from work in case of labor violations, ordering compensation for damages up to 500 rubles, referring criminal cases to the regular courts.[27]

The root function of the comrades' courts, it seems, is not to inflict punishment, but to attempt to right the injury done to the values of the community through the assumption of public responsibility for both the erring citizen's deed and for his redemption from unsocial activity. The sanctions involved tend more towards persuasion than coercion.[28]

The public order in classless society would be thus maintained by means of those public instruments stemming from the parapolice and parajudicial organizations such as are now in existence in the Soviet Union, the nation most advanced along the path to perfect communism. The transition to communism in the area of public order is to be caused and, at the same time, is to be judged successful, by the degree to which the present public militia and judicial groups increase in quantitatively greater popular self-regulation, to the degree to which the mode of sanctioning within these organizations evolves from that of coercion to that of persuasion and consequently, to the degree to which the public organizations replace rather than assist the coercive agencies, such as the police and regular courts.[29]

This, then, is an indication of what may be expected in the political sphere of a classless, perfect society according to the common Marxist theory. From the identification of the political order below, it will become evident that such an order would be very much in the forefront of the social control present in perfect communism and that classless society can truly be called political.

Analysis of Political Order

Recent attempts by social philosophers to bring greater precision to the definitions and comprehension of basic concepts of political theory through an inquiry into social control — that is, through an inquiry into those processes in society by which unity and order in the conduct of persons and groups towards the behavior patterns which make up the culture of the society are both induced and maintained[30] — have succeeded in clearing away much of the ambiguity concerning what constitutes and what differentiates the political, the social, the governmental, the legal and the ethical orders. Such distinctions were, without doubt, implicit in earlier classical political theory. Yet, because these distinctions were contained only implicitly and because many common terms of social philosophy were used in an analogous manner by the Greek and earlier Medieval political theorists, there was often an oversight of the use of analogy,[31] as well as misunderstanding and confusion on the part of some of the lesser minds which followed. The results of this confusion are, at times, still evident in social philosophy, although the conceptual tools needed to erase its traces are now at hand — thanks to the insights of current social analysis.

As a consequence of the lack of precision in distinguishing the different realms of social activity to be found among men, it is not uncommon for some political theorists either to confuse the political order with the governmental, or to improperly distinguish and relate the ethical order and the legal order.[32] Thus, when a Soviet political writer treating the classless society of the future characterizes it as having harmonious systems of bodies which are no longer "political" organizations,[33] it is in the present age, easy to see that the notion of "political" is limited incorrectly by the identification of the political order with the political group. In the case of the Soviet writer, this amounts to identifying the political order with the ruling class. Such an understanding of the political order seems to imply that membership in the political order is somehow voluntary and capable of discontinuation by revolution or other means when conditions, historical or other, allow. The political order, to be understood with some modicum of precision, however, needs to be viewed within the framework of the wider and more apparent reality of social control. From this vantage the political order can then be correctly perceived as a species of this more basic reality of social control.[34]

Among the elements of every situation of social control, the chief element is that which has been called the "dual level of operation." The first of these levels, known technically as *substantive control,* simply consists in the preferential status which any group or society spontaneously gives some values[35] over others, and the concentration of its energy on their attainment as the end or goal of the group or society. The control involved is in the first instance the preferential choosing of values, and secondly, the resulting channeling of available energies of the group or society towards these values. The control here springs from the "substantive," that is, the end, or ultimate values sought. It is thus called substantive control.

Upon this level, a second, more formal level of control supervenes. The object of this second level is that of creating and maintaining the order and conditions necessary for the pursuit of the substantive values. Thus, new values are introduced which serve as means to achieve the substantive values. These secondary values are called *formal values,* or more precisely *norms.* At this second level or operation, the control too is more formal, that is, less spontaneous than that which emerges from the concentration on a set of substantive values.

The distinction between the first and second levels of operation, between substantive and formal values and between substantive and formal control, will allow for a clearer identification of political order and its operations. It should be emphasized, however, that these two levels are not always clearly articulated in a complex society, nor is there a necessary temporal sequence in their origin. But they are distinct in principle and serve as the basic means for arriving at a precise notion of the political.

The object of social control is not as easily identified as might be thought. True, the material aspect of the object of control is the actions and interactions of men in society. The real object of social control, however, is *power*—human power—that is, the capacity of an initiative agent to stimulate response in others either with or without their consent.[36] This is, at root, the power from which all power of groups and societies by complex systems of combination is derived.

Power is present in every instance of social control in two ways. First, the object of control is power. This is to say, it is human power that is brought under control. Secondly, the control itself is power and the manifestation of power. In either case, it is the same power. The power of which control is formed and of which it is a manifestation is the same power which is the object of control. The power in social control is a feed-back of the original and constitutive power of society which, in turn, resides ultimately in the person.

In every group or society there is a spontaneous, but deliberate, seeking after the substantive values by which the group or society is defined. From this pursuit there also arises a spontaneous order from the nature of the situation by which the values are sought.[37] Yet, because of the spontaneity involved, such an ordering makes the attainment of the goal insecure. With the awareness of this weakness among the members of the grouping comes a change in the quality aspect of the control. There emerges among the group the consciousness of the *common good,* that is, the conditions or order which must prevail if the substantive values are to be attained and the spontaneous order secured. This new ordering involves the introduction of a new value, distinct in principle from the substantive values, though not in fact. This is the value of order. This order consists in the relations which must prevail among the members of the group in the light of the substantive values they pursue.

The seeds of the political order of social control are already present here at this second level of control. Once the common good, or order, has been perceived in some sense distinct from the substantive values, the process which has been designated "functional detachment"[38] has begun. To the degree to which it is perceived that the pursuit of the substantive values depends on conditions which are not implicit in, and do not emerge spontaneously from the pursuit of those values, to that extent do the conditions of *order* have a certain *independence* from the substantive values. To that extent do they become subject to their own laws, and to that extent does that part of the power of the group devoted to control direct itself towards the maintenance of the common good in an explicit fashion. And to the degree to which this functional detachment or independence is realized, the social control within the group or society and the organization which it brings into being, is to be called *political*.

The political order, then, is that dimension of the social control system which has achieved a degree of functional independence from its substantive values, and those social elements (institutions, groups, etc.) which this independence generates. As such, it is only specifically different than social control in general. The specific difference is the presence of a functional independence from the socialization process and its substantive values.

The political order is all-pervasive, and must be present at every level of social grouping,[39] for *some* perception of the common good, that is, some grasp of the conditions and order necessary for the pursuit of the substantive values, logically follows the perception of the substantive values themselves. All social groups can thus be called "proto-political,"[40] for the second level of social control is present to some degree in each. Yet there is only one political order, in the full sense, within each society. This may be termed the public order. It comes about when groups in the process of establishing relationships among themselves enter into competition for the realization of their substantive values. There is then brought into existence certain processes for achieving order in the realization of competing systems of values among the groups. Ultimately, the political order is concerned with all substantive values of society, formally however, only as they may be ordered through that control characterized above as formal values, or norms.[41] Where the locus of this political order lies is a complex question and not of immediate concern at this juncture.

From the above, it is seen that when the perfect classless society of the Marxist is viewed as one lacking the political order, this is the result of confusing the political order with rather the *formal structuralization* by which the political order separates itself from the socialization process, that is, there is a confusion of the political order with the *state*. Now it has been shown that according to the Marxist doctrine of the classless society the political order would necessarily be present in such a society as they propose.

If it is rather the formal structuralization of the political order (that is, the formalizing of political functions into static and persisting "offices" as under a "constitution" for instance — or in other words, the *state*) which the Marxist truly desires to eliminate ultimately from human society, the question of his purpose in so doing immediately arises. As has been pointed out in another place,[42] the Marxist looks upon the bourgeois state as merely exploitative in its origin and operation. As such, the social control present in the capitalist state represents a very imperfect and reprehensible form of social relationship, where the control of human power by authoritative power violates the human dignity of one class.

Even the socialist state as it now exists in the Soviet Union and throughout the communist world is considered by the Marxist exploitative, at least in regard to the bourgeoisie. Its existence is merely a necessary moment in the dialectical process towards perfect social relationships. It still has the drawback of its social control being exercised primarily for utilitarian motives and in a legalistic manner. To the extent that the utilitarian mode and what has been called the "legal-rational mode"[43] of inter-personal and inter-group relationships gives way to an affective mode based on friendship (comradeship), and where this is improbable, at least give way to a mode of relationship based on justice,[44] to that extent will the formal structuralization of the state and its organ, the law, "wither away." When these two modes, the affective and the moral, are in complete pre-eminence, human society will exist in its ideal and perfect form.

The insistence of the Marxist that the pre-eminence of friendship and justice in social relationships would result in a more truly human society, and his insistence on practical social activities to bring about this condition in existent society are, indeed, laudable. They cannot be criticized without at the same time criticizing an integral part of the Judaeo-Christian tradition and most of the major religions of the world. Yet it is also important to point up the fact that the pre-eminence of the affective and the moral modes in a society does not preclude that a government formalized under a constitution, be itself considered one of the substantive values of society to be cherished and protected.[45]

Neither does it preclude the possibility, as will be seen in the following chapter, that the other modes of human relationship, such as the utilitarian mode and "impersonal" law, can perfect society and even be essential to the attainment of the substantive values of society.

CHAPTER IX

Suggested Readings

Primary Sources

*Khrushchev, N. S., "Speech at 21st CPSU Congress," 1959.
———, "Speech to 13th Komsomol Congress," 1958.
*Lenin, V. I., *The State and Revolution*, especially Chapter V.
*Marx, K., *The Critique of the Gotha Programme*.
Program of the Communist Party of the Soviet Union, adopted by the 22nd Party Congress, 1961, Part II, Chapters I and III.
Stalin, Joseph, *Economic Problems of Socialism in the U.S.S.R.*

Secondary Sources

*Azrael, Jeremy R., "Is Coercion Withering Away?," *Problems of Communism*, XI, No. 6 (November-December, 1962), pp. 9-17.
Binkley, George W., "The Withering of the State Under Khrushchev," *The Review of Politics*, XXIII (1961), pp. 37-51.
Goldhagen, Erich, "The Glorious Future — Realities and Chimeras," *Problems of Communism*, IX, No. 6 (November-December, 1960), pp. 10-18.
Kline, George L., Hazard, John N. and Osborn, Robert, "The Withering Away of the State," *Survey*, No. 38 (October, 1961), pp. 63-90. Also in *The Future Communist Society*, W. Lacqueur and L. Labedz (eds.), N. Y., Frederick Praeger, 1962.
*Ritvo, Herbert, "Totalitarianism Without Coercion?," *Problems of Communism*, IX, No. 6 (November-December, 1960), pp. 19-29.
*Shaknozarov, Georgi, "When the State Has Withered Away," *The Soviet Review*, I (November, 1960), pp. 54-68.
*Strumilin, S., "Thoughts About the Future," *Current Digest of the Soviet Press*, XII, No. 15 (May 11, 1960), pp. 11-14.
Sukiennicki, Wiktor, "The Vision of Communism — Marx to Khrushchev," *Problems of Communism*, IX, No. 6 (November-December, 1960), pp. 1-10.

FOOTNOTES TO CHAPTER IX

1. Cf. Karl Marx and Frederick Engels, *The Manifesto of the Communist Party, Karl Marx Selected Works*, ed. V Adoratsky, 2 vols. (Moscow-Leningrad, 1935-36), I, p. 228, and Engels', *Socialism: Utopian and Scientific, ibid.*, I, p. 188, where the demise of political authority is predicted. V. I. Lenin saw the harmony of the classless society to be the effect of converting "political" functions of the state into simple administrative functions. *The State and Revolution* in *Lenin Selected Works* (Moscow, 1952), 2 vols. in 4, II, Part I, p. 305n. A contemporary Soviet political writer, Georgi Shaknozarov, holds that the Soviet public organizations are not state organs and are no longer "political organizations." Cf. "When the State Has Withered Away," slightly abridged translation of "From the State to Communist Self-Government," *Politicheskoe Samoobrazovanie*, 1960, No. 8, appearing in *The Soviet Review*, I, (Nov., 1960), pp. 64-65. Hereafter cited as Shaknozarov, *WSHWA*.
2. Shaknozarov, *WSHWA*, p. 58; emphasis added. Cf. "Lenin — znamia nashei epokhi," *Kommunist*, 1961, No. 5, pp. 7-8, as cited in John N. Hazard, "The Function of Law," *Survey*, No. 38 (1961), p. 77.
3. "Das zukünftige Staatswesen der communistischen Gesellschaft," Brief auf W. Bracke, 5 Mai, 1875, in "Zur Kritik des Sozial-demokratischen Parteiprogramms," *Die Neue Zeit*, XI, 1, p. 573.
4. *Grundsätze des Kommunismus*, in *Historische-Kritische Gesamtausgabe* (Frankfort [etc.] 1927-1932), Abt. I, Bd. 6, p. 518.
5. *The State and Revolution*, p. 306; emphasis added.
6. "Thoughts About the Future," *Oktyabr*, No. 3 (March, 1961), pp. 140-146, as reprinted in *Current Digest of the Soviet Press*, XII, No. 15 (May 11, 1960), p. 13; emphasis added.
7. Speech at 21st CPSU Congress, *Pravda*, January 28, 1959, reprinted in *Current Digest of the Soviet Press*, XI, No. 5 (March 11, 1959), pp. 13-17; emphasis added.
8. For a description of spontaneous or substantive control see p. 204.
9. Shaknozarov, *WSHWA*, pp. 64-65.
10. Cf. *The Program of CPSU*, adopted by the XXII Party Congress in Moscow, October-November, 1961, in Dan N. Jacobs (ed.), *The New Communist Manifesto and Related Documents*, 2d. ed. (New York, 1962),

p. 227, where the highly organized aspect of classless society is brought out.
11. Lenin, *The State and Revolution*, p. 292.
12. Those people guilty of anti-social activities who are sanctioned by these vehicles of public order would not be, for the most part, in a legal sense "criminals." The sanction imposed is not primarily of the nature of punishment, but rather it serves an educative and redemptive role with the assumption of responsibility by the community for the wayward's disorder and for his social salvation. Cf. *Pravda Ukrainy* (Kiev), June 10, 1962, as cited in *Problems of Communism*, XI, No. 6 (November-December, 1962), p. 12; A. I. Makarov, "The Public Organizations of Moscow's Kuibyshev Borough in the Struggle Against Violations of Soviet Law and the Rules of Socialist Society," *Sovetskoye gosudarstvo i pravo*, No. 10, 1960, in *Current Digest of the Soviet Press*, XII, No. 46 (December 14, 1960), pp. 10-12; and Herbert Ritvo, "Totalitarianism Without Coercion?," *Problems of Communism*, IX, No. 6 (November-December, 1960), p. 26. Hereafter cited as Ritvo, *TWC*.

Khrushchev thinks that if there are to be any true criminals in communist society, mental disorder will be the primary, if not the sole cause of their crime. Cf. *Pravda*, May 23, 1959, as cited in Erich Goldhagen, "The Glorious Future — Realities and Chimeras," *Problems of Communism*, IX, No. 6 (November-December, 1960), p. 16. Hereafter cited as Goldhagen, *GFRC*.
13. Speech at 21st CPSU Congress, *loc. cit*, p. 16. Cf. Jeremy R. Azrael, "Is Coercion Withering Away?," *Problems of Communism*, XI, No. 6 (November-December, 1962), p. 12 (hereafter cited as Azrael, *ICWA*), and Goldhagen, *GFRC*, p. 18.
14. Cf. P. S. Romashkin (ed.), *Fundamentals of Soviet Law*, trans. Yuri Sdobnikov (Moscow, 1960), pp. 14-20, and "The Role of Persuasion and Coercion in the Soviet State," *Sovetskoye gosudarstvo i pravo*, No. 2, 1960, as cited in Ritvo, *TWC*, p. 26.
15. Speech to the 13th Komsomol Congress, *Pravda*, April 2, 1958, as cited in Ritvo, *TWC*, p. 22.
16. Speech to 21st CPSU Congress, *loc. cit.*, p. 15.
17. *Kommunist*, No. 10, 1960. On this matter of the recent creation of the people's militia see Romashkin, *Fundamentals of Soviet Law*, p. 19, and Ritvo, *TWC*, pp. 23-24.
18. *Izvestia*, March 4, 1960; *Komsomolskaia pravda*, August 27, and October 6, 1960. Some offenses consisted of illegal night time searches to check on individuals' moral behavior, beatings administered to young people and, in one case, a citizen's death by assault. Cf. Ritvo, *TWC*, p. 24, and Azrael, *ICWA*, pp. 12-13.

19. Cf. Ritvo, *TWC*, p. 24.
20. See Chapter VI above. It may be noted in passing that the apparent failure of the Marxist to realize that certain realms of social disorder cannot be adequately controlled by means of sanctions guaranteed by agents other than the agent of the disorder himself, may become the insuperable obstacle in the process of conversion from the mode of coercion to that of persuasion in the area of social control.

At the same time, it must not be overlooked that as long as the sanction would remain entirely within the mode of persuasion, there is no area of human behavior which could, at least in theory, necessarily be excluded from the field of public control. Such a universal sanctioning principle is to be found, for example, in that much misunderstood and abused principle of Christianity known as "fraternal correction."

21. These "anti-parasite" laws, in point of fact, have never been ratified in the three largest Soviet republics (the RSFSR, the Ukraine, and Belorussia) which contain over 80 per cent of the total population. Likewise, they have been treated with considerable reserve in Soviet publications, and may be subject to further revision before they are finally accepted universally. Cf. Ritvo, *TWC*, p. 24.
22. Cf. Azrael, *ICWA*, p. 13.
23. *Zaria vostoka*, September 6, 1960, as cited in Ritvo, *TWC*, p. 24.
24. For a concise but valuable analysis of "anti-parasite" laws and the "public meeting," see Ritvo, *TWC*, pp. 24-25 and Azrael, *ICWA*, pp. 12-13.
25. Cf. Harold J. Berman, *Justice in Russia: An Interpretation of Soviet Law* (Cambridge, Mass., 1950), p. 266.
26. Khrushchev, Speech to 21st CPSU Congress, *loc. cit.*, p. 16. See also Vladimir Gsovski, *Soviet Civil Law*, 2 vols. (Ann Arbor, 1948-49), I, pp. 818 and 838; Azrael, *ICWA*, p. 13; Ritvo, *TWC*, p. 25.
27. Cf. "Draft: Model Statute on Comrades' Courts," *Izvestia*, October 24, 1959, *Current Digest of the Soviet Press*, XI, No. 43 (November 25, 1959), pp. 13-15; Solomon M. Schwarz, "The Muted Voices from Below," *Problems of Communism*, Vol. IX, No. 6 (November-December, 1960), pp. 43-44; Ritvo, *TWC*, pp. 25-26; Berman, *Justice in Russia*, p. 266.
28. For descriptions of comrades' courts in action, see Paul Barton, "The Current Status of the Soviet Worker," *Problems of Communism*, IX, No. 4 (July-August, 1960), pp. 18-27, and Harry and Rebecca Timbres, *We Don't Ask Utopia* (New York, 1939), pp. 211ff. The Timbres' description is also found in Berman, *Justice in Russia*, pp. 267-269.
29. Cf. N. Mironov, "State Security is a Cause of All the People," *Kommunist*, No. 11, 1960, pp. 39-48; Romashkin, "The Role of Persuasion and Coercion in the Soviet State," as cited in Ritvo, *TWC*, p. 26; Romashkin, "New Stage in the Development of the Soviet State," *Sovetskoye*

gosudarstvo i pravo, No. 10, 1960, in *Current Digest of the Soviet Press*, XX, No. 46 (December 14, 1960), p. 3.

30. A. Robert Caponigri, "Introduction to Political Theory" (book in preparation for publication), Chapter I. Hereafter cited as Caponigri, *IPT*. This definition of social control should be compared to several others given by Kurt H. Wolff, "Social Control," in Joseph S. Roucek (ed.), *Contemporary Sociology* (New York, 1958), p. 111.

Professor Caponigri in his forthcoming book, has utilized the conclusions reached by Ross, Cooley, La Piere and others working in the field of social control to solve the particular problem of identifying political control. In this work he clearly distinguishes political control from social control in general and defines its essential characteristics.

31. Analogy has been rightly called "deliberate ambiguity." It is simply a process of knowledge growth by which one moves from concepts that are more evident to sense experience and, therefore, better known, to a knowledge of concepts that are less evident, through the use of identical linguistic terms which then assume added imposition of meaning. Cf. Charles DeKoninck, *The Hollow Universe* (London, 1960), pp. 83-84. This approach to knowledge progression is basically Aristotelian, as is evidenced in Book V (Delta) of the *Metaphysics*, 1012b33-1025a35.

32. The better political theorists, to be sure, have properly made many of these distinctions. See, for example, Harold D. Lasswell, *The Analysis of Political Behavior: An Empirical Approach* (New York, 1948), pp. 7-8; Bertrand de Jouvenel, *Sovereignty: An Inquiry into the Political Good*, trans. J. F. Huntington (Chicago, 1957), pp. 15-25; Sebastian De Grazio, *The Political Community: A Study of Anomie* (Chicago, 1948), introduction, pp. ix,-xvii; Karl Loewenstein, *Political Power and the Governmental Process* (Chicago, 1957), pp. 13-17; R. M. MacIver, *Society: A Textbook of Sociology* (New York, 1937), pp. 12-13; Ernest Barker, *Greek Political Theory*, 3rd ed. (London, 1947), pp. 11-12.

Other distinguished European names include Gaetano Mosca, Vilfredo Pareto, Max Weber, Robert Michels, Gerhard Ritter and Guglielmo Ferrero.

33. Shaknozarov, *WSHWA*, pp. 64-65.

34. Cf. Harry Elmer Barnes, "Sociological Contributions to Political Theory," in Joseph S. Roucek (ed.), *Twentieth Century Political Thought* (New York, 1946), pp. 39ff.

Georges Gurvitch descriptively defines social control as ". . . the sum total or rather the whole of cultural patterns, social symbols, collective spiritual meanings, values, ideas and ideals, as well as acts and processes directly connected with them, whereby inclusive society, and every particular group, and every participating individual member overcome tensions and conflicts within themselves through temporary equilibria and take steps for new creative efforts." Georges Gurvitch and Wilbert E. Moore (eds.), *Twentieth Century Sociology* (New York, 1945), p. 291.

35. Value, in this context, is simply any principle which can reduce the initial or original indetermination of conscious human behavior. Within the context of social control, value, moreover, must mean group valuation, for values to which social control is orientated are socially approved or disapproved. Cf. Caponigri, *IPT*, Chapter V, and Harold D. Lasswell, *Democratic Character*, in *The Political Writings of Harold D. Lasswell* (Glencoe, Ill., 1951), p. 474. This notion of value should be compared to that of Ralph Barton Perry, *Realms of Value: A Critique of Human Civilization* (Cambridge, Mass., 1954), pp. 2-14, and *The General Theory of Value: Its Meanings and Basic Principles Construed in Terms of Interest* (Cambridge, Mass., 1950), especially, Chapters I-V.

36. Caponigri, *IPT*, Chapter III. Cf. Jouvenel, *Sovereignty*, pp. 32-33.

37. Thus, in the pursuit of intellectual values in classroom grouping, for example, there spontaneously arises an ordering or relationship between teacher and pupil. A somewhat similar ordering arises spontaneously in any human grouping for the sake of value pursuit.

38. Caponigri, *IPT*, Chapter II.

39. Cf. Jouvenel, *Sovereignty*, pp. 2n, 20 and 297, and Charles E. Merriam, *Political Power*, in Harold D. Lasswell, Charles E. Merriam and T. V. Smith, *A Study of Power* (Glencoe, Ill., 1950), Chapter II.

40. Caponigri, *IPT*, Chapter II.

41. A more complete and systematic analysis of the political order as a species of social control is to be found in Caponigri, *IPT*, especially Chapters II and III.

42. See Chapter VI, above.

43. See Max Weber's descriptive definition of this mode in "Die Wirtschaftethik der Weltreligionen," as translated in H. H. Gerth and C. Wright Mills (eds.), *From Max Weber: Essays in Sociology* (New York, 1946), p. 299.

44. For a fuller explanation of the four modes of inter-personal, inter-group relationships, see Chapter X below.

45. The concept "state" is completely neutral. We must be cautious in acceptance of those manuals and texts that hold that the state is natural to society. Rather, it seems it is the political order that is "natural" to man and his society. (It is the political order, perhaps, that is meant by the term "state" in many texts.) The state, on the other hand, would seem to be in the first and most meaningful imposition of the word, *artificial* — that is, it is the product of man's reason, a work of art. As such, not only its particular form but seemingly its very existence is dependent upon the specific substantive values chosen by the society. It is within the realm

of experience that the very form of government as set forth by a constitution can be one of the substantive values of the society, as is the case in the United States of America. This does not allow for the acceptance of the Marxist thesis that the state is somehow "intrinsically" evil, being always and necessarily exploitative. Certainly, some forms of government are patently exploitative, but there seems no inevitable cause/effect relationship between the structuralization of political functions and exploitation.

In point of fact, all societies of the past and present have had governmental forms. Is it to be concluded that such are necessary to human society? It seems not. Although it is true that government is and has been omnipresent in society, it is also true that there has never been a society in which the affective and moral modes of social relationships have been in complete pre-eminence. In the order of possibility, a particular society in which justice and friendship are pre-eminent may choose not to use statutory law, or the structuralization of political forms as set forth in a constitution and guaranteed by coercive sanction. Such a society seemingly would not be in need of a government or legal apparatus. Nonetheless, such a society would, of necessity, have within it a political order — that is, it would necessarily have within it functions which were independent of the pursuit of the substantive values of the society, and which were disposed to secure and maintain the order necessary that these substantive values be pursued. Such functions could possibly be carried out — without their becoming structuralized into permanent "offices" — by authoritative public organizations similar in nature to those described in the present chapter. It must be emphasized that such could be the case if, and only if, friendship and justice were in such pre-eminence that society could arbitrarily decide whether or not to live under the rule of law and constitutional government.

This point will be pursued further in the following chapter.

CHAPTER X

SOCIAL POWER AND CLASSLESS SOCIETY

Karl Marx looks at the perfection of society as the effect of a total absence of exploitation in the social relationships of man. Exploitation, for Marx, lay in the use of power for the maintenance of the existing mode of production for the economic, political, legal and moral dominance of one class over another.[1] As exploitation declines within the proletarian society, the state uses measures of persuasion rather than those of coercion to bring about and guarantee its end values.[2] Insofar as the persuasive mode of social control becomes pre-eminent, to that extent may the society truly be called altruistic.[3] To discover whether this last statement is able to be maintained as a thesis by the Marxist, it is imperative that the notion of *social power* be analyzed.[4] This analysis will, in the first place, make possible an understanding of the notion of *altruistic power*. Secondly, it will permit an examination of the various forms altruistic power can take. Lastly, it will allow us to judge whether such power could be the exclusive mode used in social relationships within a society.

Analysis of Social Power

Power is present in the political order in two ways. Obviously, power is first of all present as the object of political control. Such control is not directly concerned with institutions or other concrete manifestations of power, but rather, is directed towards the power itself.[5] Secondly, power is present in the political order as the very substance of that order. In other words, the political order, like every form of control, is itself power. Thus, power appears to be a natural endowment somewhat inherent in society and social control.[6] Power has a certain over-all ultimacy which all forms of social control must confront and which, moreover, tends to manifest itself in the very working of the social control itself.

From common experience, socially significant power in its broadest connotation can be descriptively defined as: *the capacity to elicit response in another with or without consent.*[7] An analysis of this definition will bring forth some valuable insight.

First of all, it is a definition of *social* power that is given. Society is composed of human persons. Social power will, of course, include only that power that has reference to the activity of persons; it is that power having its *situs* in persons acting, whether this be individually or acting in a collectivity. Impersonal forms of power, such as forces of nature or the capacity of a person to exercise sheer physical coercion, are not entirely socially irrelevant and are not to be completely excluded from the definition, but they cannot occupy a central place in the definition of social power, for history testifies that no determinate power whether economic, physical, evolutionary or psychological has been able to establish itself as the proximate motivation source in human society.[8]

Power elicits response in another. The term "elicits" includes many different modes of relationships between persons in which power can be present and effective. Another important implication is that the reality of power is to be found in the act elicited rather than in any force expended. When no response is forthcoming, it seems necessary to deny the reality of power. Nevertheless the response need not always be a fact. What is more essential to the notion of power is the capacity or the expectancy that is present. Thus, in the field of social control it is not the actual control but the capacity of control which is of the greatest importance. Power which is absolutely coextensive with actual effects is relatively sporadic.[9]

Social power is interpersonal. It is exercised by a human person or group. Likewise, the action elicited by social power is action in and of another human subject or group. Thus, social power is not technological, that is, not directed towards eliciting reaction in nature or artifacts. Hence, social power in the last instance must be termed *moral* power. This is to say, social power is truly social only insofar as the action elicited is in essence human action — *voluntary* or moral action. Insofar as the response elicited is involuntary, the power exercised to that extent ceases to be social only insofar as the action elicited is in essence human ac- power becomes impersonal; the human subject becomes an object of nature to be manipulated. There is indeed power present, but it is not to be termed social power. That such pseudo-technological power is at times present in social situations need not be argued. It exists in society in almost an infinity of degrees of intensity, beginning in a minor form in much of modern advertising, where there is an attempt to change the manner of consumer sales from that of choice to that of impulse and continuing on to the extreme forms of political exploitation characterized by use of dictatorial, tyrannical force.

Social power seems to oscillate somewhere within the two extremes of naked force or absolute coercion at one end, and complete consent in the respondent subject on the other. To the degree to which social power is exercised without consent, to that extent does it become manipulative, technological and in a literal sense, inhuman. If the consent of a human being to the exercise of power is totally absent (and this is relatively rare in social matters), then the power exercised is in no way to be designated social power, but is pure force, or violence. Power exercised without any consent whatsoever cannot be considered as social because such force simply disregards the integrity, freedom and inviolability of the human person. Such a use of power response is in a mode identical to the response of an object of nature to a natural force.[10] On the other hand, to the extent to which the consent of the responding agent is full and complete, to that degree does social power become human and, therefore, more proper or perfect within the society of man.

Full consent was termed an extreme in relation to social power, not in the sense of an excess or defect, but rather as a perfection of social power — just as naked force is an extreme in the sense of complete imperfection of human power. Social power, insofar as the response occurs with some consent, has been called a "humanization of force" or a "transcendence of force."[11] All power approaches social effectiveness as it approaches consent; social power in its perfection is the capacity to elicit complete consent. Power with consent is designated a *transcendence* of force because such power is seen to be a realization and fulfillment of what is most obviously *power,* that is, physical coercion, on a higher plane. The transcendence of force, or physical coercion, means the translation of the response to power to a higher principle — to one of several principles which will be seen to ameliorate the element of pure force.[12] Thus translated, power is re-established on a human basis, a basis rooted in the realization by society of man's dignity and inviolability; the realization that the individual himself or the group is the proper initiative cause of response to elicited action.

There are numerous modes of social relationship. There are numerous ways in which force is transcended in the exercise of social power — numerous ways by which response in others is elicited in a human way. Each of these modes is distinguished by the particular principle or value which serves as the proximate cause of the consent to respond to the elicitation of another. Among these many modes there are four which common experience manifests as especially socially effective. These four are undoubtedly the predominant ones in most societies. It is within these four modes of transcendence of force that social power is most often present.

The first of these modes may be identified as the *affective mode.*[13] Such manner of social relationship would be comparable to that described as *friendship* by Aristotle in Books VIII and IX of the *Nicomachean Ethics.* Such interpersonal, intergroup relationship would be especially characterized by a mutual desiring of the other party's well-being more for his own sake than for any lesser value that might be derived from the relationship for one's own private good or gain. It is an identification of another's well-being with one's own well-being. The motive on which this mutual identification of well-being may rest is variable, as Aristotle points out.[14] Each may wish the well-being of the other because of the assistance or usefulness which each renders the other. In such a relationship the affection arises from utility. Again, the mutual affection may arise simply because of the pleasure derived from the other's presence. Lastly, the affective mode in its perfection would consist in a persisting mutual friendship based upon the very character and personality of the persons involved irrespective of their being a source of utility and pleasure.[15] Such social relationship is relatively rare, but is to be found most often in the associations between members of the family group — and in particular in the relations between husband and wife.

Affection or friendship is easily seen to be the most effective principle by which response is elicited in the exercise of social power. It is within this affective mode that consent is most easily made complete; it is within this mode that social relationships are the most definitively "human," and the transcendence of force supreme.

The second mode of social relationship may be referred to as the *ethical mode*. Basically the relationships between persons and groups within this mode are grounded in the common notion of justice. The principle through which the consent to respond is given is the realization of the *right* of the elicitor to the response sought. This right may be in the order of material goods or may concern intangibles such as truth, honor, and so on. While the practice of the affective mode is not always within the capacity of the individual or group toward all other individuals or groups, the ethical mode may serve as a substitute for the affective mode of human relationship, while, at the same time, not seriously depreciating the specifically human mode of consent and the high degree of transcendence of force. The recognition of the right of the elicitor to an appropriate response is rooted, first of all in the recognition and acceptance by the respondent of the values, whether substantive or formal, belonging to that society or group in virtue of which there is occasioned the exercise of the particular instance of social power, and secondly, in the guarantee by the respondent that he will sanction himself if the proper response is not forthcoming.

The ethical mode offers, as does the affective mode, an effective principle of response to social power — a principle through which consent can reach a high level of perfection, and on occasion, be complete. Consequently, the pre-eminence of this form of social intercourse represents both a coveted goal for all societies and, at the same time, a valid norm by which a society may be judged by mankind.

The third mode of interpersonal, intergroup relationship may be designated the *utilitarian mode*. Within this mode the controlling principle of response elicitation is the utility resulting to the respondent from the response. Likewise, the motive of the elicitor in exercising the social power is utility. Utility in this context may be defined as "that which serves as a means to an end or goal of human activity." In the utilitarian mode, the exercise of and response to social power flows from the mutual usefulness of the elicitation and response to the individual or group values sought by the parties involved. The consent and the consequent transcendence of force is proportionate to the degree that the response serves as a means towards the achievement of the individual and social goals of the respondent. Accordingly, the range of degree of force within this mode is quite extensive and may oscillate between a total absence based on complete consent as one extreme, to almost absolute coercion or exploitation as the other extreme. The utilitarian mode is especially evident within the economic sphere of human activity where the opportunity for mutual social usefulness is prevalent.[16]

The fourth mode of social intercourse may be termed the *rational-legal mode*. When this mode of relationship is present, the principle of response elicitation is something quite impersonal and entirely extrinsic to the elicitor or the respondent. Within this mode the submission or consent is not based upon belief, personal devotion, respect for the persons eliciting, tradition or status. Rather, as Max Weber points out, the consent is based on legal authority, that is, it rests:

. . . upon an impersonal bond to the generally defined and functional "duty of office." The official duty — like the corresponding right to exercise authority: the "jurisdictional competency" — is fixed by *rationally established* norms, by enactments, decrees, and regulations, in such a manner that the legitimacy of the authority becomes the legality of the general rule, which is purposely thought out, enacted and announced with formal correctness.[17]

Thus, the submission to social power in the rational-legal mode flows from the recognition in the respondent of both a legal duty to be fulfilled by means of the response and the existence of a guarantee of "painful" coercive sanction by social authority if the response is not forthcoming. This mode, as such, permits of a range of transcendence of force beginning with a full consent based on a motive of "duty for duty's sake" through a consent based on no other motive than the avoidance of the sanction.[18]

These four modes of human relationship are not to be considered mutually exclusive. Several may be simultaneously present because of a multiplicity of response motives in any single occurrence of social power. In fact, that response within the rational-legal mode which would be made with full human consent, that is, which would be made because of a moral duty or obligation, irrespective of any fear of legal or social sanction, would seem able to be posited only through the invoking of the ethical mode simultaneously. For this reason the rational-legal mode would not seem to have the potentialities for transcendence of force as would the affective and ethical modes. Consent in accordance with the rational-legal mode is restricted by the force of the guaranteed coercive sanction. Hence, coercion is never completely transcended — except when the coercive aspects of the response are modified by persuasion to the extent that the response is guaranteed by the simultaneous recognition of, first, a duty in justice irrespective of the legal sanction and, secondly, the recognition of the legal duty and its corresponding sanction. This, however, amounts to the invocation of both the ethical and the rational-legal modes concurrently as the principles on which response to an instance of social power rests. Of itself, then, the rational-legal mode can only imperfectly transcend force.

The utilitarian mode would seem capable of totally transcending force only in the case where the goal of the individual or group responding to power, of which the response is a means, is desirable in itself. The perfection of the consent will be then lessened and take on the character of exploitation to the degree to which the goal sought through the response is considered by the respondent to be desirable only as a lesser evil then that which will occur if the response is not given.[19]

Pre-eminence of Comradeship and Social Justice

Let us now see how these different modes of social power fit into the context of Marxist classless society. Karl Marx saw the utilitarian philosophies of France and England as playing a progressive role in history in that they helped to clear the ground of feudal anachronisms. These philosophies — represented by Helvetius and Holbach on the Continent, and by Hobbes, Locke and especially later on by Bentham and Mill in England — are to be interpreted, in the eyes of Marx, as attempts to assure the full development of the individual in a social intercourse liberated from the old feudal bonds.[20] These bonds were the political, patriarchal and religious institutions of exploitation arising under feudalism and still existing in Europe to the extent that absolute monarchy was then still in vogue. Liberation from feudal exploitation could be brought about in the 18th century only by the individual being able to carve for himself a new career through which he could realize his highest capabilities. Such could come about only through competition. But a state of competitiveness could exist only when the philosophy of hedonistic utility was recognized and put into social practice. Within this philosophy, all forms of interpersonal, intergroup relationships are subsumed under and become disguised manifestations of the utilitarian mode of relationship. This relation of utility, claims Marx, has one, quite definite meaning — "I can only serve myself insofar as I deprive others of something (exploitation de l'homme par l'homme)."[21]

Historically, the 18th century brought forth this philosophy of utility, and historically the 18th century was a century characterized by this utilitarian theory becoming Western man's ideology. The different phases in the progress of the theory of utility were intimately related to the different epochs of bourgeois development — from the undeveloped bourgeoisie fighting for its freedom from absolute monarchy epitomized by Helvetius and Holbach, to the ruling and developed bourgeoisie as characterized by Bentham and Mill, where the complete coincidence of the theory of utility and political economy is achieved. To the Benthamites, the public utility reduces itself to the common utility observable in general competition where man exploits his fellow man. Through the introduction of economic relations, the definite modes of exploitation of the different classes were introduced — for the kind of competition or exploitation by which an individual brings about the common utility is dependent upon his position in life, that is, it is dependent upon one's relationship to the factors of production. Thus, while the 18th century saw the demise of feudal exploitation, the new utilitarian political economy saw a new, more progressive exploitation arise wherein the owner-bourgeoisie deprives the worker-proletariat, and the proletariat, in turn, struggles to exploit the bourgeoisie. From this point forward, Marx asserts, the utilitarian theory is of no more service to man, but yet still remains in force to serve only as a pure apologia to be used by the bourgeoisie, the dominant class, for the maintenance of existing conditions. As such, what was once the true and progressive interpretation of social facts has now become itself reactionary and detrimental to mankind's emancipation.[22]

For Marx, then, the utilitarian mode, it would seem, is no longer worthy of man. This mode of social relationship and social control represents a reprehensible form of human activity. Power exercised in this manner violates the human dignity of one class insofar as it manipulates that class for the other's benefit while, at the same time, preventing the subservient class from responding to the exercise of power in an uncoerced fashion. Human relations of the future will not include such a use of power. If social relationships based on utility must remain while the proletariat maintains itself as the dominant class in its struggle to eliminate the bourgeoisie, it is to be remembered that this is but a transitory moment — albeit a necessary one — in the dialectical process of man towards scientific freedom.

As has been pointed out,[23] Marx and Engels saw in the relationship of utility the primitive rise of the state and law. Lenin, echoing his patriarchs, maintains that the state is "a machine for upholding the dominance of one class over another."[24] As such, the purpose of the state is totally utilitarian, and all of its activities are subsumed under the utilitarian principle insofar as they tend to realize the will of the dominant class.

Since the realization of the will of the dominant class is attained with the aid of law, that is, "binding rules of conduct ordinarily in the form of legislation,"[25] law in Marxist eyes is, always and in all possible forms, an organ of utility. If, in the scientific society of the future, the utilitarian mode of social relationship is no longer to be considered a befitting form of human activity for the Marxist, this may be interpreted to mean that in a classless society utility would not be a licit or proper principle for either the elicitation of social power or for a response to it. If, too, law is considered to be but a mere organ of utility, then it follows logically for the Marxist that the rational-legal mode also would be a degradation of human dignity within the classless society. Thus, legal obligation and its corresponding coercive sanction, because it is of its nature exploitative, is likewise an unworthy principle of power response. Lacking any measure of transcendence of force, it results in mere manipulation of some people within the society for the interest of others.

Hence, it may be claimed that classless society as visualized by Marxist ideology would necessarily be characterized by the overwhelming pre-eminence of the affective and ethical modes of social relationship. The rate of advance to the stage of perfect communism in the socialist state can thus be objectively judged by ascertaining the prevalence of comradeship among the workers and the respect for social justice among individuals and groups — both private and public. The latter is most surely made evident, if we are to believe current Soviet writers,[26] by the diminution of coercive sanction and a corresponding replacement with persuasive sanction within current socialist society. This lessening of coercive sanction, as has been pointed out in the previous chapter, is brought about in Soviet society by the gradual replacement of the functions of the organs of exploitation and utility — the police, militia and courts — by parapolice and parajudicial bodies composed of volunteers whose functions are predominantly persuasive by nature.

The growth of the affective mode based on comradeship is seen by Lenin to most surely be hastened by the type of social activity best characterized by that voluntary self-sacrificing activity of certain workers practiced during the *subbotnik* movement (voluntary labor days).[27] During the dark days of the civil war in the Spring of 1919, certain communist workers and other sympathizers in Moscow organized themselves into groups and gave of their free time six hours in exhaustive work on Saturdays without pay in order that some important railroad repair work be finished. This idea quickly caught on in other districts and the subbotnik movement became an important factor in the subsequent victory of the Red Army over the Kolchakites, Denikinites and others of the White forces.[28] Work done during this movement, claims Lenin, showed a two hundred to three hundred per cent increase in productivity over labor performed for wages.[29]

Lenin looked upon the subbotnik movement as being of great import because it was initiated by the workers themselves who could not reap any possible short term gain from these voluntary actions.[30] Moreover, it was labor performed without pay, and at "an enormous increase in productivity."[31] For Lenin, who above all was interested in preserving the infant and rather sickly Soviet state during a not-too-successful stage of a civil war, the most important aspect of the subbotnik movement was the increase in productivity.[32] Nonetheless, he had the foresight to see in the self-sacrificing labors of the workers, "the *actual* beginning of *Communism*,"[33] where comradeship and concern for one's fellowmen is no longer restricted "to the workers personally or to their 'close' kith and kin, but to their 'distant' kith and kin, i.e., to society as a whole, to tens and hundreds of millions of people. . . ."[34]

The present Soviet regime likewise believes social activity similar to that of the subbotnik movement is an efficient and necessary means to break down the existing barriers between private and public life and, consequently, to progress towards the total pre-eminence of the affective as well as the moral mode of social relationship among its citizens. Accordingly, in 1958, there was a nationwide campaign to enlist workers in the *Brigades of Communist Labor,* a movement which is said to have rallied over five million workers in more than four hundred thousand brigades as of May, 1960.[35] The primary function of this "spontaneous movement" among Soviet workers is, as was the case in the subbotnik movement, to increase labor productivity through efficiency, technology and advanced methods of work. Nevertheless, the members of the brigades are also to strive to master modern scientific, technological and cultural knowledge so as to be of use to the entire collective and to society as well. Moreover, the members should cultivate in themselves the best features of the new society. They are to develop themselves both mentally and physically and to be exemplary in their daily life. They are to look upon public duty as constituting a moral obligation. Finally, they are to struggle actively for a new morale.[36] As one Soviet writer has asserted:

> Communist labor brigade members and shock workers, for the first time in the history of competition, are imposing on themselves obligations of a moral character. They pledge to combat the vestiges of the past in the consciousness of the people, to strengthen comradely solidarity and collaboration in work and living, and to be the guardians of the norms of socialist society. This is one of the most essential characteristics of the new movement.[37]

Whether the emergence of the "new Communist man" will come about through the labor brigades as predicted is certainly a moot question, even among Soviet theoreticians.[38] Nevertheless, it is clear that the goal of Marxist ideology, whatever the roads it might travel, is to be found in a classless society characterized by a scientific altruism based on a comradeship and an all-embracing justice among its component human parts.

Within Marxist writings there seems to exist a lack of recognition of even the slightest possibility for the transcendence of force within the utilitarian and rational-legal modes in the society of the future. As has been pointed out, in Marxist thought the utilitarian mode is at once both the cause and the historical brain child of bourgeois exploitation. As such, it is inexorably enmeshed in the mode of production existing in that society in which individuals privately appropriate the products and cultural benefits of social labor. And if the utilitarian mode is still in some way present in socialist society, the first stage of communism, it is so because remnants of capitalistic thought and habit still present within such a society require that the fruits of social production be apportioned according to the usefulness and value of the labor expended. Although Marx does admit a certain degree of justice in such distribution in that the workers receive in proportion to their contribution to society, nevertheless under the socialist system he maintains, some may receive more than they need, while others are receiving less than they require for a truly human existence. Hence, he cautions that distribution based on utility will not harmonize with man's social dignity and happiness in the classless society to come.[39]

For the Marxist, law and governmental activity serve as organs of utility for the dominant class. They, too, would be out of place in the society of the future. The present encirclement of socialist society by hostile bourgeois states, and the aforementioned remnants of bourgeois thought and institutions within socialist society require the existence of a state, a constitution, legal statutes and agencies of coercion for the present. However, the gradual transformation of human nature in the socialist state, as well as the revolutionary demise of the bourgeoisie, is destined to bring about in society conditions whereby the rational-legal mode of social power will be meaningless and the character of consent to be given to it degrading to the human person.

As has been seen, it is the exploitative character of these two modes of social power that allows the Marxist to view them as unworthy principles of human activity in classless society. Yet it can be argued that utility and juridical procedure, although admittedly often used purely for exploitation, nevertheless are not inexorably directed to exploitation. They might serve as principles of consent to social power by which the respondent in his consent is not thereby deprived materially or otherwise by the elicitor. A conjunction of the ethical and utilitarian principles of consent could, under certain circumstances, feasibly prove more advantageous towards attaining the values of a society than an elicitation of consent merely within the ethical mode alone.[40]

In regard to the affective mode also, utility has always had its place. As has been seen, the very reality of friendship or affection in certain instances has emerged because of the mutual utility involved in the social relationships of persons. Yet, such utility can in no way be considered exploitative since in such a friendship of utility it is the usefulness of the response to social power that causes the elicitor to desire the good fortune of the respondent, and vice versa.[41] Thus, in friendship as well as within the ethical mode, non-exploitative utility is often present. It is, apparently, advantageous towards attaining even those social values which the Marxist would consider as transcending class interest.

As with the utilitarian mode, so also with the rational-legal mode there is the possibility of a nonexploitative invocation of consent. It has been shown in another place,[42] that for the Marxist, socialist law — such as that prevailing in the Soviet Union — has a close bond with morality. One aspect of this inter-relationship lies in the empirical fact that socialist law becomes a salubrious factor in the development and confirmation of socialist moral views in the community. Through the application of the law, the citizens' consciousness of their moral obligations to the community at large and to each other are strengthened. Hence, the elicitation of human consent through the ethical principle, by the Marxist's own insistence,[43] can be greatly assured by the simultaneous invocation of the rational-legal principle. Of course, the observance of socialist law is guaranteed by the coercive sanction of the state. Insofar as the sanction is of the nature of constraint, the elicitation by means of the legal principle can be considered exploitative. Coercion in socialist society is necessary, in the Marxist mind — or at least in the Soviet Marxist mind — because of the existing remnants of a bourgeois culture and thought in the consciousness of some of the citizens of the socialist state.

In classless society, coercion is to cease and to be replaced by persuasion. It is by means of persuasion that the formal values or norms of this society are maintained. Yet the predominance of persuasion as the principal means of social control — that is, the predominance of the affective and ethical modes of social intercourse — would not necessarily preclude the simple averment of the formal values or norms within the rational-legal mode. Such a declaration of the formal values within this mode could become, by preferential choice, one of the substantive values of a society — classless or otherwise.[44] In this circumstance, the use of the rational-legal mode would "transcend" coercion and exploitation. In a society, then, of such perfection that norms are maintained by persuasion alone, the rational-legal mode could still be invoked in the political order. Such invocation would be purely arbitrary in the sense that the use of this mode would be entirely dependent upon the preferential choice of the members of the society to make "the maintenance of social order *through law*" a substantive value. It is to be continually emphasized, however, that the arbitrary choice to maintain social order *not* by means of law is open only to a society in which the affective and ethical modes are in such pre-eminence that there could be reasonable hope of maintaining social order by persuasion alone. That such a society has never existed is a patent historical fact; that such a society shall exist in the future might justifiably be criticized as a position more utopian than scientific.[45]

Nevertheless, the utopian aspect of classless society does not allow us to disclaim the attainment of such a society as a legitimate goal for mankind. The ultimate unattainability of a human goal does not destroy its licitness. An analogy with eudaemonic ethics may be of some value. For Aristotle, the ultimate goal for man, the purpose of his proper activity, is happiness.[46] Furthermore, this happiness is to be found in a life of reason in accordance with perfect virtue, along with friendship, the goods of the body and other external goods as reason prescribes.[47] Yet human experience attests that this happiness is neither attained nor maintained in its fullest perfection by any human.[48] Still, the practical impossibility of attainment of complete and unending happiness by terrestrial man does not make the attempt by man to reach this goal impractical or utopian. Insofar as man approaches the attainment of perfect virtue along with the full satisfaction of his bodily and aesthetic needs as prudence appoints, to that extent does he actually attain the ultimate goal of human activity. In the *attempt* to reach perfect happiness, he does in some measure actually possess it.

Proportionately, classless society — even if considered utopian by the non-Marxist — does not thereby become a wholly impractical or an illicit goal for man. To the extent to which society transcends force through the pre-eminence of the affective and ethical modes of human relationship, that is, insofar as social order is able to be maintained by means of persuasion rather than through coercion or threat of coercion, to that extent does this society become more truly human and more surely capable of producing happiness and contentment. Through the endeavor to attain the goals of classless society, provided the means used are in accordance with the moral and legal customs of all mankind, regardless of class interest—and on this point the world might justly take issue with the Marxist, and especially the Bolshevist—mankind can actually attain, in some measure, these very goals. It is the revitalization of these goals through practical activity that has made the Communist Movement the tremendous social force in the modern world that it is. It is, perhaps, in the reiteration of these same age-old social needs of man that Marxism has rendered its service to mankind.[49]

Suggested Readings

CHAPTER X

Primary Sources

*Lenin, V. I., *A Great Beginning.*
———, *Subbotniks: Report to Moscow City Conference of R.C.P.,* December 20, 1919.
Marx, K., *Critique of the Gotha Programme.*
*———, *Economic and Philosophic Manuscripts of 1844,* III.
Program of the Communist Party of the Soviet Union Adopted by the 22nd Party Congress, 1961, Part II.

Secondary Sources

*Denisov, A. I., "On the Relationship of State and Society in the Period of Transition from Capitalism to Communism," *Current Digest of the Soviet Press,* XII, No. 22 (June 29, 1960), pp. 17-20.
*Fetscher, Iring, "Marx, Engels and the Future Society," *Survey,* No. 38 (October, 1961), pp. 100-110.
*Mironov, N., "Persuasion and Compulsion in Combating Anti-Social Acts," *The Soviet Review,* II, No. 9 (September, 1961), pp. 54-65.
Ritvo, Herbert, "Totalitarianism Without Coercion?," *Problems of Communism,* IX, No. 6 (November-December, 1960), pp. 19-29.
Romashkin, P. S., "New Stages in the Development of the Soviet State," *Current Digest of the Soviet Press,* XII, No. 46 (December 14, 1960), pp. 3-6.

FOOTNOTES TO CHAPTER X

1. Cf. Chapter II, above.
2. Cf. Chapter IX, above. See also P. S. Romashkin (ed.), *Fundamentals of Soviet Law*, trans. Yuri Sdobnikov (Moscow, 1960), pp. 19-20; A. I. Denisov, "On the Relationship of State and Society in the Period of Transition From Capitalism to Communism," *Sovetskoye gosudarstvo i pravo*, No. 4, 1960 in *Current Digest of the Soviet Press*, XII, No. 22 (June 29, 1960), p. 17 (hereafter cited as Denisov, *RSSTCC*); Herbert Ritvo, "Totalitarianism Without Coercion?," *Problems of Communism*, IX, No. 6 (November-December, 1960), pp. 19-29. Hereafter cited as Ritvo, *TWC*.
3. N. Mironov, "Persuasion and Compulsion in Combating Anti-Social Acts," *Kommunist*, No. 3, 1961, as translated in *The Soviet Review*, II, No. 9 (September, 1961), pp. 54-65.
4. For the subsequent analysis of social power, the author is indebted to Professor A. Robert Caponigri's "Introduction to Political Theory" (book in preparation for publication), especially Chapter III. Hereafter cited as Caponigri, *IPT*.
5. Thus "Anti-Trust" laws, as one example, are only incidentally directed towards the corporations given to monopolistic policies. More basically the purpose of these laws is to control the power of which the corporations are the manifestations or concretizations. Cf. Harold D. Lasswell, *The Analysis of Political Behavior: An Empirical Approach* (New York, 1948), pp. 6-7, 37-38, 68, 76.
6. Cf. Bertrand de Jouvenel, *On Power: Its Nature and the History of Its Growth*, trans. J. F. Huntington (New York, 1949), p. 98, and Karl Loewenstein, *Political Power and the Governmental Process* (Chicago, 1957), p. 4.
7. Caponigri, *IPT*, Chapter III. Cf. Bertrand de Jouvenel, *Sovereignty: An Inquiry into the Political Good*, trans. J. F. Huntington (Chicago, 1957), pp. 32-33.
8. Marx and Engels certainly realized this in its full significance. As they point out in the first part of the *Communist Manifesto*, it is class conflict (not blind economic forces of production) that is the true proximate motor of history. On this point see Vernon Venable, *Human Nature: The Marxian View* (New York, 1945), pp. 111-112.

9. On the international scene, the military power of the great nations is manifested by the presence and capacity of their armed forces together with the expectancies these arouse, rather than by the constant use of weapons in combat.

10. It has been argued that consent, either explicit or implicit, is not a necessary condition for the exercise of social power. Force can at times be legitimately or authoritatively enacted, with the justification of the force being rooted in the objective validity of an ideal principle. This objectively valid ideal principle replaces consent as the justification for the elicitation of action. According to this opinion such power can still be designated social, for response to this principle, because it is ideal, is of the very woof and warp of truly human society.

However, it may be remarked in reply that all social power — if only because it issues from human persons — is ultimately the effect of value, for all human activity is a response to value. Now value has been rightly defined in terms of "preferential choice" of alternatives in regard to human activity. (Cf. Harold D. Lasswell, *The Analysis of Political Behavior,* p. 36, p. 65, and *Democratic Character,* in *The Political Writings of Harold D. Lasswell* [Glencoe, Ill., 1951], p. 474. Compare this notion with that of Ralph Barton Perry, *Realms of Value: A Critique of Human Civilization* [Cambridge, Mass., 1954], pp. 2-3). Thus there is a necessary relationship between value and consent. All social power, all power exercised by men on other men, is to be considered legitimate or authoritative insofar as those values toward the realization of which the social power is ordered are to *some extent* accepted by those in whom the action is elicited. The phrase "to some extent" is emphasized to point up the fact that minority groups within a society at times seemingly do not consent to some values prevalent within the social grouping. Yet even here there is at least an imperfect consent to these values when this is deemed necessary for the preservation of higher mutual values. Such would be the consent given by non-Anglican groups in England to the monarch being the head of the established church; the consent given by Republican citizens to repugnant laws passed by a Democratic Congress in the U. S. A.; the consent given to some Communist government measures by Christians behind the Iron Curtain, and so on. If the individual or group can in no way consent to the values towards which the social power is ordered, the power exercised is in the eyes of that individual or group non-authoritative and non-social — it is pure coercion.

There is the occasion where pure force must be exercised against pure force. Such would be the case in war or in the use of power to capture a hardened criminal, resisting arrest, who has rejected the values of society and is forcing his values on society. But even here, if the values towards which the power is ordered is totally rejected by the subject of the elicited action, this power in his regard could not be considered authoritative, or social — it is violence. If the one eliciting the action considers the use of such power as legitimate, it is only because he himself, or those whom he represents have consented to the values to which the use of the power is ordained. Thus it is difficult to conceive of power exercised totally without consent as being social in character, at least in regards the subject in whom the response is elicited. Consequently, when social power is defined as "the capacity to cause response in others with or without consent," the words "without consent" should be considered to mean that the consent present may be quite negligible in proportion to what could or should be present; the force involved is preponderant in relation to the consent.

11. Caponigri, *IPT*, Chapter III.
12. *Ibid.*, The word "transcendence" carries the same connotation as the Hegelian term *Aufhebung*.
13. A complete description of the modes of social relationship is found in Caponigri, *IPT*, Chapter III.
14. *Nicomachean Ethics*, Book VIII, 1156a6-1156b31.
15. Utility and pleasure are normally included in such friendship, however.
16. An obvious example of social relationship in the utilitarian mode would be that relationship ordinarily existing between a grocer and his customer. The customer exercises a form of social power to which the grocer responds because of the usefulness of this response to his financial income. Likewise, it is often the case that the grocer in turn elicits a response from the customer because of the utility of the services of the grocer in providing the customer's food supply.

There is a distinction to be made, of course, between the utilitarian mode and that aspect of the mode of friendship mentioned earlier which is based on utility. The utilitarian mode is characterized principally by the motivation on the part of each individual or group to gain something from another. This motivation is the exclusive or, at least, the prime casual element in the social transaction. The friendship of utility, on the other hand, necessarily involves the mutual willing of the good of the individuals or groups because of their usefulness to one another. Such a relationship can truly be called friendship as is evidenced by the universally accepted maxim, "A friend in need is a friend indeed."
17. "Die Wirtschaftsetik der Weltreligionen," as translated in H. H. Gerth and C. Wright Mills (eds.), *From Max Weber: Essays in Sociology* (New York, 1946), p. 299.
18. The distinction between the rational-legal mode and the ethical mode is rooted in the proper distinction between the legal realm and the ethical realm, which in turn is founded on the important distinction as

to whether the role of guaranteeing sanction for social disorder is assigned to the agent of the disorder (ethical realm) or to an agent other than the agent of the disorder (legal realm). A complete analysis of the distinction between the ethical and the legal is found in Caponigri, *IPT*, Chapter V.

19. A rather obvious example of imperfect consent within the utilitarian mode would be the response given by a person to the alleged humor contained in stories told by his employer. Such response often would be given only because absence of such response might lessen the employee's promotion potential, etc. In another instance, the consent within this mode might very well approach perfection if the response to humor in a story is given as a means of achieving affability, with this affability being considered something desirable for its own sake.

20. Cf. *Die deutsche Ideologie*, in *Historisch-Kritische Gesamtausgabe* (Frankfort [etc.], 1927-1933), Abt. I, Bd. 5, pp. 387-392. Hereafter cited as *MEGA*.

21. *Ibid.*, p. 388. Cf. *Economic and Philosophic Manuscripts of 1844*, trans. Martin Milligan (Moscow, 1961), pp. 57 and 93-97.

22. Marx, *Die deutsche Ideologie, MEGA*, Abt. I, Bd. 5, p. 392.

23. Chapter VI, above.

24. "The State," *Pravda* (No. 15), January 18, 1929. Reprinted in *Soviet Legal Philosophy*, ed. John N. Hazard, trans. Hugh W. Babb (Cambridge, Mass., 1951), p. 7.

25. S. A. Golunskii and M. S. Strogovich, *The Theory of the State and Law* (Moscow, 1940), as reprinted in part in *Soviet Legal Philosophy*, p. 365.

26. Mironov, "Persuasion and Compulsion in Combatting Anti-Social Acts," pp. 54-65; Romashkin, *Fundamentals of Soviet Law*, pp. 19-20; Denisov, *RSSTCC*, pp. 17-20.

27. V. I. Lenin, "A Great Beginning," *Lenin Selected Works*, 2 vols. in 4 (Moscow, 1952), II, Part 2, pp. 213-239.

28. *Ibid.*, p. 213.

29. *Ibid.*, p. 218.

30. *Ibid.*, pp. 230-232.

31. *Ibid.*, p. 231.

32. *Ibid.*

33. *Ibid.*

34. *Ibid.*, p. 232. Cf. Marx, *Economic and Philosophic Manuscripts*, pp. 102-105.

35. V. V. Grishin, *Pravda*, May 30, 1960, in *Current Digest of the Soviet Press*, XII, No. 22 (June 29, 1960), p. 14.

36. *Pravda*, May 31, 1960, *ibid.*, p. 16. *The "new morale" sought through*

the labor brigades can easily be interpreted, it would seem, as the preeminence of the affective and ethical modes of interpersonal, intergroup relationships over utilitarian and legalistic attitudes.

37. *Voprosy filosofii*, No. 10, 1959, p. 135, as translated in Ritvo, *TWC*, p. 23. See also, *The Program of the C.P.S.U.*, adopted by the XXII Party Congress in Moscow, Oct.-Nov., 1961, in Dan N. Jacobs (ed.), *The New Communist Manifesto and Related Documents*, 2d. ed. (New York, 1962), p. 240.

38. T. S. Stepanyan in his article, "Stages and Periods," *Oktyabr*, No. 7, 1960, complains that it frequently happens that some members of the brigades attain high production figures but do not always behave in everyday life as they should. For the translation, see Ritvo, *TWC*, p. 23.

39. Marx, *The Critique of the Gotha Programme*, ed. C. P. Dutt (New York, 1938), pp. 9-10. Cf. Engels, *Herr Eugen Dühring's Revolution in Science (Anti-Dühring)* (London, 1940), p. 123, and Lenin, *The State and Revolution*, in *Lenin Selected Works*, II, Part 1, pp. 294-298.

40. Thus, a situation in society may be imagined whereby a laggard worker may be persuaded to change his mental attitude, both because he has a moral obligation to society to give fully of his talents and, moreover, because his additional labor will reflect itself in a more complete fulfillment of his own as well as his neighbor's material needs. Such a conjunction of the ethical and utilitarian forms of social power does not seem to imply the presence of exploitation on the part of either the elicitor or the respondent. Cf. Emily Clark Brown, "The Current Status of the Soviet Worker," *Problems of Communism*, IX, No. 6 (Nov.-Dec., 1960), p. 40.

41. For example, it may be because one person offers sincere sympathy and consolation at the time of a death within the immediate family, that another person subsequently consents, most willingly, to help this individual in time of serious illness. In neither instance need the use of power be considered a form of exploitation.

42. Chapter VI, above.

43. Cf. Golunskii and Strogovich, *The Theory of the State and Law*, pp. 380-383.

44. In every legal system we find a great many "directive norms" having no sanctions. The Romans called them *"leges imperfectae."* Much modern federal legislation is more permissive than prescriptive. It neither prescribes nor proscribes a specific act; it does not depend upon punishment as a sanction. *The Area Redevelopment Act, Unemployment Benefits Act* and most of the social legislation of the early New Deal fall into this category. Cf. Lawrence Haworth, "The Standard View of the State: A Critique," *Ethics*, LXXII (1963), pp. 272ff.

Such use of the rational-legal mode is to be found also in the positive law of the Roman Catholic Church as codified in the *Codex Juris Canonici.* Here several norms, although prescribed in a legal manner, are not preceptive and carry no coercive sanction. See, for instance, Canons 859, No. 3 and 1097, No. 2.

45. On this point see T. V. Smith, *Power and Conscience,* in Harold D. Lasswell, *et. al., A Study of Power* (Glencoe, Ill., 1950), pp. 342-344.
46. *Nicomachean Ethics,* Book I, 1095a13-1096a10.
47. *Ibid.,* 1096b15-1102a4; also Book X, 1176a30-1181b23.
48. *Ibid.*
49. On this point, see Karl R. Popper, *The Open Society and Its Enemies,* 4th. ed., 2 vols. (New York, 1963), II, p. 211; Jacques Maritain, *Humanisme intégral* (Paris, 1947), pp. 232-244, trans. in *The Social and Political Philosophy of Jacques Maritain,* ed. Joseph W. Evans and Leo R. Ward (New York, 1955), pp. 326-330.

INDEX

A

Absolute, The, 60, 61
Accumulation of capital, Law of, 108-109
Aeschylus, 175
Aesthetic experience, 178. *See also* Art; Beauty; Literature
Affective mode: explained, 207, 215n45, 219-220, 228; in communism, 207, 225-226, 227, 229; coveted goal, 220, 230
Aggregate, 31, 34, 35, 36, 54n90
Alienation, 6, 157-160
Analogy, 203, 213n31
Anarchy, 1, 159, 197
Aquinas, St. Thomas, 141
Architecture, Soviet, 182-183
Aristotle, 21, 41, 58, 59, 61, 219, 230
Art: part of superstructure, 18, 135, 154, 173, 174, 179; reacts on base, 19, 154, 173, 179; and man, 104, 178, 179; and economic development, 175-176; ancient, 176-177; critique of, 177-178; realistic, 180-183; as partisan, 181-187. *See also* Aesthetic experience; Architecture; Beauty; Literature; Socialist realism
Atheism, 10, 65, 67, 71, 74; and Party, 120, 121; propagation of, 120-122. *See also* Religion
Australopithecus, 90

B

Beauty: criterion of, 175-180, 191n24; defined, 178, 179. *See also* Art
Bentham, J., 223
Berdyaev, N., 41
Bismarck, O., 120
Bogdanov, A., 41
Bourgeoisie, 28, 30-31, 32, 131-132, 223, 224
Brigades of Communist Labor, 226-227
Bukharin, N., ix, 31, 34, 35, 36, 40, 53n78, 54n92
Burgess, E., 37

C

Calvin, J., 95
Capital, 108, 110. *See also* Constant capital; Variable capital
Capital, viii, 30, 109
Capitalists. *See* Bourgeoisie
Category, 33-39 *passim*, 54n92, 60
Catherine the Great, 186
Chiang Kai-shek, 45
Citizen squads, 199-200
Civil rights, 134, 135, 149n17
Class, social: affects environment, 29-30, 34, 99; dominant, controls thought, 30, 152-153, 174; Marxist notion of, 30-32, 33-36, 37, 38, 39; defined, 31, 36-37, 38, 53n85; *an sich*, 39; *für sich*, 39; and freedom, 96-97. *See also* Bourgeoisie; Proletariat
Class conflict: motor of history, 27, 28-29, 233n8; absent in communism, 29; and distribution, 31-32, 53n80; peaceful, 43, 45;

betrayed, 46; and freedom, 96-97; and superstructure, 115, 121-122, 156, 174; origin of, 131, 152
Classless society, 2, 26, 42, 133, 141, 153, 156, 160; described, 4-6, 108, 119, 136-137, 156, 172n*61*, 211n*12;* perfects society, 33, 216, 229, 230-231; and proletariat, 34, 39; and political order, 197-208, 215n*45;* and social power, 223-231
Coercion: and communism, 141-142, 198, 199-200, 202, 211n*12,* 212n*20,* 216, 225, 230; as inhuman, 218, 234-235n*10;* as necessary, 229
Coexistence. *See* Peaceful coexistence
Common good: defined, 205, 206
Common market, 43
Communism. *See* Classless society; Communist Party; Socialism
Communist Manifesto, 8n*8,* 27, 28, 233n*8*
Communist Party, vii; 40, 42; as avant-garde, 41, 81-82, 132, 184; and religion, 120-121; and education, 163; and art, 184-187
Complementarity principle, 76
Comrades' courts, 200, 201-202. *See also* Public meetings
Concentration of capital, Law of, 109
Conditioned reflex: explained, 92-93
Conscience, Freedom of, 119
Consciousness, 11-12, 94
Constant capital, 31, 107, 109, 125n*18*
Contradiction, 64-65, 70-72, 74. *See also* Dialectics; Opposites, Law of
Cooley, C., 36

Copy theory: described, 13-14. *See also* Knowledge; Truth
Creative advancement. *See* Theoretical evolution
Croce, B., 81

D

Darwin, C., 69, 89
Decree on the Press, 186
Decroly, O., 163
Descartes, R., 14, 58, 59
De Sitter, W., 75
Dewey, J., 163
Dialectical materialism, 58-59, 64-72 *passim,* 77, 78, 79, 82
Dialectics, 27, 59, 74; explained, 60-62, 79; and truth, 73, 114, 138, 177; and morality, 114; and art, 177
Dictatorship of proletariat, 1-3, 133
Diderot, D., 59, 175
Distribution, 31-32, 53n*80,* 228
Doppler effect, 75, 76

E

Economics. *See* Mode of production
Education, 3, 73-74; part of superstructure, 150, 154; primitive, 151-152; as weapon, 156; reacts on base, 156. *See also* Polytechnism
Einstein, A., 75, 76
Encyclopaedists, 121
Engels, F.: mentioned *passim*
Ethical mode: and state, 207; in communism, 207, 225-230 *passim;* effective, 220, 230; and law, 222, 229, 235-236n*18;* and utility, 228, 237n*40*. *See also* Morality
Evolution, 69, 89-91. *See also* Theoretical evolution
Expanding universe, Theory of, 74-76

F

Factors of production, 21-23, 24
Family, 151, 152
Feudal society, 24-25
Feuerbach, L., 6, 14, 62-64 *passim*, 121
Fichter, J., 36, 37, 54n92
Forces of production, 24, 33
Formal control, 199, 204. *See also* Substantive control
Formal values, 204-206, 229. *See also* Substantive values
Founding Fathers, 40
Fourier, C., 6
Freedom, 4, 6, 106, 159, 224; defined, 5, 94-95, 185; explained, 94-97; in arts, 184-187. *See also* Human nature; Man
Friedmann, A., 75
Functional detachment, 199, 205, 206. *See also* Political order

G

Galileo, 58
Goebbels, J., 186
Goethe, J., 175
Golunskii, S., 140, 141
Great Leap Forward, 44
Green, A., 36
Group, 35-39 *passim*, 54n104, 205, 219

H

Hegel, G., 6, 58-66 *passim*, 68, 71, 72, 94
Heine, H., 175
Helvetius, C., 223
History: theory of, 17-33; determines man, 19-20, 26, 27, 97, 104; and individuals, 97-99. *See also* Mode of production
Hitler, A., 45, 98
Hobbes, T., 14, 223
Holbach, P., 223

Human nature: above animals, 12, 91; determined, 17-21, 26, 27, 42, 94-95, 97, 104; defined, 20, 21-22, 51n42, 89. *See also* Man
Hundred Flowers experiment, viii, 44

I

Idea. *See* Absolute, The
Ideinost, 181
Immortality: origin of notion, 116
Imperialism, viii, 43-46 *passim*, 109-111
Increasing misery, Law of, 109
Individual: role of, in history, 97-99. *See also* Man
Industrial reserve army, 109
Instruments of labor, 22, 23, 25, 151; ownership of, 26, 30; and education, 161

J

Jacobin clubs, 40
Jehovah, 116
Jellinek, G., 139
Johnson. H., 37

K

Kant, I., 58, 78, 149n18
Kedrov, B., 78
Kepler, J., 175
Kerschensteiner, G., 163
Khrushchev, N. S., vii, viii, 44, 45, 164, 165, 172n61, 186, 187, 198, 199, 200
Kilpatrick, W., 163
Knowledge, human: distinct from animal, 12, 91-93; and sensation, 13, 14; dialectical, 13-14; as abstraction, 14; and practice, 14-17, 181; and freedom, 94, 96, 159. *See also* Copy theory; Truth

241

Krupskaya, N., 163, 171n52
Kulturkampf, 120

L

Labor, human: and production, 22; and progress, 91, 157, 162; and value, 104, 105-106; and ownership, 105; and education, 160-162; and art, 179
Labor aristocracy, 111
Labor power: explained, 106-107, 126n18
Labor theory of value, 104-109
Langevin, P., 73
Language, 91-94 *passim*
Laski, H., 6, 104
Lavoisier, A., 107
Law: medieval, 18; as superstructure, 18, 135, 136, 150, 154; reacts on base, 19, 136, 147n11, 154, 173; theory of, 131-136, 152, 224-225, 228; defined, 133, 137, 224-225; and morality, 137-142, 229; bourgeois, 138-140; and Party, 146n8; anti-parasite, 201, 212n21. *See also* Rational-legal mode; State
Lay, W., 163
"Left" Hegelians, 62
Legal Mode. *See* Rational-legal mode
Leibniz, G., 14
Lemaitre, G., 74, 75, 87n53
Lenin, V. I.: mentioned *passim*
Literature: as superstructure, 18, 135, 154; reacts on base, 19, 154, 173; proletarian, 174, 184-187; critique of, 177; and Party, 184-187. *See also* Art; Socialist realism
Locke, J., 14, 105, 223
Lunacharsky, A., 178

M

Man: perfected by communism, 5, 33, 156, 160, 164, 207, 216; determined by history, 17-21, 26, 27, 97, 104; and production, 21; social animal, 21-22, 41, 91; maker of history, 27-28, 39, 150, 155-156; and exploitation, 32-33, 157-160, 218, 228, 234-235n10; lacks free will, 42, 94-95; tool producer, 89; his origin, 89-91; and art, 178, 179. *See also* Freedom; Human nature; Knowledge; Labor
Mao Tse-tung, viii, 44
Marx, K.: mentioned *passim*
Matter, 10-12, 62-63, 64, 70. *See also* Dialectical materialism
Mayer, K., 37
Means of production, 22, 32
Measure: defined, 68-69. *See also* Transition, Law of
Mechanists, 77
Mendelism-Morganism, 76
Menshevizing idealists, 78
Metaphysics, 58, 64, 77. *See also* Dialectical materialism
Mill, J. S., 223
Mode of production: basis of society, 17-20, 28, 97, 104, 112-113, 135-136, 150-151, 154, 173; and man, 18, 19-20, 104. *See also* Superstructure
Mohammed, 95
Monotheism, 116, 117
Montessori, M., 163
Morality: part of superstructure, 18, 112, 137, 150, 174; and freedom, 96; and labor, 104; bourgeois, rejected, 111; principles of, 111-116, 200; as a science, 113-114, 127n36, 175; not opportunistic, 127n37; and law, 137-142, 203, 229; and

education, 156; in communism, 172n61; as weapon, 174; and art, 175, 177, 186. *See also* Ethical mode

Motion, 64, 71

N

Napoleon Bonaparte, 95, 98, 186
Narodnost, 181. *See also* Partiinost; Partisanship; Truth
Nature, 21. *See also* Human nature
Nazi Germany, 45
Neanderthal man, 90
Negation, Law of, 68, 72-73, 74. *See also* Dialectical materialism; Dialectics
Nicomachean Ethics, 219
Node, 68, 69. *See also* Transition, Law of
Nuclear war, 43

O

Opposites, Law of, 68, 70-72, 74. *See also* Contradiction; Dialectical materialism; Dialectics
Orthodox Church, 122
Owen, R., 6, 160

P

Paganini, N., 191
Paper tigers, 46
Paris Commune, 2, 3, 8n9
Park, R., 37
Partiinost, 181, 184-187. *See also* Narodnost; Partisanship; Truth
Partisanship, 80-82, 181-187. *See also* Proletariat; Truth
Pashukanis, E., 147-149n12
Pauling, L., 77
Pavlov, I., 91-94 *passim*
Pavlov conference, 93
Peaceful coexistence, viii, 42-47, 56n131

People's militia, 200. *See also* Classless society; Political order
Philosophy: part of superstructure, 18, 80-82, 135, 154, 174; reacts on base, 19, 154, 173; and science, 77-82; as partisan, 80-81; as weapon, 174; utilitarian, 223-224
Pithecanthropus, 90
Pius XII, Pope, 76
Plan of Great Works, 163
Plato, 61
Plekhanov, G., 95, 96, 177, 178, 191n24
Political order: and communism, 197, 198-199, 202, 206, 215n45; analysis of, 202-206. *See also* Classless society; State
Power, social: defined, 204, 217, 235n10; analyzed, 216-222, 233n5, 234n9, 234-235n10; in communism, 223-230. *See also* Affective mode; Ethical mode; Rational-legal mode; Utilitarian mode
Polytechnism, 160-165. *See also* Education
Polytheism, 116, 117
Practice, 14-17, 151, 155, 181. *See also* Unity of theory and practice
Prayer, 117. *See also* Religion
Private property, 3, 117-118, 131
Production: basis of capitalism, 105. *See also* Mode of production
Profit, 106, 107, 108. *See also* Surplus value, Theory of
Proletariat, 2, 28, 31, 32, 131-132, 174, 224; as dominant, 32-33, 153; and communism, 34, 39; not motive force, 40, 55n110; and Party, 40-41; and truth, 80-81, 181-182, 183-184

243

Protestantism, 19, 57n*140*
Public meetings, 201, 202. See also Comrades' courts
Public order, 199-202, 206

Q

Quality: explained, 68-70. See also Transition, Law of
Quantity: explained, 68-70. See also Transition, Law of

R

Raphael, 179
Rational-legal mode: absent in communism, 207, 225, 227, 228; beneficial, 208, 229; explained, 221-222, 237-238n*44;* and ethics, 222, 229, 235-236n*18.* See also Law
Realism, 10-13 *passim.* See also Socialist realism
Relations of production, 23-24, 25, 29, 30
Relativity, Theory of, 76
Religion: part of superstructure, 18, 135, 150, 152, 154; reacts on base, 19, 104, 154, 173; war on, 62, 119-120; origin of, 116-118; serves dominant class, 117, 118-119, 152; and Party, 120; and state, 120; as weapon, 174; and art, 186. See also Atheism; Morality
Resonance theory, 77
Revisionism, 45-46
Ricardo, D., 6, 104, 105
Roman Catholicism, 57n*140,* 122, 238n*44*
Romanticism, 180-181. See also Socialist realism
Rose, A., 37
Ross, E., 36
Roucek, J., 37
Rousseau, J., 59

Rutkevich, M., 15

S

Saint-Simon, H., 6
Schmidt, C., vii, 43
Scholastics, 54n*92,* 61
Science, 65, 66-67, 70, 77-82
Shakespeare, 175
Shaknozarov, G., 197, 198, 199
Shore, M., 150
Sinanthropus, 90
Sino-Soviet conflict, 42-47, 57n*140*
Smith, A., 6, 104, 105
Social control: defined, 203, 213-214n*34;* and political order, 203-206, 213n*30,* 217. See also Formal control; Substantive control
Socialism, 1, 26, 108, 109, 132, 133, 136, 140, 141, 153, 163, 165, 207; explained, 3-4. See also Classless society
Socialism in one country, ix, 44, 148n*12*
Socialism: Utopian and Scientific, 109
Socialist realism, 177, 180-183. See also Art; Literature
Sorel, G., 81
Spartacus, 175
Spinoza, B., 14, 59
Stalin, J., viii, ix, 11, 44, 45, 64, 147-148n*12,* 162, 164, 186
State: withers 4-5, 197-202; and religion, 120; defined, 131, 207, 224; theory of, 131-133, 136, 145-146n*6,* 149n*17,* 197, 207, 214-215n*45,* 224, 228. See also Law; Political order
Strogovich, M., 140, 141
Strumilin, S., 198
Subbotnik movement, 226
Substantive control, 204. See also **Formal control**

Substantive values, 204-208 *passim*. *See also* Formal values
Superstructure: reacts on base, 136, 147n*11*, 154-156, 173-175; based on economics, 150-151. *See also* Mode of production
Surplus value, Theory of, 106-109, 125-126n*18*

T

Theoretical evolution, viii, ix, 43-44, 45, 81, 82, 109, 184
Thorndike, E., 163
Thorvaldsen, B., 179
Tools. *See* Instruments of Labor
Transition, Law of, 68-70, 74. *See also* Dialectical materialism; Dialectics
Trotsky, L., 45
Truth: theory of, 10-17; criterion of, 15-16; and practice, 15-17, 181; objective, 16; relative, 16; absolute, 16-17, 74. *See also* Copy theory; Knowledge

U

Unconditioned reflex: explained, 92
Unity of theory and practice, vii, 17, 80, 155, 160, 164, 181. *See also* Practice
Utilitarian mode: absent in communism, 207, 225, 227-228; beneficial, 208, 228, 237n*40*, 237n*41*; explained, 221, 222, 223, 235n*16*, 236n*19*; and ethics, 228, 237n*40*; and friendship, 228-229, 237n*41*. *See also* Utility
Utility: basis of values, 105; and friendship, 219, 228-229, 235n*16*, 237n*41*; defined, 221; and history, 223-224, 227. *See also* Utilitarian mode

V

Value, 37-38, 39, 42, 80, 105-108 *passim*, 214n*35*, 234n*10*; Exchange, 105; Use, 105. *See also* Formal values; Labor theory of value; Substantive values
Variable capital, 31, 107, 109, 125n*18*
Venable, V., 27, 58
Vyshinsky, A., ix

W

Wages: unjust, 106, 108
War, 43, 46, 110-111
Warner, W., 37
Weber, M., 221

Z

Zhdanov, A., 186